INTELLECTUAL FREEDOM

A Reference Handbook

INTELLECTUAL FREEDOM

A Reference Handbook

John B. Harer
Texas A & M University Library

CONTEMPORARY WORLD ISSUES

ABC-CLIO

Santa Barbara, California
Denver, Colorado
Oxford, England

Library of Congress Cataloging-in-Publication Data

Harer, John B.
   Intellectual freedom : a reference handbook / John B. Harer
      p. cm.—(Contemporary world issues)
   Includes bibliographical references and index.
   Freedom of speech—United States—History.   2. Freedom of religion—
   United States—History.   3. Freedom of the press—United States—
   History.   4. Assembly, Right of—United States—History.   5. Censorship—
   United States—History.
   I. Title.   II. Series.
   KF4770.Z9H3   1992   324.73'0853—dc20   [347.302853]   92-35565

ISBN 0-87436-669-0 (alk. paper)

99 98 97 96 95 94   10 9 8 7 6 5 4 3 2

ABC-CLIO, Inc.
130 Cremona Drive, P.O. Box 1911
Santa Barbara, California 93116-1911

To my parents, Robert J. and Sherry Harer,
for teaching me the value of learning and reading

Contents

Preface, ix
Acknowledgments, xiii

1 Introduction, 1
Intellectual Freedom, 1
The Theories of Intellectual Freedom, 3
Historical Foundations of the First Amendment:
   From 1215 to 1791, 5
The First Amendment in U.S. History, 8
   Freedom of Religion, 9
   Freedom of Speech, 12
   Freedom of the Press, 20
   The Right to Assembly, 24
Intellectual Freedom and Censorship, 26
Current Issues in Intellectual Freedom, 31

2 Chronology, 37

3 Biographical Sketches, 53

4 Laws, Legislation, and Court Cases, 65
Judicial Review and the Court System, 66
Understanding Case Law Citations, 67
Cases Involving Freedom of Religion, 68
Laws and Cases Involving Freedom of Speech, 74

Laws and Cases Involving Freedom of the Press, 108
Cases Involving the Right to Association and
    Assembly, 122
Laws Regulating the Free Flow of Information, 130

5 Directory of Organizations, 135

6 Selected Print Resources, 161

Reference Works, 161
    Bibliographies and Guides, 161
    Indexes and Abstracts, 163
    Directories, 165
    Yearbooks, Dictionaries, and Encyclopedias, 166
    Special Issues of Periodicals, 168
Monographs 170
    General, 170
    Freedom of Religion, 181
    Freedom of Speech, 186
    Freedom of Press, 218
    Freedom of Association, 226
Periodicals, 227

7 Selected Nonprint Resources, 241

Films, Videocassettes, and Filmstrips, 241
Databases, 265
CD-ROMs, 269
Television Programs, 271
Educational Software and Simulation Games, 274

Glossary, 279
Index, 293
About the Author, 315

Preface

"Stone walls do not a prison make, nor iron bars a cage" is a famous Shakespearean quote about the struggle for freedom of the intellect. It expresses the belief that ideas will stay alive no matter what level of oppression takes place. History shows that humankind not only holds ideas dear but also expresses them passionately. However, there is an ample body of history documenting the suppression of beliefs, particularly beliefs that are expressed or when attempts are made to make them become reality.

Thomas Jefferson and the creators of the Bill of Rights recognized this fundamental lesson. They feared the unchecked power of authority to suppress ideas and knew this to be a threat to freedom. The Bill of Rights represents the realization that freedom for humankind can only be preserved if ideas can be expressed, not merely owned by the believers. But what forms of expression enable ideas to flourish for the general good, and what limits, if any, are reasonable for the protection of freedom itself and for humankind? The following text is a guide to these very questions.

The founding fathers wrote into the Bill of Rights four fundamental types of expression to be protected: freedom of religion, freedom of speech, freedom of the press, and the right to assembly. These were seen as distinct and separate forms of expression but ones that were intrinsically related. How each of these freedoms would manifest itself was not defined by the Constitution. That was left up to society, to the process society might use to resolve conflicts over these freedoms, and the provisions of the constitutional process.

Our four expressive rights are not the result of lofty intellectual pursuit but instead reflect the basic struggle of our people to survive and to grow through human interaction. The Bill of

Rights did not solve this battle between expressive rights and authority in favor of individual rights against the public order. Instead, it is and has been a guidepost for intellectual freedom. As this text is examined, the historical progression of each of the rights is detailed. Our history is replete with both successes and injustices in the protection of individual and expressive rights. Especially in the introduction and the chapter on case law, the text shows that the four freedoms have been greatly expanded over time and that Americans today enjoy a superior level of freedom to hold beliefs, to speak their minds, to print their views, and to meet with others of like mind. This has come about gradually. Society remains troubled by the outcomes of challenges to expressive rights granted to individuals and continues to push for retractions or at least redefinitions of those rights as they continue to be interpreted and practiced. Despite the generally positive direction of the courts in defining the boundaries of intellectual freedom, battles continue on virtually a daily basis. These conflicts will never be entirely solved; there is no single answer. It is a constant process with many of the same issues being revisited over and over again—highlighting the need for a continuous study and examination of intellectual freedom.

The introductory chapter of this book is designed to provide as accurate a definition of intellectual freedom as possible though there are severe limitations to a clear and concise one. An examination of the philosophical approaches to expressive freedom provides a framework for gauging the direction and rationale of historical events as well as legislation and case law. These theories put the remainder of the text in proper perspective. The first chapter also outlines a very rich history of each of the four freedoms as our nation has endeavored to define them within the context of everyday life in each era. In this, as well as all other chapters, the organization of the text is designed to follow the order of the First Amendment—beginning with the freedom of religion and ending with the right to assembly. In the final section of this chapter, a current review of issues in intellectual freedom provides an up-to-date history of expressive rights.

One of the most unique aspects of our American form of government is judicial review. The executive and legislative branches of government are capable of providing protection for expressive rights, but the courts have more often been champions of the First Amendment or at least primary interpreters of its meaning. Chapter 4, devoted to case law and legislation, thoroughly examines this topic. It also provides an introduction to the way the constitutional review and legal process works, essential to understanding the cases listed.

Controversial subjects often divide people, and some present-day controversies, such as abortion or capitalism versus communism, result in well-defined opposing camps. However, intellectual freedom, especially viewed in terms of the First Amendment, does not present as clear choices. Chapter 3, biographical sketches, and Chapter 5, organizational descriptions, make no attempt to provide clear distinctions either. Each entry is written in a straightforward manner, avoiding value judgments as much as possible. Most individuals and organizations intimately involved in pursuing some aspect of intellectual freedom profess to defend the First Amendment. However, individuals on one side believe there are limits to expression, especially to preserve public order or traditional values, and that a strict interpretation of the Constitution is proper. The other side argues that few, if any, limits are justified so that expressive rights are preserved even from inadvertent suppression. These two chapters reflect these two diverse views.

The last two chapters provide a body of resources useful for research and study of this topic. The literature of intellectual freedom is considerable. The annotated bibliography of Chapter 6 presents many of the most recent publications as well as a selection of the most important retrospective texts. It also includes important relevant journal titles that cover at least some aspect of one or more of the four freedoms. Chapter 7, an annotated bibliography of nonprint resources, goes beyond a compilation of audiovisual materials. This chapter has sections on videos, databases of relevance, CD-ROM products, and television programs chosen as prime examples of the practice of free speech as well as programs that seem to have an impact on how society administers these rights.

The glossary at the end of the book is an extremely important tool for this text as well as for studying this topic. The highly legal nature of intellectual freedom presents a large number of terms that are not part of everyday speech, or that take on a unique meaning in a legal context. This chapter can be consulted whenever needed, but it is especially useful in discussions of case law or legislation. A subject/author/title index rounds out the book.

Acknowledgments

Numerous individuals have helped to bring about this book. Most importantly, I thank Steven Atkins of Texas A & M University's Evans Library, without whom this book would not have been accomplished. A colleague, friend, and conference roommate, Steven is a consummate professional.

During the creation of this work, several colleagues and friends lent advice and support, in both substantive and emotional terms. Jay Martin Poole has been my mentor and counsel since rejoining the staff of the Evans Library at Texas A & M University. His leadership has been essential to my continued success. I could not have completed this task without the advice of my good friend and colleague Suzanne Gyeszly. Her contributions are truly appreciated. My staff at the Evans Library is to be commended for their support and understanding, often expressed even under adverse conditions; special thanks go to Evelyn Aldred, Sandra Cooper, Tommy Schaffer, and Susan Scott. Also, the student assistants who provided much of the typing support, Tara Austin and Kim Tubbs-Nelson, are due my heartfelt gratitude. I thank the Graduate School of Library Science at Clarion University of Pennsylvania, especially Dr. Bernard Vavrek, for my solid grounding in librarianship and the principle of intellectual freedom.

Last, I must take this opportunity to thank my family, especially my wife, Sue Meisel-Harer, for their support.

1

Introduction

Intellectual Freedom

THE FIRST AMENDMENT TO THE UNITED STATES CONSTITUTION reads, "Congress shall make no law respecting an establishment of religion, or prohibiting the free exercise thereof, or abridging the freedom of speech, or of the press; or the right of the people peaceably to assemble, and to petition the Government for a redress of grievances." The founding fathers meant the First Amendment to embody the freedoms and rights basic to a free people. However, they did not define what they meant by these freedoms and rights; they only stated that the government could not limit such rights.

Though the First Amendment does not define freedom of religion, freedom of speech, freedom of the press, and the right of assembly, it does provide the basis for later definitions. It is these definitions that have come to be grouped under the category of intellectual freedom—the unrestricted ability to think or reason as we wish and to express our ideas. A conceptual framework of freedom plays an important role here. The noted Civil War historian Bruce Catton once said: "If any one word tells what America really is, it is the one word—Freedom. . . . The secret of the American tradition is freedom—freedom unabridged and unadulterated, freedom that applies to everybody in the land at all times and places, freedom for those with whom we disagree as well as for those with whom we do agree."[1] Freedom, then, is free choice: the control of one's self. An individual has the freedom to control his or her own actions, thoughts, beliefs, and reasoning.

Freedom, then, is "the absence of necessity, coercion, or constraint in choice or action" (*Webster's Ninth New Collegiate Dictionary*) and pertains to the self, physically and mentally. Freedom of the physical self is also addressed by the Bill of Rights, as well as by parts of the Constitution, but freedom of the intellect is the essence of the First Amendment.

As to intellect, Justice Louis Brandeis said in *Gilbert v. Minnesota*, "in a democracy every citizen has a right to teach the truth as he sees it."[2] The search for truth is grounded in the capacity to think, reason, and believe. Yet, the initial concept of what constitutes a "protected" intellect was "truth" on a higher order or, in other words, factual, unimpeachable statements. Therefore, libel and slander laws were established to govern speech and press because fidelity in both thought and word was seen as necessary for an orderly society.

However, "truth" limited only to factual, unimpeachable statements presents a serious dilemma for humankind. Too often, life requires decisions and actions before all the facts can be discovered. In such cases, people must rely on opinions. Eli Oboler states, "There is a great temptation for any believer in intellectual freedom to equate the belief in and practice of freedom of expression with some kind of perfect state, perfect world, perfect life. It is a manifestly unattainable ideal, which in no way affects its practical and immediate value as the only way to come even close to that essential of a livable life, truth."[3] Even more so, the imagination of most humans has been captured by philosophies that form the foundation of most interactions between people. Opinion and philosophy open up the door to differences between individuals, and often violent objections and power struggles over competing ideas. To go beyond "truth" recognizes that more is valuable than what can be proven within the range of human reasoning and that the "truth" is not necessarily absolute.

Furthermore, ideas, beliefs, and expression are seen as valuable as truth because they increase the range of reason. Through this ability to expand reason, innovation and change transform society for the good. Alexis de Tocqueville, who chronicled democracy in the United States in the early 1800s, said that if democracy has one failing, it is that the tyranny of the majority has the tendency to strike down opinion "strong enough to chill innovators, and to keep them silent and at a respectful distance."[4]

Ideas, opinions, and beliefs are seen as valuable because they are considered unique to the human species. No other species has been shown to form ideas, opinions, and beliefs in the way that humans do. Consequently, freedom to develop such thoughts is worth preserving so as to avoid what de Tocqueville said would have humans waste their "strength in bootless and solitary trifling."[5] In other words, such a license of freedom would protect the quality of ideas. Humankind would be free to develop and discuss high, profound and philosophical concepts of religion, politics, the economy, and culture. Without this protection, the relations between people are severely limited to noncontroversial topics like the weather.

The definition of intellectual freedom is, then, a complex conceptualization of the human right to hold truths, ideas, opinions, and beliefs freely and without control and to express such thoughts so that innovation and change can occur for the benefit of humanity and society. But, as Eli Oboler states: "The intellectually free are those who honestly try to find the truth on any issue as dispassionately, objectively, and fully as human failings of the mind and body permit. Any barriers to threading the maze of opinion and argument and agreement and disagreement are only achievable hurdles, not impassable walls or blind alleys."[6] Therefore, it must be remembered that our above definition implies that intellectual freedom embraces not only unquestionable ideas, opinions, and beliefs but also questionable ones. Put another way, our definition includes not only ideas, opinions, and beliefs with obvious value but also those with no apparent value.

The Theories of Intellectual Freedom

Because ideas step beyond the confines of a stable, acceptable platform of "truth," the extent to which intellectual freedom and expression pervade human interaction has created numerous theoretical bases. It is important to consider the more prominent theories of freedom of expression because these theories provide a framework for examining a rhetorical definition within the context of the real world. Theories also enlighten the understanding of these concepts and give them a richness of reasoning that enables society to build, grow, and change for the better. Here are the six major theories:

1. Marketplace of ideas
2. Social exchange
3. Social utility
4. Self-government
5. Expression versus action
6. Communications context

The first major theory comes from the writings of John Milton in his *Areopagitica*. Milton argues that the expression of ideas needs a *marketplace* to enter where people can pick and choose, as they see fit, for their own needs and with their own biases.[7] To Milton, truth will be in competition with all other ideas. Until the best idea is identified, suppressing any idea involves the risk that the best idea will not be available in the marketplace and thus denies people the opportunity to choose that idea.

John Stuart Mill's theory on freedom of expression (*social exchange*) is similar to Milton's philosophy. In a society with free expression guaranteed, a false idea can be traded for a true one. Mill believes that if the right to express an opinion is denied, both those who agree and those who disagree with that opinion suffer because the opportunity to judge true or false ideas also is denied.[8]

The concept of *social utility* is the third major theory. Zechariah Chafee sees two kinds of expression: one that is of interest to the individual and one that is important to society, or the social interest.[9] The latter is more precious to Chafee because it serves society as a whole and, in the long run, for the good. But to Chafee, there is a point where expression for social interest clashes with society's need for public order. He argues strongly that expression and order must be balanced but more importantly that the balance generally must tip toward expression much more than order. The point where the balance must tip toward order is the point of social utility. For Chafee, social utility becomes the overriding concern when expression gives rise to unlawful acts that threaten social order.

Another theory of freedom of expression stresses that expression that furthers *self-government* should be absolute. Espoused by Alexander Meiklejohn, this theory of self-government recognizes two forms of expression, private and public.[10] It is the public form that contributes to self-government and therefore must be protected. Private expression, on the other hand, is not within the scope of the First Amendment, and as a result Meiklejohn argues that private expression can be regulated.

Thomas Emerson originated the precept that *expression and action* should be distinguished from each other. Emerson believes the First Amendment should protect and maintain four social values: assuring individual self-fulfillment, attaining the truth, ensuring participation in the decision-making process, and providing a balance between stability and change.[11] To achieve these four social values, expression must be fully protected under the First Amendment.

The sixth major theory, articulated by Franklyn Haiman, recognizes that expression takes place within a *communications context*: expression of any type or category must be judged by the setting within which it takes place.[12] Haiman rejects a categorical approach to free speech. Instead, he suggests that the limits of expression may be determined within four specific contexts:

1. Communication about other people
2. Communication to other people
3. Communication and social order for people to make free and informed choices
4. Government involvement in the communication marketplace

These six theories demonstrate that intellectual freedom is more than merely the ownership of an idea and, more importantly, that it is inherently valuable because ideas advance reason and the ascent of reason contributes to the common good of humankind. It logically follows that to be valuable—in other words, to advance the common good—ideas must be expressed.

Historical Foundations of the First Amendment: From 1215 to 1791

The American Revolution embodied the American colonists' desire for their rights as Englishmen and its success enabled the first great modern democracy. English rights, on the other hand, had been established through at least two major revolutionary events. In 1215, the Magna Carta became the first great document to establish the beginnings of a codification of representative or parliamentary government. King John was forced by his noblemen to sign the Magna Carta because of his capricious decision making and his lack of respect for feudal law. Primarily, he increased taxes without gaining the consent of the barons, contrary to feudal custom, and demanded more military service from them than had been done in the past. John also often suspended the right to trial by jury. The Magna Carta was the first step away from the belief that kings had a divine right to rule and toward rule by the people, though it took centuries for this process to reach fruition.

Although English common law was refined over the next 400 years and the rights of English citizens grew, another revolution occurred in 1688. Under King Charles II, certain rules were designed to favor Catholics, and this angered many Protestants. The king's brother, James II, continued these policies until he was forced to flee England after parliamentary forces secured the reign of William of Orange, a Dutch prince, and his wife, Mary. Mary, being the daughter of James II and a Protestant, was a legitimate heir to the throne and both represented the return of the Reformation and peace to England.

This has become known as the Glorious Revolution for its lack of bloodshed and for establishing parliamentary rule in England to a greater degree than ever before. It also resulted in the Toleration Acts and the Bill of Rights for English citizens. The Toleration Acts addressed the struggle for religious freedom and toleration of different sects that had suffered greatly after the establishment of the Anglican Church by allowing at least all Protestant sects to worship as they believed. The Bill of Rights dealt directly with self-governance.[13]

These historical events were the lessons for the leaders of the American Revolution, which occurred less than 100 years after the Glorious Revolution. The Glorious Revolution also inspired John Locke's *Two Treatises on Civil Government,* and it was Locke's writings that had the most impact on the great minds of the American Revolution, especially Thomas Jefferson and James Madison. Locke's work also is probably the single most important philosophical source for the Bill of Rights to the United States Constitution. His *Letter for Toleration* and *Essay Concerning Human Understanding* also contributed to the philosophical foundations of individual and religious liberty supported by the creators of the U.S. Bill of Rights. Locke argued that government was established through the consent of the people and was not a divine right that stemmed from God.[14]

The events of the American Revolution also bear out the roots of the Bill of Rights. By 1765, the English Parliament had passed the Revenue Act and the Stamp Act, creating a furor in the American colonies over British taxation policies. As a result, the discontent in the colonies grew across all class lines and in each colony. In 1772, for example, Boston citizens drew up "A List of Infringements and Violations of Rights." Each colony had its own charter, which established its form of government and its relationship with the mother country, (1) as a proprietorship where the colony was controlled by a prominent person, often because of favors owed by the king, or (2) as a royal colony safely controlled by the king, or (3) as a corporate colony controlled by a company's stockholders. Several had their own Bill of Rights, and all the colonies considered themselves a government of English citizens with full English rights.[15] What they were experiencing instead was in direct opposition to those rights and indicative of the kind of arbitrary power these documents were intended to control. The Boston "List" recorded the indignities suffered by the Massachusetts colonists including the writs of assistance used to arbitrarily search homes and seize property, the quartering of troops in colonists' homes at the colonists' expense in a time of peace, threats to the principle of trial by a jury of peers as the military held trials of civilians, and a fear of the loss of religious equality as the English government pressed to establish the Anglican church as the state religion.[16]

The Declaration of Independence was the final act of a community of frustrated people who believed they had no other choice in obtaining their rights as individuals and Englishmen. Stephen B. Presser calls the Declaration of Independence "the most important single statement of American political philosophy" and says that it "sets forth the enduring key ideals of American politics: the notions of the equality of individuals before God and the law; the belief in the divinely sanctioned and inalienable human rights; and a preoccupation with the life, liberty, and pursuit of happiness of the individual."[17] The declaration set the new nation on a course, first of war, then of self-government where legitimacy and power arises from the consent of the governed, and finally to the establishment of individual rights.

Though the main text of the United States Constitution lacks a bill of rights, it does enumerate some individual rights such as prohibitions against *ex-post facto* laws and bills of attainder. A full bill of rights was not included primarily because the Constitutional

Convention was formed to rectify the inadequacies of the Articles of Confederation in providing a governmental structure. Furthermore, the convention was long and arduous, and it concluded its business when a basic document was apparent. Rather than continue on even longer over a bill of rights, the delegates closed off debate despite such an attempt by George Mason in the concluding moments, leaving establishment of a bill of rights up to the ratification and amendment process.[18] The citizens of the new states were divided between the Federalists, who wanted a strong government, and the Jeffersonian democratic-republicans, who feared the intrusion of a strong government in individuals' lives. A bill of rights was seen by the Jeffersonians as the insurance against the excesses of a government capable of dictatorial rule, and without the assurance of its creation, so eloquently made in the Federalist Papers, several states would not have ratified the new Constitution.

The First Amendment in U.S. History

The opposition to the new Constitution in 1787 was by no means limited to its lack of a bill of rights. However, it was clear to the Constitution's supporters that this fact could be and was being used to prevent the Constitution's ratification. Accordingly, James Madison introduced into Congress a bill of rights, and twelve articles were approved and sent on to the states for ratification in September 1789. By December 15, 1791, ten amendments were ratified; these ten are now known as our Bill of Rights. The two remaining articles, dealing with rules for Congress, were never approved.[19]

Of the ten amendments that constitute the Bill of Rights, the First comprises the doctrine for intellectual freedom, which consists of the following four freedoms:

1. Freedom of religion. Two clauses constitute the wording of this freedom in the First Amendment. The first clause is called the "establishment" clause and states that "Congress shall make no law respecting an establishment of religion." This means that no religion can be established as the official religion of any government body, including a city, county, state, or the whole

country. The second section is known as the "free exercise" clause, and it prevents government from prohibiting the free exercise of any religion.
2. Freedom of speech.
3. Freedom of the press.
4. The right to assembly. The First Amendment elaborates on this last right by saying "or the right of the people peaceably to assemble, and to petition the Government for a redress of grievances."

These four rights have become codified in U.S. law and society through various events and court cases.

Freedom of Religion

It is not accidental that freedom of religion is listed first in the First Amendment. Some scholars argue that the other rights emanate from this freedom and that without it a free and democratic government cannot stand. Jefferson saw the dangers of a state supported or sanctioned religion and expressed them in his 1787 letter to the Danbury Association of Baptists, in which the first mention of a wall of separation between church and state is made. It is these remarks that frame the modern-day debate on the separation of church and state.

On one side, it is argued that the "wall" was the intent of the framers of the First Amendment and that Jefferson meant this wall to be very high, thus removing all government intrusion into religion.[20] On the other side of the debate stood Judge Joseph Story, a Supreme Court justice and member of the Court during Chief Justice John Marshall's term of office. He argued, in his *Commentary on the Constitution of the United States,* that the founding fathers meant to encourage and support the practice of religion, especially Christianity, and only to prevent rivalry among the sects or the dominance of one sect over others.[21] Furthermore, this argument also makes a case that the phrase "Congress shall make no law" limits the wall to federal, congressional action and does not extend it to state governments.

Regardless of the approach, whether it be a wall of separation between church and state or a system of government that encourages all religions and remains sect-neutral, the Supreme Court has ruled on both the establishment clause and the free exercise clause. For instance, in *Watson v. Jones* 20 L. Ed. 666 (1871), a congregation had divided over a denominational rule that a person who aided the Confederacy in the Civil War or still believed in the institution of slavery could not be a member or minister unless he or she renounced these positions. The Court, in deciding which half of the congregation legally controlled the church property, declared that independent congregations must decide such matters by majority vote and that congregations subordinate to a higher church body must defer to that authority, rather than to the government.

The most important actions by the Court on freedom of religion pertain to either the establishment clause or the free exercise clause, and often both issues are involved in the same case. The most prominent establishment clause cases to be mentioned deal with a religious test for public office, entanglement of church and state, and religion in the public schools. Many of the public school cases, as well as the distribution of religious literature and conscientious objector cases, have elements of both clauses.

The first important case we consider regarding freedom of religion is *Reynolds v. United States.* Though George Reynolds lost his bid to remove his conviction for polygamy, because it was committed under religious motivation since the Mormon Church held polygamy as an important precept, the case was the first to recognize that religious belief was protected by the First Amendment. The Court purposely made a distinction between belief, which is protected, and overt deed, which is not protected by the First Amendment. The establishment clause was tested as well in *Torcaso v. Watkins,* which struck down the use of a religious test for public office. The Court made it clear that the federal and state governments had to remain neutral and that this included being neutral between belief and unbelief. Also, in *Walz v. Tax Commission of the City of New York,* entanglement in church matters was seen as an establishment concern. Taxes on church property brought on more entanglement; therefore, tax exemptions for church property strengthened the separation of church and state.

The cases of religion in public education often involve intertwining establishment and free exercise issues. The most important case to examine is *Everson v. Board of Education.* In this case, three fundamental arguments were made by Justice Hugo Black, writing for the majority of the Court. He enumerated a very clear statement on the wall of separation, listing several prohibitions against establishing a state religion, tax support or aid to one or any religion, or legislation or government action forcing citizens to attend church, among other issues. He then argued that every citizen was entitled to benefit from established welfare legislation and ruled that in this case the law authorizing rebates to parents whose children used public transportation to get to school must be applied to families with children attending religious schools as well. Last, this was the first decision to make the First Amendment applicable to the states under the provisions of the Fourteenth Amendment in such cases.

Other important opinions regarding religion in the public schools deal with both the establishment and the free exercise clauses. Chief among these are the prayer-in-public-schools case, *Engel v. Vitale* in which several parents, including Steven Engel, objected to the use of the New York State's Board of Education's Regent's Prayer in the public schools; the *Bible* readings case, *Abington School District v. Schempp,* in which the Edward Schempp family successfully challenged a Pennsylvania law requiring a passage in the *Bible* to be read in school each day; and the released-time cases, *McCollum v. Board of Education* and *Zorach v. Clauson,* both decisions pertaining to school policies that allowed children in a public school to be released early to attend religion classes.

In each of these, except for *Zorach,* the Court found significant entanglement by the schools that threatened the free exercise of religion by at least some students. In *Zorach,* however, released time was permitted because it was privately financed, totally voluntary, and not conducted on school premises.

In other free exercise litigation, the Jehovah's Witness faith has played a major role. In the early 1940s, two lawsuits over regulations mandating the recitation of the Pledge of Allegiance and the salute to the flag were brought to the Supreme Court by Jehovah's Witness parents. In *Minersville School District v. Gobitis,* the Court supported a local school district in its attempts to promote citizenship. However, three years later, the Court reversed itself when the state of West Virginia attempted to impose the same rule on all school districts in *West Virginia State Board of Education v. Barnette.* Also, several distribution of religious literature cases were brought by the Jehovah's Witnesses, most notably *Cantwell v. Connecticut* and *Murdock v. Pennsylvania.* In each case, ordinances prohibiting the distribution of religious literature were declared unconstitutional.

Freedom of Speech

Despite its position as the second freedom in the Bill of Rights, the exercise of speech has had the most significant impact on the U.S. way of life. All speech can be categorized in a legal sense, as either *protected* or *unprotected* speech, in what Joseph Hemmer calls a "two-tiered approach."[22]

Tier one, unprotected speech, includes certain forms of dissent, such as the advocacy of the immediate overthrow of the government by force or violence, provocative speech or "fighting" words, obscenity, libel, and commercial speech, which primarily consists of advertising. Tier two, protected speech, consists of activities such as news, political expression, certain forms of dissent, any objection that does not advocate the violent overthrow of the government (such as an argument made in a town meeting against a proposed or existing law), and associational expression (such as public assemblies and petitions). These distinctions are by no means either clear-cut or consistent, and many factors have created numerous exceptions. However, generally feasible standards have been established through an extensive body of case law over the past two centuries.

These two tiers materialized as a result of the Supreme Court's attempt to address how society desires to limit speech. In our system of government, the legislative-executive process manifests these desires of the majority by enjoining the activities of individuals and their right to speak freely. The courts, on the other hand, constrain government and other authorities, in a system of checks and balances, and have created the tests for protected and unprotected speech that define these limitations.

There are four essential categories in which free speech may be limited: libel, dissent, obscenity, and commercial speech. To regulate civil relations among individuals, *libel* and *slander* laws have historically controlled speech about or between people since the advent of English common law. Libel is a defamatory statement, attacking a person's qualities of character, that is written down or broadcast. Slander is the same as libel, only spoken and not written down or broadcast.

To maintain loyalty to the nation and its institutions and to ensure civil order, restrictions on *dissenting* speech and symbolic (wordless, or nonverbal) "speech" have been established. Issues of academic freedom are a corollary to dissenting speech. When educational institutions establish regulations contrary to the principles of academic freedom, they do so to impose some control over members of the faculty.

To maintain a concept of morality acceptable to a majority of citizens, regulations on *obscenity* are established. Finally, information disseminated to sell a product is not seen as information needed for self-government. Because self-government is a precious activity and commercialism is not, *commercial* speech is not a protected form of expression.

Libel: Limitations on Individual Civil Relations

Libel is generally a nonprotected form of speech. Libel is a statement that is published or broadcast with the intent of harming another person's reputation or good name. Slander is a spoken form of defamation, but because it is not published or broadcast, it is not permanent and cannot be transmitted to a larger audience as effectively. Therefore, only libel is prosecuted in most cases. However, not all libelous statements can be considered an unprotected form of speech.

There are three mitigating distinctions in determining whether or not a statement that harms another person is protected. In libel case law, the first major distinction involves intent. Intentional defamation, or harm, must be demonstrated. A falsehood can be the primary means of harming someone, and intentionally using a false statement to damage another person's standing or reputation is libelous. However, the truth of a statement is not necessarily a defense for libel, either. Some states permit proving the truth of a statement as a complete defense, but others require that a nonmalicious motive must also be shown to use truth as a defense.[23]

The next distinction differentiates between a private citizen and a public person. The Supreme Court has ruled in several cases that a public figure, such as a television or radio personality or an elected official, does not enjoy the same libel protection as a private citizen. For such public persons, the *New York Times v. Sullivan* doctrine of actual malice requires public officials to show that a potentially libelous statement was made with "reckless disregard" for the truth. This doctrine also applies to private persons who become involved in an event of public interest, such as a spokesperson for a local group lobbying for a cause. In another important case, a public official had to show more than a reasonable belief that he was defamed to win a case of libel (*Garrison v.*

Louisiana). Speech important to a "robust debate," or those discussions needed by citizens to understand all sides of a controversial issue, is also protected (*Greenbelt Publishing Association v. Bresler*).

The final distinction to understand concerning libel cases is that a class of individuals, not just one person, can be libeled. The *Beauharnais v. Illinois* case is the first and most important ruling recognizing that a whole class of individuals can be defamed. In *Neiman-Marcus Company v. Lait,* the Supreme Court also recognized that corporations can be defamed.

Dissent: Limitations on Speech Challenging Authority

Dissent also can be either protected or unprotected speech. The distinction is made only under certain conditions and for certain forms of dissent. Dissenting speech is one of the most complicated issues of the freedom of speech. Dissenting opinion, and its expression, is a mark of democratic societies. Because dissent can pose a challenge to the existing order, it has often been viewed as a threat to entrenched regimes. Authoritarian states suppress dissent to perpetuate their power. Democratic societies tolerate dissent because it is a change agent that can promote the general welfare and because democracy recognizes that diversity needs to be protected in order to guard against shifting political winds. For example, in nondemocratic nations, especially in historical times, as a popular political viewpoint or action lost favor with the majority, or more often ceased to be supported because of a military coup or other power struggle, those who held that viewpoint when it was acceptable found themselves persecuted, jailed, or even executed. Dissent most often takes form in either the spoken word, symbolic speech, or the written word. Controlling dissent in educational institutions often threatens academic freedom, as well. Limitations of dissent are allowed if they are necessary to maintain peace, order, and protection for the form of government.

Over the years, the Supreme Court has produced six major tests for distinguishing between protected and unprotected dissenting speech. Some of these tests have waxed and waned as the makeup of the Court has changed, whereas others have remained steadfast.

The most significant test for protected dissent is the "clear and present danger" doctrine. This appeared as a Court opinion first in the case *Schenck v. United States.*[24] A "clear and present danger" exists if the words are capable of bringing out an immediate "substantial evil" the government wishes to prevent. Numerous dissenting speech cases have validated or clarified this monumental test over the years, but two other very important cases should also be examined carefully to understand this concept. In *Bridges v. California,* the Court held that to allow limitation of dissenting speech the circumstances must involve a substantive evil and the result that is expected must be very serious. The danger must also be very imminent. By 1951, the Court found the need to clarify "clear and present danger" again in *Dennis v. United States.* In this case, the Court stated that the "gravity of the evil" can be used to assess a clear and present danger that may not meet the element of an imminent danger.

In the 1920s, the Court promulgated the "bad tendency" test in *Gitlow v. New York.* Under this less stringent test, speech can be limited if it has a tendency to lead to a substantial evil. This standing was finally reversed in *Bridges v. California.*

Also in the *Dennis* case, a distinction is made between "advocacy of ideas," which is protected, and "advocacy of action," which is not. Though Eugene Dennis was convicted for advocacy of the overthrow of the U.S. government, the Court in later cases, particularly *Yates v. United States,* sanctioned the assertion of ideas but found calls for acts of sedition to be a threat to order and authority in the new test known as "advocacy of action."

The "balancing" test and the "preferred position" test are two more recent, competing doctrines. In the balancing test, non-speech rights, such as those covered by other amendments in the Bill of Rights (for example, the right to a speedy trial) and speech rights are weighed in cases where they conflict with each other and then balanced to see which of the rights has priority. However, Justice William O. Douglas created the preferred position doctrine, in *Murdock v. Pennsylvania,* which is similar to the balancing test in that it weighs competing rights, but in this test the argument is tipped in favor of the First Amendment. The rights provided in the First Amendment are considered the preferred position to the state's power, although circumstances may require a choice favoring the government in some cases.[25]

Justices Douglas and Black also figure prominently in the final test to be considered. Known as the "absolutist" principle, it has never been supported by a majority of the Court. Black describes it as providing no restrictions on expression whatsoever. Black believed that "the men who drafted our Bill of Rights did all the 'balancing' " that was necessary.[26]

The clear and present danger test has remained a staple of free speech decisions throughout the Court's recent history, and every indication is that it will continue to be important. The other tests may figure prominently in the rhetoric of some justices at any given time, with the possible exception of the bad tendency test, depending on the particulars of the case and the philosophical inclination of the justice rendering the opinion.

Beyond the general tests governing dissent in a speech activity, the Court has also addressed the regulation of specific types of speech or words often heard in dissent. These words are classified most often into fighting words, provocative words, threatening words, and offensive words.

In *Chaplinsky v. New Hampshire*, the Court declared that fighting words do not enjoy protection under the First Amendment. Fighting words, or "such words, as ordinary men know, are likely to cause a fight," are seen as a threat to order; therefore, the state may regulate or prohibit them.[27]

Provocative words are more problematic. The Court ruled in *Terminiello v. Chicago* that when a crowd contributes substantially to the disorder, then the provocative words are only a mitigating circumstance and the speaker cannot be denied his or her right to speak. However, in *Feiner v. New York*, when the speaker was viewed as contributing substantially to the disorder by his provocative words, it was decided that these words were not protected by the First Amendment. The circumstances behind who creates the disorder, then, determine whether or not provocative words are protected.

The Court has also considered threatening words to be beyond the scope of protection under certain circumstances. In *Watts v. United States*, remarks about killing President Lyndon Johnson were seen to be within a context of political hyperbole, so Watts was not held in violation of the speech limitations regarding threatening words. However, in *Kelner v. United States*, the threatening words were seen as unprotected because Russell Kelner's stated intent to harm Yasir Arafat was genuine. The Court considers threatening words to be unprotected if there is an intent to harm but not if the statements are "political hyperbole."

Last, in the seminal case *Cohen v. California*, offensive words, such as vulgarity, used within a dissenting speech context are considered to be under the protection of the First Amendment. Paul Cohen had worn a jacket with the words "Fuck the Draft" on the back into the Los Angeles County Courthouse. The Court made it clear in this case that offensive words such as these can be protected as long as they do not fall into any unprotected class, such as fighting words, and are not intended to appeal to prurient interest.

The effect of these rulings is that in free speech cases the courts rely on these various tests in determining whether a particular form of speech can be considered constitutionally protected. Speech that presents a "clear and present danger" and speech that "advocates action" are not protected, but speech that "advocates ideas" is protected. Furthermore, certain classes of words, at least under some situations, are not protected. "Fighting words" do not enjoy any protection under the First Amendment, nor do "threatening words" unless they are expressed within the context of political hyperbole.

Dissent without Words: Symbolic Speech

One of the most controversial debates on freedom of speech regards dissent that is not pure speech. Symbolic speech is the representation of ideas in a form other than spoken or written words. On one hand, symbolic speech is a form of expression that can effectively convey an idea more graphically than words alone. On the other hand, some scholars and jurists argue that the founding fathers only intended to protect pure speech with the First Amendment.[28] In recent years, the Supreme Court has been faced with cases in which freedom of symbolic speech is pitted against acts that threaten or destroy the symbols of our democracy or acts that defy the authority of the government to maintain our system of governance. These cases have principally fallen into draft card–burning cases or flag-burning cases.

The most famous flag-burning case, *Street v. New York,* declared that the act of flag burning is an expression of ideas. This decision has been upheld over the years, most recently in *Texas v. Johnson,* but a significant minority opinion has consistently argued that the act of flag burning is a property crime as well as the destruction of a treasured national symbol.[29] In the most significant draft card–burning case, *United States v. O'Brien,* the Court upheld the Selective Service regulations against destruction of draft cards. The Court has uniformly ruled that possession of the draft card is a responsibility for male citizens.

Dissent in Schools and Colleges: Academic Freedom

The American Association of University Professors defines academic freedom as "freedom of inquiry and research; freedom of teaching within the university or college; and freedom of extra-mural utterance and action."[30] The rights of faculty need protection to ensure integrity in instruction and to prevent the danger of a state-controlled "truth" being taught within the classroom. However, academic freedom also involves the right to dissent and to question educational authorities, whether in a public school or a college. Academic freedom is the foundation of our democratic educational institutions and is essential to true scholarship and intellectual discovery.

The free speech rights of teachers and students generally enjoy protection under the First Amendment. In *Slochower v. Board of Higher Education*, for example, the Court required at least an initial investigatory hearing for dismissal proceedings against faculty. Such a hearing must be held to have an official record of the facts and give the employee a chance to defend him- or herself. Harry Slochower was dismissed after the college where he taught learned he had refused to testify at a U.S. Senate committee hearing.

Several cases, most notably *Sweezy v. New Hampshire, Givhan v. Westernline Consolidated School District*, and *Mt. Healthy City School District v. Doyle*, have built a fundamental right of faculty to exercise their freedom of speech in expressing their opinions as citizens and as faculty, as well as their right to hold unpopular views.

However, school administrators can set some limitations on certain speech activities in the schools. The Supreme Court allows schools to set guidelines for speakers on campus and for acquiring and removing books from the library. The cases *Board of Education, Island Trees Union Free School District v. Pico* and *Hazelwood School District v. Kuhlmeier* are the two most important cases enumerating administration rights in establishing guidelines for the school library and for the student newspaper, respectively.

Without a doubt, the two most important student rights cases are *Tinker v. Des Moines Independent Community School District* and *Hazelwood School District v. Kuhlmeier*. The *Tinker* case is the first major decision recognizing that students enjoy civil liberties as do adults. However, the more recent *Hazelwood* case has apparently reversed the *Tinker* decision in its ruling that school authorities can censor the school newspaper because of the newspaper's place in the instructional program. Other important cases to study about student rights include *Healy v. James,* concerning a student's right to association, and the *Pico* school library book censorship case, which includes a strong argument for student rights.

Obscenity

Obscenity is ordinarily considered a nonprotected form of speech. The welfare of a nation is provided for by government in a number of ways, including crime prevention, health regulations, protection for physically and mentally abused adults and children, and many similar measures. Morality is also seen as necessary for the welfare of society by a significant portion of the populace. What constitutes morality, however, differs from individual to individual. The primary method of limiting obscenity comes through the prosecution of obscene materials under the tests and the guidelines of the Supreme Court.

The three most significant tests for obscenity are historically sequential. The first, and earliest, is the *Hicklin* rule. Arising out of an English court case, *Regina v. Hicklin,* this very strict interpretation permits courts to declare a whole work obscene even if only one passage is ruled obscene. This measure was finally reversed in *Roth v. United States* in 1957. Under *Roth,* a very liberal period of obscenity prosecutions held sway. *Roth* requires that a work be judged as a whole and use a national standard, or in other words, that the moral standards of the citizens of the U.S. be used to gauge how or if the work is offensive.

The current test, from *Miller v. California* (1973), is a more conservative standard, although the work must still be judged as a whole. With *Miller,* the more liberal view, which determines obscenity by whether a work is "utterly without social redeeming value," was replaced by a test for "serious literary, artistic, political or scientific value." Furthermore, the national standard of morality under *Roth* was dropped in favor of a local or state standard.

Other, more specific governing variables help determine whether a potentially obscene work is protected. The most important of these are prior restraint, pandering, guidelines concerning youth, and privacy. *Prior restraint,* if activated, prohibits the publication or showing of an allegedly obscene work before there has been a hearing to determine whether the material is obscene. The existence of prior restraint normally reverses any obscenity conviction, though it does not necessarily protect a work from further obscenity prosecutions. Prior restraint is also an important freedom of the press issue.

Pandering is the intentional use of an erotic appeal to sell allegedly obscene materials and is not constitutionally protected.

Youth have always been considered to be vulnerable to the ill effects of obscenity, so *guidelines for youth* have a long history. As the Supreme Court's decisions unfolded, certain standards became clear. An adult cannot be convicted of selling a work that appeals to adults simply because children might be exposed to the material. However, in *Ginsberg v. New York,* the Court ruled that it is illegal to sell an obscene work to a youth. In the wake of the national uproar over child pornography, several pieces of federal legislation were attempted and enacted in the 1980s, such as the Child Protection and Obscenity Enforcement Act of 1988.

The Supreme Court has also ruled that the production and sale of child pornography is prohibited (*New York v. Ferber*) and that the possession of child pornography, even in the privacy of one's own home, is illegal (*Ohio v. Osborne*). Notwithstanding the *Osborne* decision, private possession of obscene materials other than child pornography is protected as long as it is within the confines of one's own home (*Stanley v. Georgia*).

Commercial Speech: Limitations on Private Speech

Commercial speech can be a form of unprotected expression similar to libel, dissent, and obscenity. Corporations and individuals can advertise, but a free speech defense of advertising against regulations or prohibitions of content and format has much less validity than in other free speech arguments. The first great test of commercial speech remains *Valentine v. Chrestensen,* which permits limits to such commercial speech as advertising and gives greater protection to noncommercial speech such as debates and political discussions. Several subsequent cases have given more First Amendment protection to commercial speech, however. The main concern regarding commercial speech is deceptive advertising. Though the maxim of caveat emptor is a standard business justification for advertising claims, the Supreme Court has consistently ruled against clearly deceptive advertising practices.

Freedom of the Press

Freedom of the press, the third freedom of the First Amendment, is inextricably linked to freedom of speech. Virtually all of the four allowable limitations of speech—those regarding libel, dissent, obscenity, and commercial speech—are also limitations of the press. However, there are differences.

A printed work has much greater impact than the spoken word because it has the potential to reach and influence a much larger audience. Second, there are many aspects of producing the press's output that affect the expression of ideas and truths that, if regulated or prohibited, can place the act of expression in danger even though the regulations do not necessarily address the published remarks directly, primarily the method of gathering news, especially by informant sources. Third, with the advent of new forms of media, such as radio, television, and computer networks, many issues have arisen concerning the format of expression as well as the actual content.

In the United States, the original means for controlling the press was through libel suits. The first notable example is that of John Peter Zenger in 1743, an editor of a New York colonial newspaper that often published articles critical of the colonial governor. Zenger successfully argued that publishing the truth should be a defense and thus defied the conventional wisdom and ended colonial intrusion into freedom of the press.[31]

To clarify any confusion between publication of speech and publication by the press, the issue of the press must be understood in terms of the dissemination of news. Book and magazine publishers produce works of fiction and nonfiction that can be subject to challenges of the ideas and language they use and convey. They also publish news and newsworthy items. News is normally considered a protected form of speech. The emphasis here is more on the act of publishing rather than on the content of the work; however, these lines can be intertwined and blurred. A content approach is more properly a freedom of speech issue. Broadcasting issues in radio and television are a different media format for both speech activities and the dissemination of news. There are different issues regarding producing broadcasts versus publishing the news that also must be addressed.

The publication of news has been considered a fundamental right of the press. In the many cases applicable to this issue, a number of guidelines have arisen from the Supreme Court's rulings. The most important of these is the concept of prior restraint. This is the same axiom for free speech matters; however, prior restraint has been the major method for controlling the press in the past. The landmark case *Near v. Minnesota* established the unconstitutionality of prior restraint, which is a ban on publishing a work before the work is actually created and distributed.

J.M. Near had written highly critical articles against the police and was denied the right to publish these articles by a 1925 Minnesota law.[32]

A similar type of guideline has been the subject of recent cases regarding the publication of books about the Central Intelligence Agency (CIA), which involve the federal government's pre-publication review regulations. Under these government rules, CIA agents, among other individuals, must submit any publication, written either while they are serving as agents or after they leave the employ of the agency, for review before it can be published. The government can constitutionally delete those parts of the text considered classified information or too sensitive (*Snepp v. United States*).

Politics has always been a contentious point for the press. Objectivity is usually expected of the news, but a political viewpoint is inherently biased because it generally takes a stand on at least one issue. It is also expected that the news will keep the public informed and provide the widest access to all viewpoints, issues, and information. The guidelines for information with a political theme, then, have traditionally emphasized access to all points of view and fair, balanced coverage of the issues, candidates, and opinions. In the case *Mills v. Alabama*, an example of the attempt to control the press concerning political news, the Supreme Court struck down regulations banning election eve editorials.

In addition to guidelines on the publication of news, a more grave set of rulings has governed the gathering of news. These cases have had widespread implications for the free flow of information. An examination of the body of case law governing news gathering seems to indicate that the Court does not place a high degree of value on the privileges of news reporters.[33]

The most prominent news reporter decision, *Branzburg v. Hayes*, has left the issue of reporter's privileges in serious doubt. The majority of the Court generally denies journalists the right to refuse to reveal sources of information to an official investigatory body, but deep divisions amongst the jurists' opinions have led to a few other courts upholding such privileges over the years. Several states have also attempted to address this difficulty by passing shield laws protecting reporters and their sources, but all shield law cases before the Supreme Court have ended in a denial of such privileges for the correspondents involved.

Similarly, reporters are prohibited from interviewing prison inmates or gathering information directly from them. The

Supreme Court has held that the government has a legitimate interest in deterring crime with such prison regulations and also that reporters have full access to information available to the general public, which is seen as sufficient to protect freedom of the press. Only in executive privilege cases has the Supreme Court ruled consistently for news gathering. Several cases have arisen out of the Watergate affair because President Richard Nixon claimed he could withhold information as the Chief Executive of the United States, holding these materials were vital to his leadership of the nation. The Court has consistently struck down these claims and opened up this information to news agencies.

Newspapers have been supplanted as the sole source of news by the broadcasting industry. This information medium is rapidly becoming the news delivery system of choice, and it carries far greater impact on society. However, unlike newspapers, which are only read by those who wish to receive them, radio and television utilize the airwaves that anyone can access and any person can receive unknowingly. Accordingly, the Federal Communications Act of 1934 created both the codes governing use of the airwaves and the Federal Communications Commission (FCC) to enforce the statute. Enforcement is carried out primarily through the licensing process.[34]

The Federal Communications Act established five primary rules that govern the airwaves: the equal-time rule, the candidate-access rule, the fairness doctrine, the personal-attack rule, and the limited-access doctrine. All pertain to the conduct of public affairs on the air.

The *equal-time rule* requires all broadcasters to provide equal time to all qualified candidates in an election if at least one candidate is given any time for a broadcast. The rule has two primary caveats. First, no station is required to seek out candidates but simply must provide time if requested. Second, any station can deny broadcast time to a candidate by denying all such candidates the use of station facilities.

The *candidate-access rule* gives the FCC the power to revoke a station's license if the station fails to give a reasonable amount of time to a legally qualified candidate. This rule is sustained by a case brought to the Court by President Jimmy Carter (see *Columbia Broadcasting System v. FCC*).[35]

The *fairness doctrine* grew out of three FCC hearing decisions on charges of bias in programming. By 1949, the FCC had created this doctrine to provide objective coverage of public issues. The fairness doctrine requires that broadcasters provide a reasonable percentage of broadcast time to public issues and that during these broadcasts opposing views must be presented. The difference between the fairness doctrine and the equal-time rule is that the latter pertains to political candidates in an election, whereas the former governs any public issue of importance other than candidate views and political campaigns (see *Brandywine-MainLine Radio v. FCC*).[36]

With the landmark case *Red Lion Broadcasting Company v. FCC*, the Supreme Court also supported the *personal-attack rule*. This FCC regulation requires broadcasters to give individuals a chance to reply to any on-air personal attack by another individual or group. This rule applies to anyone, not just political candidates as does the equal-time rule.

The *limited-access doctrine* is a corollary of the fairness doctrine and permits stations to deny access to all petitioners, whether they request paid time or free access, as long as the requirements of the fairness doctrine are met.

In addition, the Federal Communications Commission has been faced with several issues concerning programming formats and content. Though the commission does not regulate programming directly, many of these issues play major roles in the decision to renew a station's license. Programming-format matters range from providing productions of interest to local audiences to the type of programming or a change in format. In one of the most famous broadcasting cases, *FCC v. Pacifica Foundation*, better known as the "filthy words" case, the FCC was accorded the right to either deny a license or set program limitations when concerns about obscenity are brought against a station. The effect of these guidelines is to regulate broadcasting far more heavily than print media.[37]

The Right to Assembly

The fourth freedom of the First Amendment is the right to assembly and association. As written, this right includes assembly and the right to petition for a "redress of grievances." The First Amendment does not actually mention association. This right has come about through interpretations by the Supreme Court, especially in the landmark case *National Association for the Advancement of Colored People (NAACP) v. Alabama*. However, each of these elements is important to intellectual freedom.

Freedom of speech guarantees an individual the right to express ideas. The freedom of the press guarantees an individual the right to disseminate ideas. The right to assembly and association is a guarantee that ideas can be shared with other individuals, not only with those who hold common beliefs but also with those who do not hold similar views in an attempt to influence and educate them. The right to petition is a fundamental process for making government responsive and effective.

There are several Supreme Court trends in the protection of the right to assembly. The Court has clearly recognized this right, and authorities must follow certain requirements when granting requests by groups who wish to assemble in public places. One of the earliest and most crucial cases, *Hague v. Congress of Industrial Organizations,* addresses the practice of arbitrary ordinances concerning assemblies and the discriminatory application of such ordinances to unpopular groups. However, other cases, most notably *Cox v. Louisiana,* permit governmental bodies to set regulations regarding the use of public facilities to maintain peace, order, and the welfare of all citizens, although they may not ban any activity outright.

More importantly, the right to association has been recognized by a series of cases, the first being the *NAACP* case mentioned above, that protect the integrity and safety of the association. Any requirement forcing associations to reveal their membership lists is patently unconstitutional. Furthermore, associations have been granted the right to recruit new members (see *Thomas v. Collins*) and to raise funds.

Sometimes groups or associations can be quite volatile, especially in their interactions with others. Overt acts for various purposes such as soliciting members, protests, and even fund-raising often pose threats, real and imagined, to public order. Under the concept of the right to petition, such activities as picketing, boycotts, and demonstrations have been used to bring about change, as well as the more usual practice of gathering signatures on petitions. The Supreme Court has also provided guidelines for these activities. The right to picket was granted in the case *Thornhill v. Alabama.* However, several other decisions by the Court have drastically limited this right. The most crucial limitations are regulations that govern time-place-manner for picketing (see *Hughes v. Superior Court of California*).[38]

The NAACP also figures prominently in a case on economic boycotts. The Supreme Court upheld such practices when the businesses of a Mississippi community brought suit against the NAACP for losses incurred during a civil rights boycott.

Demonstrations have also been subject to a two-tiered set of guidelines. On one hand, demonstrations cannot be restricted on the basis of content, as in the case *Police Department of Chicago v. Mosley.* On the other hand, restrictions can be set regarding excessive noise near certain institutions such as schools, and private property can enjoy more protection than public property.[39]

Intellectual Freedom and Censorship

Censorship is the act of examining material to suppress or delete any part of that material considered objectionable. When individuals fully exercise their rights, an inevitable conflict arises. The line where one individual's rights end and another's rights begin becomes blurred. Open expression challenges convention and the ideas held dear by others. Additionally, some expressions are seen as threatening to the public welfare and order. Censorship of speeches, books and other printed works, art, and media, especially films, often becomes the by-product of this conflict.

Many intellectual freedom cases resulted from a form of censorship that tended to spring from official, governmental action. However, censorship can come from almost any source. Librarians and school curriculum specialists may fear the consequences of purchasing a particular book and therefore may commit an act of self-censorship by not purchasing it or by placing it on a restricted shelf, which the British call the "poison shelf."[40] A parent or other library patron may file a complaint with the school or library. A special interest group may lobby the town council or state government to ban certain types of books or to establish laws aimed at individuals with unpopular political views. A crowd may object to a speaker at an indoor or outdoor rally or demonstration. All of these instances represent the attempt by an individual or a group to restrict or eliminate the expressed ideas of another individual or group.

The consequences of these acts vary. At times, such acts may be justified, at least in the view of a majority of individuals or the legal system, given the circumstances and time period. Sometimes no serious consequences at all occur and an issue disappears due to a lack of merit or interest. Still other situations reach various levels of authoritative action, from a decision by a library or school committee on up to the Supreme Court.

It is important to recognize that acts of censorship are commonplace. Those that have reached some prominence, such as the cases included in this book, are not isolated instances but represent the episodes in U.S. history that have been the most troubling or have been used as a vehicle for social change by the government, the courts, or social forces.

In 1930, for example, Mary Dennett set out to give her two junior-high-age sons a lesson in sex education. After consulting over 60 sources unsatisfactorily, she wrote her own lesson and then had it published as a pamphlet, "The Sex Side of Life." Its distribution was limited to interested parents and a few social agencies. However, Dennett was charged with sending obscenities through the mail and fined $300. The conviction was reversed by a federal appeals court, which found the pamphlet to be useful instructional material.[41] Throughout much of U.S. history, such incidents have occurred over matters of sex and erotica, unpopular political opinion, and religious beliefs considered heretical. Prior to 1900, books, visual art, and public performances were the most challenged formats. With the advent of film as a medium, challenges expanded into this art form for much the same reasons, especially over obscenity.

One of the earliest challenges grew out of the publication of John Cleland's *Memoirs of a Woman of Pleasure,* one of the most famous erotic novels in all history. The novel was published in the United States for the first time in 1821 and promptly banned. Various publishers, both underground and legitimate, have attempted its publication since, until the work was finally declared acceptable under the *Roth* standard in 1966. Literary works of every type, both acclaimed and with little value, have been subject to attack throughout history. In 1885, Mark Twain's *The Adventures of Huckleberry Finn* was banned in Concord, Massachusetts, because of "objectional language."[42] Though tame by today's standards, what was seen as sordid tales of drunkenness and frank language of everyday events such as "I say orgies, not because it's the common term, because it ain't—obsequies bein' the common term—but because orgies is right term" about a funeral event, shocked many in society of the day.

Many of the more important historical incidents of censorship in the United States have focused on literary classics or highly acclaimed work. Anthony Comstock attempted to declare both Henry Fielding's *Tom Jones* and Jean-Jacques Rousseau's *Confessions* obscene.[43] During the 1920s, attempts at publishing and distributing the unexpurgated edition of D. H. Lawrence's *Lady Chatterley's Lover* failed, and the complete edition was not successfully published until 1966. Charles Darwin's *Origin of the Species* was the center of the Scopes trial controversy in 1927. One of the few successful entries into the country of this genre of censored works was James Joyce's *Ulysses*. Prosecutions for its publication in the United States began in 1919, but in 1933 Random House challenged the Tariff Act provisions prohibiting the book's importation. A federal appeals court ruled that the book was not obscene, establishing the *Ulysses* standard in the opinion.

Not all censored works in this time period could be characterized as valuable or classical literature. Pornographic novels had become the staple of many Victorian era writers and readers, and several attempts to publish and import them into the United States were undertaken. The alternative press publisher Jack Kahane, operating the Obelisk Press, was responsible for distributing many of these works. He published such noted sex novels as Frank Harris's *My Life and Loves*, the autobiography of a Victorian era libertine, and Sheila Cousins's *To Beg I Am Ashamed*, about her life as a prostitute. Kahane's son, Maurice Girodias, carried on his legacy as the publisher of the Olympia Press, which produced such pornographic pulp novels as Terry Southern's *Candy* and Pauline Reage's *The Story of O*.[44]

Nor has U.S. literature been spared the censor's knife. Of the many works experiencing difficulties, Henry Miller's novels *Tropic of Cancer* and *Tropic of Capricorn* have had the longest struggle. These two works were written overseas, and attempts to import them into the United States began in 1934. Steamy by the era's standard, the books were not free from customs seizures and outright bans until the Grove Press published them in 1961. In 1882, Massachusetts banned Walt Whitman's *Leaves of Grass* for its frank language,[45] particularly passages referring to a homosexual relationship, such as "and it seems to me if I could know those men better, I should become attached to them, as I do to men in my own lands, It seems to me they are as wise, beautiful, benevolent, as any in my own lands; O' I know we should be brethren and lovers, I know I should be happy with them." Theodore Dreiser's works, including *Sister Carrie, The Genius,* and *An American Tragedy,* have constantly been attacked for their portrayal of seedy lifestyles. Other critically acclaimed U.S. authors who experienced censorship attacks in the first half of the twentieth century included Sinclair Lewis for *Elmer Gantry,* Ernest Hemingway for *The Sun Also Rises,* and John Steinbeck for *The Grapes of Wrath.* [46]

Periodicals have also been the subject of suppression. Anthony Comstock, the most noted nineteenth-century anti-obscenity crusader, made numerous attempts to censor the *Woodhull and Claflin Weekly,* a journal of women's rights. During World War I, *The Masses,* a socialist monthly magazine, was closed under the Espionage Act of 1917. However, the magazine that has come to epitomize soft-core pornography, Hugh Hefner's *Playboy,* is one of the most censored periodicals because it features nude models and was the first widely popular men's magazine to do so. It has been the object of numerous anti-pornography campaigns. In one such case, the Playboy Corporation sued Attorney General Edwin Meese for circulating a blacklist of "soft-core pornography," including *Playboy,* to retail outlets.[47]

Motion pictures are another major media format that has come under assault regarding obscenity and political content. D. W. Griffith's monumental film *Birth of a Nation* has the distinction of being considered the most censored film because it has the most recorded incidents (over twenty) of censorship.[48] Its favorable treatment of the Ku Klux Klan has angered many communities. Several films shown in the early 1950s, however, contributed greatly to bringing about broader protection of the film as an art form. In 1952, the Supreme Court ruled that *The Miracle* by Roberto Rossellini was not obscene and declared film to be a form of expression that would be treated, constitutionally, in the same manner as books.[49]

After the 1957 *Roth v. United States* decision, a period of liberalization occurred whereby a broader range of obscene materials were produced and distributed. In one major event, pornographic film producers distributed *Deep Throat* in 1972 and benefitted from a brief period of wider acceptance of pornography known as "art porn." *Deep Throat* was eventually declared obscene but not before it achieved national prominence and spawned two other major art porn films, *Behind the Green Door* and *The Devil in Miss Jones.* [50] By the 1973 release of the later two films, the new *Miller v. California* standard placed greater restrictions on obscenity. This standard was first tested with the Mike Nichols film *Carnal Knowledge,* but the Supreme Court found that mere coverage of sex in a film did not necessarily make the film offensive.

Some more recent films have come under scrutiny for their political or religious content, rather than for obscenity. Frederick Wiseman's *Titicut Follies* is a documentary on a mental institution in Massachusetts. Its stark footage embarrassed state officials, and the film's distribution is now limited to a well-defined list of professionals.[51] The British film *Monty Python's Life of Bryan* and the more recent film *The Last Temptation of Christ* have been picketed by religious groups at showings around the nation because these groups consider the films blasphemous and degrading to their beliefs.

We have discussed classic literature and pornography as the subjects of censorship attacks, but L. B. Woods has shown in his 1979 book *A Decade of Censorship in America* that censorship is a common occurrence against all forms of literature available to most students and the general public in school and public libraries.[52] His study shows, at least for the 1960s and 1970s, that the five most censored books are J. D. Salinger's *Catcher in the Rye*, Eldridge Cleaver's *Soul on Ice*, Claude Brown's *Manchild in the Promised Land*, the anonymously written *Go Ask Alice*, and Joseph Heller's *Catch-22*.[53] Magazines on the censorship list with at least three challenges or complaints as compiled for this study included *Time, Newsweek, Playboy, Scholastic Scope* (a version of *Junior Scholastic* for the developing reader) and *Evergreen Review* (a left-wing political journal).

Woods found that the most censored film was *The Lottery*, an adaptation of the short story by Shirley Jackson about a town that kept a tradition of stoning to death a member of the community picked by a yearly lottery. Other films included on the list were *Birth of a Nation, Deep Throat*, and *Pink Flamingo*. The most censored children's books were *Inner City Mother Goose, Sylvester and the Magic Pebble*, and *Little Black Sambo*.[54]

Woods's research also indicates that the sources of censorship attempts from within educational institutions are most often administrators and trustees. Students, teachers, and librarians also raise challenges but much less frequently. Of the individuals outside educational institutions, parents and other citizens are by far the most significant sources of censorship, followed by governmental entities. The findings also list such organizations as the John Birch Society, Parent-Teacher Association (PTA), American Legion, National Association for the Advancement of Colored People (NAACP), and Citizens for Decent Literature as the greatest sources of attacks by groups.[55]

Current Issues in Intellectual Freedom

The current climate for intellectual freedom has been influenced by the conduct of public affairs during the Reagan and Bush administrations. Though book censorship continues to plague many local institutions, on a more visible level the censorship of art and music has taken center stage. This has arisen, primarily, because of political lobbying by noted, conservative representatives and senators, especially Senator Jesse Helms, Republican of North Carolina, and representatives Dana Rohrbacher and Robert Dornan, both Republicans from California.

The greatest, most sustained controversy has revolved around funding for the National Endowment for the Arts. Virulent objections have been voiced over grants for artistic works with graphic sexual content and sacrilegious overtones, especially one work by Robert Mapplethorpe depicting a crucifix submerged in a jar of urine. This controversy has spawned the unsuccessful prosecution of a Cincinnati art museum director for exhibiting obscenity with the display of Mapplethorpe works. In addition, massive protests have been mounted by the art world to reject allocated funds, and John Frohnmayer, executive director of the National Endowment for the Arts, resigned during the 1992 presidential campaign after numerous conservative groups and political figures openly criticized him and his support for what was seen as offensive art.

The most serious issue at the heart of this controversy concerns the logic of federal funding for specific programs, otherwise known as sponsorship. Similar to those who argue against federal funding of abortion clinics for the indigent on the grounds that the government should not be in the position of promoting abortion, opponents of art funding object to such federal grants on the grounds that these grants will promote obscenity. This argument was also used as the prime reasoning of Chief Justice William Rehnquist to uphold the gag rule for federally funded abortion clinics in the *Rust v. Sullivan* case. The gag rule reverses the thoroughly grounded concept of "absolute privilege" for medical professionals which recognizes the special relationship a doctor has with his or her patient and grants immunity from libel prosecution. The Rehnquist Court promotes the argument that the federal government can choose to sponsor or reject sponsorship of any service or benefit based on the ideological will of

Congress. Current predictions about the extension of this logic to other areas of intellectual freedom are a mixed bag of pessimism and a "wait-and-see" reaction, though Rehnquist did allude to academia as a possible protected institution.

An examination of the more well-known cases that came before the Supreme Court during the late 1980s and early 1990s also points to a fuzzy picture of the future. On a positive note, flag burning as symbolic speech was protected by the Court again in *Texas v. Johnson.* This decision carries little predictive value, however, because a conservative justice has replaced a liberal justice since this 5–4 split decision was rendered.

In other notable cases, there are more clear signs that the Court, at least, has begun to validate a very conservative, philosophical trend. As a result of *Hazelwood School District v. Kuhlmeier,* a major reversal of the student rights case *Tinker v. Des Moines Independent School District,* school authorities are now permitted to censor student newspapers because of the instructional role these papers are designed to play. The Court also reversed another landmark decision in *Ohio v. Osborne.* In the mounting national campaign, both in the legislative and judicial branches, against child pornography, the protection of the privilege of the privacy of one's home provided for in *Stanley v. Georgia* has been struck down, at least regarding the possession of child pornography.

As Nadine Strossen states, "Eschewing the Supreme Court's established role as the guarantor of individual liberties—including the paramount liberty of free expression—the Rehnquist Court increasingly has deferred to judgements of majoritarian governmental branches in support of speech-limiting measures."[56] Other rhetoric of Chief Justice Rehnquist supports authoritarian control of individual rights along conservative, ideological grounds. Arguments about obscenity, school administrative rights, and symbolic speech have leaned heavily on right-wing ideals in Rehnquist's utterings and written opinions. Justice Rehnquist also openly supports a concept of religious freedom that rejects a high wall of separation between church and state, preferring to argue that original intent means that the founding fathers promoted a Christian but sect-neutral state. There is reason for alarm about the protection for First Amendment rights. Not only is Chief Justice Rehnquist an influential voice among the justices, but also the Court now has a substantial conservative majority appointed by two conservative presidents.

The potential difficulties in the Supreme Court during the 1990s and into the year 2000 will require free speech advocates to be more politically astute to effect change at the legislative and executive levels. The future of intellectual freedom relies upon the shifting winds of judicial and political opinion, but such freedom seems in grave doubt for the foreseeable future.

Notes

1. Robert B. Downs and Ralph E. McCoy, eds. *The First Freedom Today*. Chicago: American Library Association, 1984, p. xiii.

2. Nat Hentoff. *The First Freedom*. New York: Delacorte Press, p. 128.

3. Eli M. Oboler. *Defending Intellectual Freedom*. Westport, CT: Greenwood Press, p. 5.

4. Alexis de Tocqueville. *Democracy in America*. New York: Century Co., 1898, vol. II, p. 322.

5. Ibid., p. 323.

6. Oboler, *Defending Intellectual Freedom*, p. 8.

7. John Milton. *Areopagitica and Tractate on Education*. New York: P. F. Collier & Son, 1909, p. 239.

8. John Stuart Mill. *On Liberty, and Other Essays*. New York: Book League of America, 1929, p. 21.

9. Zechariah Chafee, Jr. *Free Speech in the United States*. Cambridge, MA: Harvard University Press, 1967, p. 31.

10. Alexander Meiklejohn. *Free Speech and Its Relation to Self-Government*. New York: Harper & Brothers, 1948, p. 2.

11. Thomas I. Emerson. *The System of Freedom of Expression*. New York: Random House, 1970, pp. 6–7.

12. Franklyn S. Haiman. *Speech and Law in a Free Society*. Chicago: University of Chicago Press, 1981, p. 425.

13. Robert Allen Rutland. *The Birth of the Bill of Rights*. Boston: Northeastern University Press, 1991, p. 5.

14. Catherine Gilbert and Stephen B. Presser. "John Locke." In *The Guide to American Law*. St. Paul, MN: West Publishing Co., 1984, vol. 7, pp. 213–216.

15. Rutland, *Birth of the Bill of Rights*, p. 25.

16. Ibid.

17. Stephen B. Presser. "The Declaration of Independence." In *The Guide to American Law*. St. Paul, MN: West Publishing Co., 1984, vol. 4, pp. 53–55.

18. Rutland, *Birth of the Bill of Rights*, p. 117.

19. Ibid., pp. 214–215.

20. O. Carroll Arnold. *Religious Freedom on Trial.* Valley Forge, PA: Judson Press, 1978, p. 21.

21. Ibid., pp. 20–21.

22. Joseph J. Hemmer, Jr. *The Supreme Court and the First Amendment.* New York: Praeger, 1986, p. 409.

23. Ibid., p. 160.

24. *Schenck v. United States.* 39 S. CT. 247 (1919), p. 249.

25. Hemmer, *Supreme Court and the First Amendment,* pp. 6–7.

26. Ibid., p. 8.

27. *Chaplinsky v. New Hampshire.* 62 S. CT. 766 (1942), p. 770.

28. Robert Bork. *The Tempting of America.* New York: Free Press, 1990, p. 127.

29. Ibid.

30. Walter P. Metzger, ed. "General Report of the Committee on Academic Freedom and Academic Tenure." In *The American Concept of Academic Freedom in Information.* New York: Arno Press, 1977, Section 2, p. 20.

31. Rutland, *Birth of the Bill of Rights,* pp. 22–23.

32. *Near v. Minnesota.* 51 S. CT. 625, 1931.

33. Hemmer, *Supreme Court and the First Amendment,* p. 269.

34. Jonathan Green. *Encyclopedia of Censorship.* New York: Facts on File, 1990, p. 91.

35. Hemmer, *Supreme Court and the First Amendment,* p. 360.

36. Leon Hurwitz. *Historical Dictionary of Censorship in the United States.* Westport, CT: Greenwood Press, 1985, p. 101.

37. Ibid., pp. 112–113.

38. Hemmer, *Supreme Court and the First Amendment,* p. 51.

39. Ibid., p. 60.

40. Green, *Encyclopedia of Censorship,* p. 237.

41. Ibid., p. 279.

42. Anne Lyon Haight, updated and enlarged by Chandler B. Grannis. *Banned Books, 387 B.C. to 1978 A.D.* New York: R. R. Bowker Co., 1978, p. 50.

43. Ibid., p. 360.

44. Green, *Encyclopedia of Censorship,* p. 163.

45. Haight, *Banned Books,* p. 45.

46. William Noble. *Bookbanning in America.* Middlebury, VT: Paul S. Eriksson, 1990, p. 92.

47. Ibid., p. 259.

48. Edward DeGrazia and Roger K. Newman. *Banned Films: Movies, Censors and the First Amendment.* New York: R. R. Bowker Co., 1982, p. 180.

49. Ibid., p. 231.

50. Ibid., p. 355.

51. Ibid., p. 312.

52. L. B. Woods. *A Decade of Censorship in America.* Metuchen, NJ: Scarecrow Press, 1979.

53. Ibid., p. 91.

54. Ibid., pp. 91–93.

55. Ibid., pp. 103–105.

56. Nadine Strossen. "The Free Speech Jurisprudence of the Rehnquist Court." In *The Free Speech Yearbook* (1991), p. 91.

2

Chronology

1215   Noblemen force King John of England to accept the terms of the Magna Carta. After years of discontent with Richard I and John, the feudal barons force John to grant privileges, including trial by jury, consent by the barons on taxation and royal decrees, and freedom for the church from royal interference, as a concession to all freemen. The Magna Carta will become one of the major influences on the doctrine of individual rights in English and U.S. law.

1650   William Pynchon's *The Meritorious Price of Our Redemption* is publicly burned, becoming the first book in the history of the American colonies to be censored. Pynchon was one of the founders of the Massachusetts Colony, but his book is highly critical of Puritan orthodoxy. Pynchon is also publicly censured and banished to England.

1686   John Locke publishes his *Two Treatises on Government,* which will provide the basis for the theory of the rights of humankind and support the Glorious Revolution that brought William and Mary to the throne of England. Locke's philosophies on individual rights will have a tremendous impact on the leaders of the American Revolution, especially Thomas Jefferson, and will become the foundation of the main concepts of the Declaration of Independence and the Bill of Rights.

1787   The Constitution of the United States is created by a convention of leaders of the American Revolution and U.S. statesmen, establishing a unique form of representative government.

1791   The first ten amendments to the U.S. Constitution, known as the Bill of Rights, are ratified by the states. The First Amendment becomes the basis for all expressive rights and freedoms, including freedom of religion, freedom of speech, freedom of the press, and the right to assembly and association.

1798   The Alien and Sedition Acts are passed by the Federalist-controlled Congress and signed into law by President John Adams. This is the first instance of a peacetime anti-sedition act and the first major suppression of free speech and free press after the adoption of the Bill of Rights. Concerned about the growing hostility with France over the XYZ affair and angry with the criticisms by the Jeffersonian Democratic-Republican Party, the Federalists design these acts to control dissent. These measures are then enforced largely on the basis of political opinion. Only a number of Democratic-Republican editors and writers are prosecuted under the law.

1821   The first publication of John Cleland's *Memoirs of a Woman of Pleasure,* or *Fanny Hill* is attempted in the United States and is banned by the Massachusetts courts. Several attempts will be made for the next 140 years until Putnam publishes two unexpurgated paperback editions in 1963 and their sale is upheld by the Supreme Court in the *Memoirs* case of 1966.

1825   In one of the first libel cases in the United States, the *Commonwealth v. Blanding* decision declares that the truth of a libelous statement does not make it acceptable if the intent is to harm an individual. Richard Blanding had published in a newspaper a "scandalous and libelous" attack on the character of an innkeeper, Enoch Fowler. Although Blanding offers to prove the truth of the statements, the Massachusetts court rules that the publication of a truth for the sole purpose of damaging another's good name is still libelous.

1865   The first postal act banning the distribution of obscene materials through the U.S. mail is passed by Congress. This act, as codified by the Comstock Act of 1873, will be responsible for most federal convictions for obscenity.

1868   The *Hicklin* judicial test for obscenity is established in the British case *Regina v. Hicklin.* Though an English court decision, the *Hicklin* standard will be the rule for all cases of obscenity in U.S. courts until it is modified by the *Ulysses* standard in 1933 and overturned by the *Roth* test in 1957. Under the *Hicklin* rule, a

1868
cont.
work is not judged as a whole but can be ruled obscene even if just one passage is so declared. Furthermore, the work does not have to offend the "average person" but only must be found to have a bad effect on susceptible classes of individuals such as children, abnormal adults, or any member of a subgroup of society outside the mainstream, such as a criminal.

1873
The Society for the Suppression of Vice is founded by Anthony Comstock. Comstock uses the society to campaign for strict federal and state laws controlling obscene material and later in the same year is successful with the passage of the Comstock Act, also known as the Federal Anti-Obscenity Act, which codifies into federal laws the original Postal Act of 1865. Comstock is appointed a special agent to the U.S. Post Office and crusades against obscenity in this capacity for 40 years.

1879
Reynolds v. United States becomes the first major test of the free exercise of religion clause of the First Amendment. Though the Supreme Court rules against polygamy within a Mormon faith, the Court upholds the right to hold religious views and to exercise legally acceptable beliefs.

1913
The first board of film censors is established by the Ohio State Legislature on April 16, 1913. The legislature creates a Board of Censors to screen every film to be shown in Ohio prior to the film's release to theaters. Guidelines of the board permit only films with moral or educational value, or that are entertaining and harmless.

1915
The controversial film classic *Birth of a Nation* is first shown on February 8. D. W. Griffith's film of the Civil War and the Ku Klux Klan will become the most censored film in the United States, with over 100 challenges by 1980.

1919
The "clear and present danger" test for the protection of dissenting speech is established in the case *Schenck v. United States*. Speech that represents a clear and present danger, which means speech that may cause immediate harm if acted upon, is not protected by the First Amendment. Charles Schenck had called for resistance to the draft during World War I.

1920
The American Civil Liberties Union (ACLU) is founded by Roger Baldwin. The ACLU will become the leading civil liberties group in the United States, entering numerous court cases in support of the First Amendment rights of such diverse

1920
cont.
groups as the NAACP and the American Nazi Party, among many others.

1925
In *Gitlow v. New York,* the doctrine of "bad tendency" is espoused by the Supreme Court to prohibit dissenting speech that by its nature poses a threat to the breach of peace. The Court argues that a clear and present danger is not always clear but that speech that shows a bad tendency may be banned.

1927
The illustrious "Monkey" trial, *Scopes v. State,* a Tennessee case, pits two celebrated U.S. lawyers, William Jennings Bryan and Clarence Darrow, in a nationally watched trial over the teaching of evolution in the public schools. The trial later will be immortalized in the book and film of the same name, *Inherit the Wind.*

1930
The Tariff Act of 1930 permits the U.S. Customs Service to seize any obscene material coming into the United States. By the end of the decade, such literary works as Henry Miller's *Tropic of Cancer* will be seized and refused distribution rights in the United States.

1931
The concept of "prior restraint," or the prohibition on speech or publication before it actually occurs, is determined to be unconstitutional in the Supreme Court case *Near v. Minnesota ex. rel. Olson.* The Court sees such prior censorship, even of the openly anti-Semitic newspaper published by J.M. Near, as contrary to the founding fathers' belief in freedom of the press.

The first Motion Picture Code is implemented by the Motion Picture Producers and Distributors Association (MPPDA), also known as the Hays Office. The code requires every script to be submitted to the MPPDA for review under the guidelines established by Martin Quigley, publisher of the *Exhibitor's Herald,* a leading industry journal. The code is later revised in 1956 and again in 1966.

1933
On the evening of May 10, 1933, shortly after Adolf Hitler becomes chancellor of Germany, students burn an estimated 20,000 books in a square near the University of Berlin. This is the first of many mass book burnings orchestrated by Josef Goebbels, the Nazi propaganda minister. Book burning is now often likened to Nazi tactics by opponents of censorship.

1934
The Federal Communications Act establishes the Federal Communications Commission. The act provides for equal time in

1934
cont.
broadcasting for political candidates and creates the "fairness doctrine." This rule requires broadcasters, both radio and television, to provide equal coverage to all sides of a controversial topic.

The *Ulysses* standard states that in attempts to determine obscenity, a work must be judged as a whole. In *United States v. One Book Entitled Ulysses,* an appeals court reverses one of the main tenets of the *Hicklin* rule, which permitted a work to be judged obscene even if only an isolated passage was determined to be obscene. Random House Publishers successfully use James Joyce's monumental work *Ulysses* to challenge the *Hicklin* rule.

Obelisk Press, later known as Olympia Press, attempts the first importation and sale of Henry Miller's *Tropic of Cancer.* The books are promptly seized by the U.S. Customs Service. A similar fate will befall Miller's *Tropic of Capricorn* in 1939, and both books will be generally unavailable until Grove Press publishes new editions in 1961.

1939
In the seminal case *Hague v. Congress of Industrial Organizations,* the constitutional right to assembly is upheld. This case was brought because the mayor of Jersey City, New Jersey, had enforced an ordinance prohibiting public meetings in public places against the CIO labor organization.

The Library Bill of Rights becomes the policy of the American Library Association. Designed to set down the most fundamental principles for library services and the delivery of information, the Library Bill of Rights is the primary vehicle for the protection of the rights of library users and for the defense of intellectual freedom in information institutions.

1940
Congress enacts the Smith Act, the first peacetime anti-sedition law since the Alien and Sedition Acts of 1798. This law is later modified in 1948 and again in 1957. It will remain the U.S. federal sedition law, prohibiting advocation of the overthrow of the U.S. government by force or violence as well as any act that would overthrow the government in the same manner.

The Supreme Court upholds the right of a school district to require that all students salute the flag of the United States and recite the Pledge of Allegiance, even over objections based on religious principles. In *Minersville School District v. Gobitis,* the Court rejects the claim by the parents of two children who are

1940
cont.
Jehovah's Witnesses that the salute and the pledge violate their constitutional rights. Instead, the Court argues that the public school district has a legitimate right to promote citizenship.

In *Cantwell v. Connecticut,* the free exercise of religion is upheld by the Supreme Court. The Court rules that the distribution of religious literature on public thoroughfares is protected by the First Amendment.

1942
"Fighting words" are declared not to be under the protection of the First Amendment in the landmark case *Chaplinsky v. New Hampshire.* The Court considers epithets or personal abuse to not constitute a communication of information and rules that such words are offensive if the average person sees the words as able to cause a physical fight.

1943
The 1940 flag salute case, *Minersville School District v. Gobitis,* is reversed by the Supreme Court in *West Virginia Board of Education v. Barnette.* Using the opposite argument, the Court declares that mandatory regulations requiring students to salute the flag or recite the Pledge of Allegiance are a violation of the free exercise of religion clause of the First Amendment.

1949
The United Nations Protocol of 1949 adopts the International Convention for the Suppression of the Circulation of and Traffic in Obscene Publications. The convention, originally a product of the League of Nations, is created to combat the international spread of pornography.

1950
Senator Joseph McCarthy of Wisconsin charges that the U.S. Department of State is infiltrated with "known Communists" in the first of several national attacks on liberals, the army, and the entertainment industry. McCarthy's anti-Communist crusade ushers in an era of repression, including the blacklisting of liberal Hollywood actors and writers. The McCarthy era spawns numerous instances of censorship of college professors' viewpoints through administrative harassment and dismissal hearings for those who are believed to hold left-wing or communist ideas. Television and film writers on a blacklist produced by the American Legion and other supporters of McCarthy are forced to use pen names to sell scripts, and many blacklisted actors, such as Zero Mostel, find securing parts difficult.

1951
J. D. Salinger writes the quintessential alienated youth novel *The Catcher in the Rye.* By 1976, the well-known study *A Decade of*

1951
cont.
Censorship will show that *The Catcher in the Rye* is the most censored book in schools and libraries.

1952
In a case involving the Roberto Rossellini film *The Miracle,* the Supreme Court reverses the 1915 *Mutual Film Corporation v. Industrial Commission of Ohio* decision and declares for the first time that film is a form of expression protected by the First Amendment.

1953
Playboy magazine hits the newsstands as the first popular men's magazine featuring pictorials of nude female models. Hugh Hefner, founder and publisher, uses the magazine to promote his philosophy of intellectual freedom and develops the Playboy Foundation to provide financial support against censorship challenges to books, free speech, and a free press.

The European Convention on Human Rights is signed by member states of the Council of Europe. Born as an attempt to prevent repetition of the atrocities committed during World War II, Article 10 of the convention is written to guarantee freedom of expression to all citizens of the signatory states.

1957
The *Roth* standard replaces the *Hicklin* rule as the test for obscenity with the Supreme Court case *Roth v. United States.* Under *Roth,* an era of liberalization with a greater acceptance of erotic and obscene publications begins. The *Roth* standard states that for a work to be banned, that work, taken as a whole, must be determined to appeal to prurient interests and must be judged obscene by contemporary community standards. The Court defines "prurient interest" to be terms that excite lustful thoughts or that are "lewd" or "lascivious."

1958
The right to association is affirmed by the Supreme Court in *N.A.A.C.P. v. Alabama.* In this landmark civil rights case, the Court holds that no state or other authority can require an organization to reveal the membership or names of members held confidential.

1964
On October 19, the Lincoln, Nebraska, school system orders all copies of Hazel Bannerman's *Little Black Sambo* removed from the open shelves of the schools' libraries. Responding to the charge of inherent racism in the book, the school district orders all copies put on a "reserved" shelf, making this the first incident of censorship of this book.

1964   Amid a climate of civil rights conflicts, the Supreme Court
cont.   establishes the "actual malice" test for libel involving a public
figure. In the case *N.Y. Times v. Sullivan,* the Court rules that a
public figure (a Montgomery, Alabama, city commissioner in
this case) must show either actual malice or the intentional publication of a statement known by the publishers to be false
before libel can be proven.

1965   The first major conscientious objector case, *United States v.
Seeger,* is decided by the Supreme Court. Under *Seeger,* conscientious objector status can be granted even if the objector does
not hold a belief in a supreme being as long as his or her
religious views on conscience are sincerely held.

1966   The Freedom of Information Act (FOIA) is passed by Congress.
FOIA is designed to open public documents once shielded from
public view. Files kept on individual citizens are also made available to those individuals by this law.

A well-known publisher of pornography, Ralph Ginzburg, is
convicted of pandering for attempting to operate a mass-mail
advertising campaign for erotic literature through the Intercourse and Blue Ball, Pennsylvania, post offices.

1967   The Universal Declaration of Human Rights becomes the official United Nations document for the worldwide protection of
human rights. Article 19 of the declaration states that "everyone
has the right to freedom of opinion and expression." By U.N.
agreement, this declaration extends intellectual freedom to all
peoples of the world.

The *Memoirs* standard, as a test of obscenity, refines the *Roth*
standard, in the Supreme Court case *A Book Named "John Cleland's Memoirs of a Woman of Pleasure" v. Attorney General of Massachusetts.* With the *Memoirs* decision, the Court rules that the
three *Roth* tests must be applied independently. *Memoirs of a
Woman of Pleasure,* also known as *Fanny Hill,* is the first noted
pornographic novel, and attempts to legally publish it in the
United States up to this date have spanned 142 years. In this
case, G. P. Putnam's Sons produces the first successful, legally
sanctioned edition, showing that the work has become accepted
by society with a record number of sales to universities, libraries,
and the Library of Congress. The book is judged not obscene
for the first time because it is not "unqualifiably worthless,"
although it is determined to have little social value.

1967
cont.
Loyalty oaths as a condition of employment for teachers and professors are declared unconstitutional in the case *Keyishian v. Board of Regents*. In this landmark academic freedom case, the Supreme Court rules that the classroom is a "marketplace of ideas" and that loyalty oaths threaten to undermine the robust exchange of ideas.

The President's Commission on Obscenity and Pornography is established by President Lyndon Johnson. It is created to study the laws governing obscenity and the sale and distribution of pornography as well as pornography's effects on society. The 18-member panel includes scholars, business leaders, members of the clergy, and lawyers.

1968
In *United States v. O'Brien*, the Supreme Court rules that in a situation where both speech and nonspeech elements exist, the government can regulate the nonspeech, or symbolic speech, activities. In this case, the act of burning a draft card as a form of protest is declared not protected by the First Amendment.

In *Epperson v. Arkansas*, the Supreme Court declares the first repeal of a statute forbidding the teaching of evolution in the public schools. Though *Epperson* primarily involves the establishment of religion clause, the Court also rules on free speech grounds in declaring such statutes unconstitutional.

1969
Mere "advocacy of action" that does not call for illegal action is declared to be protected speech in the landmark dissenting speech case *Brandenburg v. Ohio*. The *Brandenburg* case reverses 40 years of judicial sanctions against political dissent.

1970
In *Red Lion Broadcasting Co. v. Federal Communications Commission*, the fairness doctrine of the Federal Communications Commission is affirmed. The Court orders radio station WGCB in Red Lion, Pennsylvania, to give equal time to an author to rebut charges made by the Reverend Billy James Hargis that the author's book is intended to smear Senator Barry Goldwater during the 1964 presidential campaign.

A "zone of privacy" is declared as existing within an individual's own home in the landmark case *Stanley v. Georgia*. Robert Stanley had been convicted of possession of pornography in his home after a raid for gambling devices. On appeal, the Supreme Court declares that a state has no business telling anyone what he or she can read in the confines of his or her home.

1970
cont.
Symbolic speech, in the form of flag burning, becomes a protected act in the seminal Supreme Court case *Street v. New York*. Sidney Street had been arrested for burning a flag after he heard that James Meredith, the first black student at the University of Mississippi, had been shot and killed.

The landmark student rights case *Tinker v. Des Moines Independent Community School District* is decided by the Supreme Court. John F. Tinker and his sister, Mary Beth, as well as other students had worn black armbands to school to protest the Vietnam War, and school authorities had suspended Tinker when he refused to remove the armband.

The most celebrated trial of the anti–Vietnam War protest, known as the trial of the Chicago Seven, takes place in Chicago. The eight defendants are charged with rioting as a result of the protest marches during the 1968 Democratic Convention. Bobby Seale, the only black defendant, is bound and gagged during the trial and is considered a separate defendant by both the court and the press.

1971
In the famous Pentagon Papers case, the Supreme Court denies the federal government's attempt to prevent the publication of sensitive government documents concerning the Vietnam War. Daniel Ellsberg, a former Defense Department analyst, had turned the papers over to the *New York Times* and the *Washington Post*, both of which published excerpts contradicting publicly announced U.S. foreign policy.

In *Cohen v. California*, the Court rules that a protest using a vulgar word cannot be considered offensive speech. To be offensive, the words must appeal to a prurient interest. In this case, Paul Cohen had worn a jacket into the Los Angeles County Courthouse that had a vulgar phrase protesting the draft.

The Mike Nichols film *Carnal Knowledge*, starring Jack Nicholson and Candace Bergen, is banned in Georgia. The case resulting from this ban, *Jenkins v. Georgia*, becomes the first test of the new *Miller* obscenity standard.

1972
The film *Deep Throat* popularizes pornographic film and begins a brief "art porn" era. Although the film later will be judged obscene after several prosecutions in 1975, record audiences across the nation view this film and two others, *Behind the Green Door* and *The Devil in Miss Jones*, before the "art porn" phenomenon dies out.

1972
cont.
The first national study of the effects of obscenity and pornography is issued by the President's Commission on Obscenity and Pornography. The report finds no link between pornography and antisocial behavior and recommends that pornography be decriminalized. A minority report of the commission denounces the findings.

1973
The still current test for obscenity is enunciated in the landmark case *Miller v. California.* The "prurient interest" rule is changed to "patent offensiveness" as judged by state or local standards, not by the national standard of the *Roth* tests. *Miller* ushers in a conservative wave of obscenity prosecutions.

1974
The Privacy Act is created by Congress to protect individuals. The act permits anyone to see any file kept on them by any federal agency and to have corrected any errors contained in the file. The Privacy Act fails to have an impact after the public uses the provisions of the Freedom of Information Act to obtain the same information.

1976
Federal commissions and regulatory agencies are required to hold open meetings under the provisions of the Sunshine Act. The act greatly extends the free flow of information to the public that was begun under similar laws such as the Freedom of Information Act.

1978
After a series of nationally reported incidents, the "Whistleblowers Act," or Civil Service Reform Act, provides for the protection of government employees who report errors or misdeeds in the management of federal agencies.

In a major broadcasting case, *F.C.C. v. Pacifica Foundation,* the Supreme Court declares that reasonable regulations are acceptable for broadcasts deemed inappropriate for some viewers and listeners. After radio station WBAI in New York played a monologue of comedian George Carlin's "The Seven Words You Can't Say on TV" in 1973, a father complained to the FCC that his son overheard this vulgar language. Later referred to as the "filthy words" case, this ruling permits the FCC to enforce regulations requiring that such programming be aired after midnight.

1979
The landmark school book censorship case *Board of Education, Island Trees Union Free School v. Pico* declares that public schools have the discretion to determine what can be owned by the schools' libraries but that they cannot make such decisions based on partisan or political ideology. In this case, the Court also affirms the First Amendment rights of students.

1982   The Intelligence Identities Protection Act is passed by Congress. Concerned by reports that exposé books by former CIA agents may contribute to the deaths of clandestine CIA agents abroad, the federal government makes it a crime to publish the name of any covert agent or any other identifying information.

1983   The prosecution of pornography in the cities of Minneapolis and Indianapolis is undertaken using feminist arguments against pornography's exploitation of women. Laws drafted with the advice of feminist writer Andrea Dworkin that permit obscenity prosecutions on the grounds of the exploitation of women are used successfully in Indianapolis under Mayor William Hudnut.

1985   Under lobbying pressure from the Parent's Music Resource Center, the U.S. Senate holds hearings on the content of music lyrics in recordings and music videos. The recording industry voluntarily agrees to encourage producers to label recordings as a means for parents to evaluate purchases for and by their children.

Attorney General Edwin Meese is sued for ruling a Canadian film on acid rain to be political propaganda. In *Keene v. Meese,* the Supreme Court rules that Meese's action, taken to prevent the showing of the film in the United States, violates the First Amendment right to free speech.

The Meese Commission, also known as the Attorney General's Commission on Pornography, is established by Attorney General William French Smith. The commission is brought about as a result of discontent by many conservatives with the findings of the President's Commission on Obscenity and Pornography (1970). Smith soon after resigns, and the new attorney general, Edwin Meese, gives the commission more impetus for completing its task. The panel includes scholars, housewives, and antipornography crusaders. Due to a limited funding base, the commission does not use any independent research but instead relies heavily on testimony given at public hearings in six cities, a review of published articles, the work of the commission's staff, and letters to the commission from the public at large.

1986   The second major report on the societal impact of obscenity and pornography is issued by the Attorney General's Commission on Pornography, also known as the Meese Commission. The commission's report is diametrically opposed to the report pro-

1986
cont.
duced by the 1970 President's Commission on Obscenity and Pornography. It concludes that there is a link between the pornography industry and organized crime. Furthermore, the report shows a causal relationship between violent acts and pornography depicting violence or sadomasochism. A minority report by two members of the commission charges that the evidence presented to the hearings was skewed toward violent materials. One of the more controversial sections of the report gives advice to citizens' groups on how to conduct a grassroots campaign against obscenity and pornography.

1988
In *Hazelwood v. Kuhlmeier*, the Supreme Court reverses its argument made in the *Tinker* case and rules that school officials have the authority to censor school newspapers because the papers serve an instructional purpose. The *Hazelwood* case signals a major change in the Court's thinking about student rights.

In a continuation of the crises in the Middle East stemming from the rise in fundamentalist Islamic fervor, the Ayatollah Ruhollah Khomeini of Iran issues a death warrant in absentia for the author Salman Rushdie. Khomeini incites the Moslem world against Rushdie's book *The Satanic Verses* for what is seen as an affront to the Islamic faith. Mass public burnings of the book occur throughout the Moslem world. Major U.S. bookstore chains announce the removal of the book from their shelves, though ultimately a temporary decision, for fear of violence and Islamic retribution. Rushdie is forced into hiding to protect his life, and he will not emerge until 1992 under heavy security in New York City to denounce worldwide censorship.

1989
The U.S. Congress passes the first of two Child Protection Acts to combat child pornography. The original act requires producers of any obscene material or works using models or actors to keep extensive records on the ages of those models and actors. The act also defines a distributor as any individual, organization, or group that sells or lends at least two obscene works. This provision causes alarm among publishers, booksellers, and libraries because the broad language means the definition easily can be applied to such institutions, as well as to distributors of adult books. A second attempt at a new bill is made later in 1989 with little change in the language.

In Church Hill, Tennessee, a parent attempts to remove her child from school to avoid the child's exposure to the *Impressions* readings series. Several national groups, including the Eagle

1989
cont.   Forum and the American Family Association, join in a suit against the school for use of the series because of its secular humanist approach. The courts ultimately rule in the school district's favor, but not before the objecting parent withdraws her child from the public school in protest.

1990   The National Endowment for the Arts (NEA) requires artists receiving NEA grants to sign a pledge that no obscenity or pornography will be produced with the funds. Rising out of objections by Senator Jesse Helms (R-NC) to antireligious art funded by an NEA grant, the pledge creates a furor in the art and academic worlds, with several funded artists refusing or returning their grants in protest.

The Motion Picture Association of America unveils its latest revision in the rating code for films. The new designation NC-17 replaces the former X rating.

Obscenity charges are brought against the rap group 2 Live Crew for performing the music from their album *As Nasty As They Wanna Be*. In addition, several record store clerks are prosecuted for selling the album. 2 Live Crew is acquitted, but a store clerk in Florida is convicted of selling the album when the jury in that case rules the album obscene.

In *Ohio v. Osborne*, the Supreme Court rules that the private possession of child pornography is not constitutionally protected. During a police search of his home, Clyde Osborne had been found to have photographs of nude, adolescent boys in suggestive poses. In this appeal of his conviction for possession of child pornography, Osborne claims that the Ohio statute is overly broad and violates the private possession standard set in *Stanley v. Georgia*. The Court rejects this argument and declares that the state may regulate private behavior of this nature to protect children.

Concerns about academic freedom and the constitutionality of personnel records are raised in *The University of Pennsylvania v. The Equal Employment Opportunity Commission*. The Supreme Court upholds the EEOC's regulation requiring the disclosure of peer review documents during a discrimination suit, originally brought forward by a woman faculty member in a tenure dispute.

1991   The cable music television channel MTV, under fire by parents' groups for the sexual and violent content of music videos on the

1991
cont.

channel in general, comes under severe criticism for airing a Madonna video highly critical of censorship that also is erotic and sexually suggestive.

A movie by the emerging black film director John Singleton, *Boyz N the Hood*, is removed from theaters in several cities after riots by gang members at two California openings result in injuries. A critically acclaimed film about black ghetto life and growing up with an absent father, the film reopens without incident several days later.

The Supreme Court, in the Indiana case *Barnes v. Glen Theatre*, reverses the 1975 *Doran v. Salem Inn* case and declares that nude dancing is not a protected form of expression.

In the abortion-related case *Rust v. Sullivan*, the Supreme Court rejects the First Amendment arguments that doctors and patients have an absolute privilege from prosecution—in other words, that they cannot be compelled to testify as to the contents of their conversation—and that patients have the right to information on abortion. Instead, the Court declares that in federally funded clinics the government can set regulations on what information can be given because the government sponsors the clinic through funding.

In *Simon & Schuster v. New York State*, the Supreme Court strikes down the New York State "son of Sam" law, which was originally enacted to prevent David Berkowitz, the "son of Sam" mass murderer, from collecting royalties for the sale of his sensational story. Simon & Schuster had sued over the state's attempt to apply the law to the publication of *Wiseguy*, the biography of mafioso Nicholas Pilegi, subject of the movie *Goodfellas*. The law had raised concerns among publishers over the possible chilling effects on publishing such firsthand accounts.

3

Biographical Sketches

THE STUDY OF INTELLECTUAL FREEDOM is a study of interest groups, political pressure, and legal action. Though several individuals have influenced the principles of intellectual freedom and the climate of censorship, many are associated with an organization as either a founding member or an active participant in the process of maintaining intellectual freedom. Chapter 5 should be examined along with the biographies of the people listed here for a more thorough understanding of the role of individuals in establishing and preserving intellectual freedom. These biographical sketches cover the more important modern-day individuals noted for their role in issues concerning intellectual freedom.

Roger Nash Baldwin, 1884–1981

Founding member and executive director of the American Civil Liberties Union (ACLU), Roger Nash Baldwin is the foremost name in the defense of civil liberties in the United States. Born in Wellesley, Massachusetts, and educated at Harvard University, Baldwin began his career teaching sociology and as a social worker in St. Louis, Missouri. During World War I, he was the director of the American Union Against Militarism and spent a year in prison as a conscientious objector. In 1920, the ACLU was founded with Baldwin as its director. He served in this capacity until his retirement in 1950 and continued as an indefatigable champion for civil liberties until he died in 1981. Baldwin wrote numerous pamphlets and articles on civil liberties as well as the books *Civil Liberties and Industrial Conflict* and *A New Slavery: Forced Labor.* He was also chairman of the board of the International League for the Rights of Man.

David K. Berninghausen, 1916–

One of the leading authorities and scholars on intellectual freedom, David Berninghausen has been a lifelong educator and librarian active in the defense of intellectual freedom. Berninghausen received a bachelor's degree in 1936 from Iowa State University and went on to earn a degree in librarianship from Columbia University and a master's degree from Drake University. He has held numerous library positions, including director of the library at Cooper Union, a private college in New York City, and professor of library science at the University of Minnesota. His most well-known book, *Flight from Reason: Essays on Intellectual Freedom in the Academy, the Press and the Library,* is a quintessential text on intellectual freedom.

Hugo Lafayette Black, 1886–1971

Supreme Court Justice Hugo Black is considered by many legal scholars to be one of the greatest Supreme Court justices and a foremost champion of the First Amendment. Born and raised in Alabama, Black obtained a law degree from the University of Alabama Law School at Tuscaloosa in 1906. While an attorney in Birmingham, he joined the Ku Klux Klan in 1921 for political expediency. He resigned from the Klan in 1925 when he ran for the U.S. Senate. Elected in 1926, Black remained in the Senate until 1937, when President Franklin Roosevelt appointed him to the Supreme Court. His legal opinions strongly supported First and Fifth Amendment rights in most cases. One serious deviation from these stands was the World War II Japanese-American relocation case *Korematsu v. United States,* in which Black defended the decision to relocate Japanese-Americans into internment camps during the war. Among his most famous judicial decisions were the majority opinion in *Marsh v. Alabama,* which permitted Jehovah's Witnesses to distribute religious literature, and *Wesberry v. Sanders,* which inaugurated the "one man, one vote" precedent. Black also rendered the decision in *Youngstown Sheet and Tube Co. et al. v. Sawyer,* which struck down President Harry Truman's seizure of the steel industry in 1952. Black's judicial opinions and legal writings argue for a near absolute freedom of speech.

Dorothy M. Broderick, 1929–

Editor of *Voice for Youth Advocates,* a young adult library services periodical, Dorothy Broderick has had a long, distinguished career as a youth services librarian and advocate for intellectual freedom. Her career has included serving as a librarian in several New York City public libraries as well as being a professor of librarianship at Case Western Reserve and Dalhousie University. Broderick has written several books on young adult literature and on intellectual freedom, most notably *The Image of the Black in Children's Literature,* based on her doctoral dissertation; *Library Work with Children;* and *Intellectual Freedom and Young Adults.* She is an active member of the American Library Association (ALA), was a 1977 ALA presidential nominee, and has chaired the Intellectual Freedom Committee of ALA's Young Adult Services Division.

Alan Dershowitz, 1938–

Law professor and First Amendment scholar and attorney, Alan Dershowitz is the premier counselor for free speech cases in the United States today. Dershowitz obtained a bachelor's degree from Brooklyn College in 1959 and was elected to Phi Beta Kappa. At Yale University Law School, he became editor of the *Yale Law Review* in his second year. Offered a position at Harvard University Law School upon graduation, he clerked for several federal judges instead, including Supreme Court Justice Arthur Goldberg. Dershowitz became a Harvard law professor in 1964 and was the youngest law professor to earn tenure in the university's history, at the age of 28. He joined the Massachusetts ACLU and argued many of the most famous and controversial free speech cases of the 1960s and 1970s. Among his clients were Dr. Benjamin Spock, baby doctor and antiwar activist; Bruce Franklin, a militant leftist professor at Stanford University; and the racist genetic theorist William Shockley. William Kunstler prevailed upon Dershowitz to write the appeal for the "Chicago Seven." In one of the most important cases of his career, he defended Frank Snepp, a former CIA agent and author of *Decent Interval,* a book critical of the evacuation of Saigon in 1975. Dershowitz has also been the defense counsel for two of the most famous pornographic film cases, successfully arguing against the ban of the Swedish film *I Am Curious (Yellow)* and in 1976 defending Harry Reems, the principal male actor in the art porn film *Deep Throat,* against charges of conspiracy to promote and distribute obscenity.

Dershowitz's best-selling book *The Best Defense* espouses his legal philosophy and provides an in-depth look at the cases he has argued.

Dr. James C. Dobson, 1936–

Member of the Attorney General's Commission on Pornography and founder of Focus on the Family, James Dobson is a leading researcher and author on traditional family values and child psychology. Dobson earned a bachelor's degree in psychology from Pasadena College in 1958 and his master's and doctorate from the University of Southern California in child development and research design. He has held appointments as clinical professor of pediatrics at the University of Southern California School of Medicine and on the attending staff of the Children's Hospital of Los Angeles. Dr. Dobson founded the Focus on the Family, a non-profit special-interest group dedicated to preserving traditional family values. He hosts a weekly 30-minute radio program covering various topics of concern to the maintenance of traditional family values. Focus on the Family publishes the magazine *Citizen*, which regularly features articles on such issues as abortion, pornography, and public school curriculums. Dobson is also the author of numerous books, most notably *Dare to Discipline, The Strong Willed Child,* and *Fighting for the Minds of Our Children: America's Second Civil War.*

William Orville Douglas, 1898–1980

Supreme Court Justice William O. Douglas was the leading liberal jurist during the Earl Warren and Warren Burger Court years. Born and raised in Yakima, Washington, he attended Whitman College and Columbia University Law School. Later he befriended the distinguished jurist Harlan Stone, and when Louis Brandeis resigned from the court in 1939 President Franklin Roosevelt tapped Douglas to fill the vacancy. Throughout his career on the Supreme Court, Douglas was a powerful philosophical force. He greatly influenced Earl Warren, among other justices, and contributed significantly to the liberal decisions of the Warren Court during the 1960s. He played a major role in the desegregation case *Brown v. Board of Education,* in several freedom of religion cases such as *Abingdon School District v. Schempp,* and in the obscenity cases of the era, most notably *Roth v. United States.* His obscenity decisions argued for the absolute freedom of speech and press.

Two impeachment movements were launched against him. The first one occurred after he granted a temporary stay of execution for Julius and Ethel Rosenberg, convicted of spying for the Soviet Union and providing the Soviets with secret documents on the atom bomb. The second came after the publication of his radical text *Points of Rebellion*, which argued that there are circumstances when a citizenry should rebel against a legitimate government, in 1970. Along with Hugo Black, he is considered, among Supreme Court justices, to be the greatest champion of the Bill of Rights.

Andrea Dworkin, 1946–

Feminist writer and anti-pornography crusader, Andrea Dworkin brought about the Dworkin-McKinnon bills, anti-pornography statutes in several cities, most notably Indianapolis and Minneapolis. Dworkin was born in Camden, New Jersey, and graduated from Bennington College in 1968. She has written numerous books and is especially known for the 1986 novel *Ice and Fire* and several feminist and anti-pornography treatises, including *Woman Hating, Pornography: Men Possessing Women,* and *Right-wing Women.* She was also a contributing author for *Take Back the Night: Women on Pornography,* a well-known feminist text. Dworkin's theories on the exploitation of women by men in the production of pornographic works impressed Mayor William Hudnut of Indianapolis. He was able to fashion local legislation using this feminist logic and with the backing of Dworkin and her attorney, Catherine McKinnon, to create a vehicle for pornography prosecutions. Both Dworkin and McKinnon lecture against pornography and provide assistance to other governmental authorities who wish to write anti-pornography legislation.

Ira Glasser, 1938–

Executive director of the American Civil Liberties Union, Ira Glasser carries on the legacy of Roger Baldwin as head of the foremost civil liberties organization in the United States. Glasser was born in New York City and earned his bachelor's degree in mathematics from Queens College and a master's from Ohio State University. While studying philosophy at the New School for Social Research, he became associate editor of *Current*, a liberal public affairs journal. In 1967, he joined the staff of the New York Civil Liberties Union, becoming its director in 1970. In 1978, he replaced Aryeh Neier as executive director of the national ACLU,

In the 1980s he charged the Reagan administration with perpetrating a "broad and systematic attack on our political freedoms" and the Supreme Court under Warren Burger and William Rehnquist with abandoning the traditional defense of civil liberties.

Danny Goldberg, 1950–

Founder of the Musical Majority, Danny Goldberg has been leading the fight to combat censorship of modern music. Goldberg is most noted for managing several rock-and-roll stars, especially Belinda Carlisle of the Go-Go's and Andy Taylor of Duran Duran. He co-produced the *No Nukes* concert film of 1980. In addition to directing the Musical Majority, he is president of Gold Mountain Records, a rock-and-roll label. The Musical Majority was founded in response to the growing influence of the Parent's Music Resource Center and to combat record labeling.

Jesse A. Helms, 1921–

U.S. senator from North Carolina and the leading anti-obscenity legislator in the country today, Jesse Helms has been responsible for more anti-obscenity legislation than any other politician. Born and raised in North Carolina, he has been variously the city editor of the *Raleigh Times,* administrative aide to U.S. senators Willis Smith and Alton Lennon, and executive director of the North Carolina Bankers Association. He gained his political fortunes as head of WRAL television and the Tobacco Radio Network. Helms regularly attaches an anti-obscenity amendment to most major legislation. His somewhat successful efforts have brought the passage of the "dial-a-porn" amendment, which restricts 900 pay-for-sex numbers, and severe restrictions on the funding of the National Endowment for the Arts (NEA) along with the creation of the anti-obscenity pledge for artists receiving grants from the NEA.

Nat Hentoff, 1925–

Columnist, writer, and social critic, Nat Hentoff has been a major force in the advocacy of intellectual freedom. Born and raised in Boston, he attended Northeastern University in Boston, where as editor of the student newspaper he experienced censorship of his work for the first time. Hentoff is a regular columnist for the *Village Voice,* where he often addresses arguments germane to current intellectual freedom topics. He is a prolific author of books for young adults and adults. His book *Our Children Are Dying* is a highly acclaimed treatise on the plight of inner-city schools. Among his novels for young adults, *The Day They Came to Arrest the Book* has a censorship theme. *The First Freedom* is his best text on intellectual freedom. Hentoff can often be seen on national broadcasts speaking as an advocate for intellectual freedom.

Reed John Irvine, 1922–

Cofounder of Accuracy in Media and Accuracy in Academia, Reed Irvine has carried on a long struggle against liberal bias in the media. During World War II, Irvine worked as a Japanese language officer for the Marines. He received a bachelor's degree from St. Catherine's Society at Oxford University in the United Kingdom and worked for the Federal Reserve System as an economist until the late 1970s. Along with John McLean, publisher of the *Underground Conservative*, and Abraham Kalish, who worked for the U.S. Information Agency, Irvine founded Accuracy in Media (AIM) in 1969. The publication *The AIM Report* refutes various news media for what is seen as reporting with a liberal bias. AIM also has practiced what some critics claim are disinformation campaigns in which multinational firms have been attacked. AIM published reports that Orlando Letelier and his aide, Chilean diplomats in exile after Augusto Pinochet came to power in 1973, were secretly Communist agents, among other news stories. Accuracy in Media also published the book *Target America: The Influence of Communist Propaganda on the U.S. Media* by James Tyson, Jr., in 1981. In 1985, Irvine founded Accuracy in Academia after complaints by some academics of a liberal bias in university teaching. Irvine vowed to place Accuracy in Academia members in classrooms to report firsthand on professors with excessive liberal bias in their lectures, but none of this reporting has surfaced as yet.

Karen Kennerly, 1940–

As executive director of PEN American Center, the U.S. arm of the international civil liberties and civil rights organization International PEN, Karen Kennerly manages one of the primary civil liberties groups in the United States today. Born in New York City, she earned her bachelor's degree from Pembroke College. She also is an author; her book *The Slave Who Bought His Freedom* has an intellectual freedom theme.

Dr. Jerry Kirk, 1931–

President of the National Coalition Against Pornography and chair of the Religious Alliance Against Pornography, an arm of the national coalition, Dr. Jerry Kirk is one of the nation's leading spokespersons against the proliferation of pornography. Having earned his bachelor's degree in education at the University of Washington, Kirk went on to receive a master's of divinity and a master's of theology from Pittsburgh Theological Seminary. Kirk has been a Presbyterian minister in Cincinnati for more than 20 years. He began the National Coalition Against Pornography in response to the report by the 1970 President's Commission on Pornography and Obscenity. Kirk is the author of *The Mind Polluters*, a treatise against pornography.

Richard Kleeman, 1922–

Chair of the Association of American Publishers (AAP) Freedom to Read Committee, Richard Kleeman is a leading spokesperson for intellectual freedom today. Kleeman earned a bachelor's degree from Harvard University, graduating Phi Beta Kappa. He began his career as a journalist and was the Washington correspondent for the *Minneapolis Tribune* for several years. He joined the AAP in 1972 and served as the organization's senior vice-president until his retirement in 1987. He remains a consultant on intellectual freedom issues for the association and chair of the AAP Freedom to Read Committee.

Judith Fingeret Krug, 1940–

Director of the American Library Association's (ALA) Office for Intellectual Freedom, Judy Krug has been the chief officer of the most active organization for combatting censorship challenges to libraries and other institutions. Krug holds a bachelor's degree in political theory from the University of Pittsburgh and a master's degree in library science from the University of Chicago. She held various library positions before being appointed director of the ALA's Office for Intellectual Freedom (OIF) in 1967. Krug also holds an appointment as executive director of the Freedom to Read Foundation. As one of her many OIF duties, Krug is editor of *The Newsletter on Intellectual Freedom,* the prime reporting source for censorship challenges and related intellectual freedom news. In 1977, she became the executive producer of the controversial

ALA film *The Speaker,* concerning the opposition to a presentation by a scientist who argues that blacks are naturally inferior. Krug is often called upon by the media to represent the pro–intellectual freedom viewpoint in nationally televised debates. She has testified before Congress on numerous occasions about pending legislation of relevance to intellectual freedom concerns. Recipient of the Robert B. Downs Intellectual Freedom Award, Krug also has received the Carl Sandburg Freedom to Read Award. She is very active in support of librarians under challenge or pressure by censorship groups, providing advice and resources wherever possible.

Norman Milton Lear, 1922–

A successful television producer, Norman Lear parlayed his household name into the establishment of one of the most influential intellectual freedom interest groups, People for the American Way. Lear began his career as a comedy sketch writer for TV shows, went on to produce several feature films, and then created the immensely successful *All in the Family* television series. In 1980, in response to the growing successes of conservative politicians, especially Ronald Reagan, and to the rising tide of conservative backlash against civil liberties, Lear established People for the American Way. The organization aims its efforts at counteracting the conservative political special interest drives, usually by financing national advertising campaigns and providing resources to other groups needing such assistance. People for the American Way regularly publishes studies and surveys on censorship and other civil liberties issues.

Barry Lynn, 1948–

A leading attorney for the American Civil Liberties Union (ACLU), Barry Lynn is in the forefront of most major civil liberties issues today. Lynn attended Dickinson College in Pennsylvania, earned his master's degree in theology from Boston University, and earned his law degree from Georgetown University in Washington, D.C. He has represented clients of the ACLU in several civil liberties and First Amendment cases. He is also one of the leading spokespersons for ACLU positions. He was a contributor to the National Coalition Against Censorship's booklet *The Meese Commission Exposed* and has been the commission's most vocal critic. Lynn is also an ordained minister in the United Church of

Christ. He recently received the Playboy Foundation's First Amendment Award.

Kenneth Dale McCormick, 1906–

Founder and first chair of the Association of American Publishers (AAP) Freedom to Read Committee, Ken McCormick has been a leading crusader for intellectual freedom for more than 30 years. McCormick earned his bachelor's degree from Willamette University in 1928. He has held various positions with Doubleday and Company since 1930 and is currently a senior editor with the firm. McCormick lectures widely on books and intellectual freedom and is a regular contributor to the magazine *Publisher's Weekly.*

Leroy C. Merritt, 1912–1970

A lifelong librarian and leading crusader for intellectual freedom until his death in 1970, Leroy Merritt developed the *Newsletter on Intellectual Freedom* of the American Library Association (ALA) into a major source on censorship challenges. He earned his library degree at the University of Chicago in 1936 and a Ph.D. in library science in 1942. He held various library positions, most notably professor and later dean of the School of Librarianship at the University of California at Berkeley. Merritt wrote *Book Selection and Intellectual Freedom,* a major text addressing library collection development and intellectual freedom. He also was editor of the *Newsletter on Intellectual Freedom* from 1962 until his death in 1970.

Pat Robertson, 1930–

Founder of the Christian Broadcasting Network (CBN) and creator of the television show *The 700 Club,* Pat Robertson is one of the most prominent televangelists in the nation today. Robertson is the son of A. Willis Robertson, a senator from Virginia from 1947 to 1967, and has a law degree from Yale University. Robertson's ministry has always stressed conservative family values and evangelical Christianity. Programming on his network, CBN, includes news analyses and guest interviews on such topics as abortion, pornography, the occult, and political issues of the day. In 1981, he founded the Freedom Council to recruit other Christians for political action to influence public policy. Robertson's National Legal Foundation has supported a number of challenges to school and library materials, particularly the 1989 Alabama textbook controversy, in which Judge Brevard Hand declared that the

Impressions textbook series promoted secular humanism and violated the freedom of religion. Robertson sought the Republican nomination for president in 1988.

George Seldes, 1890–

An international newspaper reporter and crusader for freedom of the press, George Seldes has been an eyewitness to many significant world events since the 1920s. Born in New Jersey and raised in Pittsburgh, he is the brother of the noted author and former editor of *Dial* magazine Gilbert Seldes. George Seldes began his newspaper career at the *Pittsburgh Leader*. By World War I, he was an international reporter for Colonel Robert McCormick's *Chicago Tribune*. While in France in the 1920s, Seldes befriended many literary giants of the "lost generation," especially Ernest Hemingway. To combat censorship of the press, he founded the magazine *In Fact* in 1940, which lasted for ten years. He has written books on censorship, including *You Can't Print That* and *Freedom of the Press*, as well as his recent autobiography *Witness to a Century*.

Oren J. Teicher, 1949–

President of the American Booksellers Foundation for Free Expression, Oren Teicher is a leading spokesperson for intellectual freedom and the freedom to read. Teicher earned a bachelor's degree from George Washington University in 1971. He has held several positions for Representative Richard Ottinger (D–New York), including administrative assistant and campaign manager. Teicher currently directs the intellectual freedom activities of the American Booksellers Association (ABA), including monitoring challenges to bookstores and booksellers and keeping the association membership aware of trends and issues.

Studs Terkel, 1912–

Born Louis Terkel in New York City, Studs Terkel is a prolific and noted author of popular oral histories, especially *Working: People Talk about What They Do All Day and How They Feel about What They Do, Hard Times: An Oral History of the Great Depression,* and *The Good War: An Oral History of World War II.* Terkel also is a strong advocate for intellectual freedom. He began his career as an actor and has hosted the regular interview show "Wax Museum" on radio station WFMT in Chicago since 1945. He hosted the television show *Studs' Place* in the 1950s, but investigations by the House Un-American Activities Committee into the liberal causes he supported ended both the show and his television career. In 1990, Terkel won the Robert B. Downs Intellectual Freedom Award. He took the name "Studs" from James T. Ferrell's fictional character Studs Lonigan in such works as *Judgement Day, The Young Manhood of Studs Lonigan,* and *Young Lonigan.*

Donald E. Wildmon, 1938–

Minister and television reformer, Donald E. Wildmon founded the Coalition for Better Television in 1981. Born and raised in Mississippi, he graduated from Millsaps College in 1960 and obtained a masters of divinity degree from Emory University. Wildmon founded the Coalition for Better Television to pressure the networks using advertiser boycotts so that more wholesome shows would be broadcast and in an attempt to reduce the themes of sex and violence. He has written several inspirational and religious books such as *Stand Up to Life: A Man's Reflection on Living.* Wildmon also is president of the American Family Association, which has conducted a number of challenges to films and television, including the Saturday morning cartoon *Mighty Mouse* and the film *The Last Temptation of Christ.*

Frank Zappa, 1940–

A rock-and-roll musician and songwriter, Frank Zappa has been in the vanguard for the defense of the music industry in the 1980s and into the 1990s. Born in Baltimore and raised in Lancaster, California, Zappa began his career writing film music scores, the first for the movie *Run Home Slow.* Influenced by the zany music of Spike Jones as well as by the rise of rhythm and blues in the 1950s, Zappa formed the Mothers of Invention with fellow music "freak" Don Van Vliet. They produced several albums of avant-garde music, but Zappa's penchant for strange and crazy musical style kept him off the charts until the 1980s, when the hit single "Valley Girls," featuring his daughter Moon Unit, reached the Top 40 unexpectedly. With the advent of the record labeling campaign under the aegis of the Parent's Music Resource Center, Zappa crusaded for the record industry. He testified against labeling schemes and censorship of music lyrics before the U.S. Congress and several state legislatures.

4

Laws, Legislation, and Court Cases

THE FOUR FREEDOMS OF THE FIRST AMENDMENT were designed to protect intellectual rights. Philosophers have recognized that the body can be imprisoned but the mind can still hold ideas. The founding fathers reasoned that ideas provided the sustenance needed for civilization to thrive. But to survive and contribute to the welfare of people and society, those ideas had to be expressed. From the lessons of history and the more direct experiences of British rule, including licensure laws to control the press and laws prohibiting religious practices other than of the Anglican church, the expression of ideas has proven to be troublesome to authority. In adopting the First Amendment, the founding fathers intended to ensure that expression be given as wide a berth as possible.

The laws and court rulings included in this chapter form the body of legal thinking concerning intellectual freedom. Each of the four freedoms constituting the First Amendment is, in some way, an expressive right. Freedom of religion is in some respects a more narrow expressive right because it is the expression of one category of ideas. However, religion is so strongly woven into the fabric of culture and humankind that the creators of the First Amendment felt it necessary to enumerate this freedom as a right distinct from the expression of other ideas in any form. The freedom of speech is the protection for the most fundamental form of expression, the spoken word. The right to state a point of view or idea is the first break in the imprisonment of ideas. The freedom of the press is a natural extension of the freedom of speech. The right to express ideas in print is crucial to intellectual rights and also has the potential to reach many more people than the spoken word. The right to assembly and association is also an expressive right, for it guarantees that ideas held and said can be heard by others and that mutual support can be maintained by those with the same beliefs.

The cases and laws listed here establish the legal context for each of these four expressive rights. Attempts to place any limitation on these rights or to establish the legitimate regulation of such behavior by the nation or state often bring government into direct conflict with individual citizens. The U.S. Constitution provides for the interpretation of any of its provisions, including any amendment, by the Supreme Court. Because the First Amendment is worded quite simply, the Constitution offers no guidance to the ordinary citizen as to where the rights of individuals end and the state's right to maintain law and order begins. When such conflicts arise, the only recourse is judicial review by the courts, especially the Supreme Court, to examine the intent of the framers of the Bill of Rights as well as the legal precedents established by the courts over the years that draw the line between these two legitimate, competing rights. However, there is also a rich history of legislation that regulates the expressive behavior of individuals and, conversely, the regulatory behavior of the state in drawing limits and barriers to expression.

This chapter provides an annotated list of laws and legislation of importance in this society's continuous attempts to establish the rights of individuals as well as the limits of free expression for the benefit of the nation. The list is arranged in five sections with the first four corresponding to one of the four freedoms of the First Amendment. The fifth section contains legislative initiatives that, although not directly related to one of the four freedoms, are designed to provide for the free flow of information from the federal government that is imperative to an informed citizenry and the maintenance of the four freedoms.

Judicial Review and the Court System

Case law is composed of judicial decisions that have the force of law. In our federal system of government, there are three tiers of courts: local, state, and national (or federal). Each level of the courts may adjudicate a conflict regarding the rights of an individual. However, an interpretation of a constitutional guarantee that has the force of law can only come from the appropriate state or federal court. Local courts are only the initial phase for hearing a case, and they decide which party is in the right. Most states have their own Bill of Rights and protection of freedoms written into their state constitutions. These Bills of Rights provide the same constitutional guarantees but only for the citizens of the respective state. The upper levels of the state judicial system, culminating in the state supreme court, can establish case law on the expressive rights of individuals within that state only. The First Amendment to the U.S. Constitution applies to all U.S. citizens. Generally speaking, most issues concerning the abuse of personal freedoms are decided in the federal court system.

The U.S. Supreme Court is the ultimate point to reach in determining the constitutionality of a law or the fairness of an authoritative action. The Supreme Court established the power of judicial review, which is the ability to interpret the Constitution, in the landmark case *Marbury v. Madison,* written by the first great chief justice, John Marshall. Supreme Court interpretations have the force of law and can only be overturned by the Supreme Court in a subsequent case or by an amendment to the Constitution.

Understanding Case Law Citations

In the court case listings in this chapter, the official title of the case appears first. The first name in the title is the party who charged a violation of a law or who wishes a lower court decision to be reversed. This party is known as the plaintiff. The second party is known as the defendant and is the party who has been charged with some wrong or who must argue that a lower court decision was valid.

The title is written to indicate that the parties are adversaries, or plaintiff versus (notated "v.") defendant. The title is followed by the case reporter citation, which tells where the decision can be found. A case reporter is a set of books listing judicial decisions. The title of the case reporter is in abbreviated form and set between two numbers. The number before the abbreviation is the volume of the case reporter, and the number after the abbreviation

TABLE 1

Abbreviation	Full Title	Publisher
U.S.	United States Report	G.P.O.
S.Ct.	Supreme Court Reports	West
L.Ed.	Lawyer's Editions	Lawyers Cooperative
USLW	United States Law Week	Bureau of National Affairs
F.	Federal Reporter	West (for District Court cases)
F. 2d	Federal Reporter	2nd West Series (for Appeals Court cases)
F. Supp.	Federal Supplement	West (for Circuit Court cases)

is the first page of the judicial decision in that volume. For example, for the case *Minersville School District v. Gobitis* 60 S.Ct. 1010 (1940), Minersville School District is the plaintiff who sought to reverse a lower court ruling, and Gobitis is the defendant. The case can be found in the *Supreme Court Reports* case reporter in volume 60 beginning on page 1010. The date in parentheses is the year the decision was made, which is often different from the year that the incident leading to the case occurred. Most case reporters are published by the government, the West Publishing Company, or the Lawyers Cooperative Publishing Company. Table 1 provides a list of abbreviations used in this chapter. Most case reporters can be found in any bona fide law library, but most of them do not own all of the case reporters. If a particular reporter is not available, *Shepard's United States Citations* lists all case citations and translates the proper citation for all other reporters. Use this source to locate the citation for the available reporter.

Cases Involving Freedom of Religion

Freedom of religion is the expressive right to hold a belief in a faith, to exercise that belief, and to associate with others who hold the same belief. It is no accident that freedom of religion is the first freedom enunciated in the First Amendment. By 1791, the 13 United States had a 200-year experience with freedom of religion. Several of the original American colonies were founded either as a direct result of religious persecution or to establish religious tolerance within their borders. The founding fathers recognized this right as fundamental to freedom of expression and to the stability of the nation. The following is a list of the most salient cases enumerating the religious rights of all citizens.

Reynolds v. United States
25 L.Ed. 244 (1879)

The *Reynolds* case was the first test of the First Amendment's free exercise clause. George Reynolds, a devout Mormon, was convicted in the territory of Utah of breaking a law enacted by Congress in 1862 prohibiting bigamy. The Supreme Court upheld the conviction. In the Court's opinion, an act committed even under religious motivation was not to be allowed by the government against the interest of the state. The justices took this opportunity to make a distinction between religious belief and overt action. They said that holding a belief is protected by the Constitution but that acts considered to be illegal are not, even though these acts are an outgrowth of a specific religious belief.

Cantwell v. Connecticut
310 U.S. 296 (1940)

In this seminal case, the Supreme Court clearly established a wall between government and the right of the religious faithful to disseminate information and to evangelize. Furthermore, the *Cantwell* case is the first religious freedom decision to incorporate the Fourteenth Amendment into the First, thus making the free exercise of religion a guaranteed right of individuals applicable at the state level. Newton Cantwell and his two sons, all Jehovah's Witnesses, played records and sold books in a predominantly Catholic neighborhood in New Haven, Connecticut. All three were convicted of breach of the peace and violation of a law prohibiting solicitation of money or services for an organization not given permission for such solicitation by the secretary of the public welfare. The Supreme Court ruled that these convictions were a clear infringement of the Cantwells' rights under the free exercise clause of the First Amendment and overturned the convictions.

Minersville School District v. Gobitis
60 S.Ct. 1010 (1940)

The first famous flag-salute case, *Gobitis* upholds the authority of a school district to require students to say the pledge of allegiance even over religious objections. Lillian and William Gobitis were expelled from the Minersville, Pennsylvania, schools for refusing to say the pledge of allegiance to the U.S. flag. Both were practicing Jehovah's Witnesses and believed that such pledges were forbidden by the Bible.

Their father brought suit to exempt his children from the practice, but the Supreme Court disagreed. The justices believed failure to abide by this rule would cause difficulties in discipline and would weaken the beliefs held by other children in the value of the exercise. Just three years later, this decision was reversed in the *Barnette* case.

Murdock v. Pennsylvania
319 U.S. 106 (1943)

Similar to the *Cantwell* case, in *Murdock* the Supreme Court struck down license fees to distribute religious literature as a barrier to the right of the free exercise of religion. Robert Murdock, a Jehovah's Witness, was charged a license fee by the Jeannette, Pennsylvania, town government. The difference between *Cantwell* and *Murdock* is that a permit was required in *Cantwell* and was seen as a direct limitation on the exercise of religious belief, because such permits could be granted on a discriminatory basis. In *Murdock*, the fee represented a barrier to exercising the right to address others about the religious views held, and this was considered an abridgment of the First Amendment freedom of religion.

West Virginia State Board of Education v. Barnette,
319 U.S. 625 (1943)

The mandatory pledge of allegiance as a group recitation in school ceremonies and as initial school day formalities was ruled an infringement of the free exercise clause of the First Amendment. This ruling overturned the *Gobitis* decision. As in *Gobitis,* several children were expelled from school for refusing to recite the pledge of allegiance to the flag as a required routine each day. However, in this case, instead of a local school district's rule, the incidents involved a state board of education's regulation requiring all public school students in the state to comply. In the opinion written by Justice Robert Jackson, the Court held that individual freedom of mind was preferred over officially disciplined uniformity and that no vital function of a board of education could take precedent over constitutional rights. The public schools' right to instill national unity and loyalty was not questioned by the Court, but the justices doubted that requiring the pledge of allegiance was an appropriate means to achieve this end.

Engel v. Vitale
370 U.S. 421 (1962)

This is the famous prayer-in-the-schools case in which the Supreme Court ruled an infringement of students' rights to the free exercise of

religion on an individual's right to choose how to exercise his
or her faith. In 1951, the New York State Board of Regents
established a prayer to be read after the Pledge of Allegiance. It
was not compulsory, nor were local school districts forced to use the
proscribed prayer. One local board adopted the prayer and was sued
by a group of parents on the grounds that use of the prayer violated
their First Amendment rights. A local court and the New York State
Court of Appeals believed the procedure to be acceptable in that
saying the prayer was not required and that it was a nonsectarian
prayer (which means it did not use the particular language of any
one faith). However, the Supreme Court, in a nearly unanimous
decision written by Justice Hugo Black, ruled that such prayers were
an act of the establishment of religion and that having the prayer
recited in school placed undue pressure on others to participate even
though their religious beliefs might be in conflict with the prayer or
its meaning.

Abington School District v. Schempp
374 U.S. 203 (1963)

This monumental decision declared that the practice of reading
selections from the Bible as part of school ceremonies or initial
school day routines is an unconstitutional infringement on religious
freedom. The Schempp family were members of the First Unitarian
Church of Germantown, in Pennsylvania. As part of their children's
regular morning school exercises, the Lord's Prayer, a verse selection
from the Bible, and the flag salute were required by law. The
Schempps sued the school district as a test case of the constitutionality
of this practice. In an opinion written by Justice Tom Clark, both
required Bible reading and the recitation of the Lord's Prayer in
public school were declared unconstitutional. The grounds for
this decision were that both practices are an act of the establishment
of religion and that such rules dictated to children a certain form
of exercise of faith that may not be accepted by their religious
beliefs. Justice Clark did, however, recognize that the study of the
Bible for its literary and historical qualities was allowed by the First
Amendment.

United States v. Seeger
380 U.S. 163 (1965)

The *Seeger* case permits a conscientious objector to refuse to serve in
the military even if the objector does not believe in a "supreme being,"
as long as the objector's religious views are sincerely held. This was the

first case to expand the limitation of the conscientious objector status beyond certain identified sects such as the Quakers. Daniel Seeger was convicted in a New York district court of refusing induction into the military. Though he claimed conscientious objector status, Section 6(J) of the Universal Military Training and Service Act required that such objectors had to hold a belief in a supreme being. Seeger's conviction was reversed by the court of appeals, and that reversal was affirmed by the Supreme Court. The Court held that Seeger's decision was based on sincerely held views and that this was a sufficient test to meet conscientious objector exemptions to the military induction law. To the Court, Seeger's views occupied a significant portion of his life equal to that occupied by views of God held by other persons who would qualify for the exemption.

Epperson v. Arkansas
89 S.Ct. 266 (1968)

The 1928 Arkansas law forbidding the promotion of Charles Darwin's theory of evolution was struck down in this case, which was the first Supreme Court case to declare such laws unconstitutional. The Court argued that the law did not permit institutions to develop a climate where a plurality of religious beliefs were encouraged. Until 1965, all Arkansas public schools used biology textbooks that did not include any mention of Darwin's theory of evolution. School authorities at the school where Susan Epperson was teaching biology purchased a new text in 1965 that included Darwin's theory and told her to use that particular text. Faced with violating either the law or an order to the contrary from the school principal, Epperson sued successfully in court. This administrative rights case also had elements of free speech as part of the constitutionality considered in the opinion.

Welsh v. United States
398 U.S. 333 (1970)

In this case conscientious objector status was defined more clearly and the *Seeger* case was reaffirmed. Elliott A. Welsh did not have any strong, formal religious training such as that usually cited by conscientious objectors, including Seeger. He was convicted of refusing military induction under the Selective Service Act of 1966. The Supreme Court reversed an appeals court ruling upholding Welsh's conviction on the grounds that his views on killing and violence had the strength of more traditional religious beliefs.

Gillette v. United States;
Negre v. Larsen
39 USLW 4305 (1971)

The belief that a specific war should be grounds for conscientious objector exemption from military service was rejected by the Supreme Court in these companion cases. Guy P. Gillette was convicted of failure to report for induction into the military, and Louis Negre attempted to obtain a discharge from the service after receiving orders for Vietnam. Both sued on the grounds that the Vietnam War was immoral and both expressed a conscientious objection to that war, but not to all wars in general. The Supreme Court upheld the government's right to conscript men into the military service and denied the contention that objection to a specific war fell within the doctrine of religious freedom as guaranteed by the Constitution.

Stone v. Graham
101 S.Ct. 192 (1981)

In another issue concerning religious activity and school authority, the Supreme Court struck down a school's requirement that a copy of the Ten Commandments be posted in each classroom. A Kentucky statute required the posting of the Ten Commandments, and State Superintendent of Public Instruction James Graham defended the law in court, arguing that the posting was a secular activity and was financed with private money. The Court disagreed, reasoning that the religious aspects of the commandments were unique to Judeo-Christian doctrine and therefore that the commandments could not be regarded as secular.

Grove v. Mead School District No. 354
753 F.2d 1528 (1985);
cert. denied, 106 S.Ct. 85 (1985)

According to the *Grove* decision, the use of a specific book as part of the curriculum, even though some students might find the book in conflict with their religious beliefs, is not a violation of the freedom of religion clause of the First Amendment. Cassie Grove believed the book *The Learning Tree,* a required text in her English class, to be objectionable because she felt it promoted secular humanism in opposition to her Christian beliefs. The school assigned another book to her upon complaint, but her family filed suit to halt the practice of requiring certain texts. The appeals court found that because the book was a novel with a very minute religious component in the story, it did not deal with secular humanism. Also, because Cassie Grove was offered another choice, she was afforded protection regarding both the free exercise clause and the establishment clause. In refusing to hear the case, the Supreme Court upheld the appeals court ruling.

Wallace v. Jaffree
105 S.Ct. 2479 (1985)

The concept of a "moment of silence" to facilitate the opportunity for prayer in the public schools without providing an establishment of religion was struck down by the Court as a violation of the First Amendment. Ishmad Jaffree, among several parents, filed suit against the Alabama State education authorities for promoting religious activities with the creation of a "moment of silence" as part of the regular school day. The Supreme Court struck down the Alabama statute on the grounds that it established a situation where the state government and local authorities were not practicing complete neutrality and thus were encouraging religious activities that may violate individuals' rights to practice their faith as they see fit.

Laws and Cases Involving Freedom of Speech

The First Amendment states, "Congress shall make no law respecting an establishment of religion, or prohibiting the free exercise thereof, or abridging the freedom of speech." The simplicity of this statement is marred by nearly 200 years of debate about its meaning and its application in a modern society. On its face, it seems to provide an absolute right to say anything. Constitutional authorities, however, have recognized that there are limitations. A government has a legitimate interest in maintaining order to protect its citizens from harm that they bring on themselves, from harm that may be perpetrated by a foreign government, and from harm caused by a governmental authority such as the state itself. Those limitations to the freedom of speech are the subjects of the cases and laws that follow. Also included in the concept of speech is a more controversial issue of "symbolic speech." The following is by no means an exhaustive list, but it does cover the major issues governing free speech.

Libel and Slander Laws

Libel and slander are civil wrongs regulated through state laws. These laws have their roots in English common law. Libel and slander laws are directed at the historical problem of defamation, or communicating false information and thereby causing injury to a person's good name and reputation. Libel and slander laws represent the traditional form of limiting free speech and free press. Slander is rarely prosecuted because it is difficult to produce convincing evidence of slander. Libel used to have both criminal and civil remedies, but general practice today is to sue for civil damages. Court cases define the limitations of expression as regards libel more readily.

Criminal Syndicalism Laws

Several states have enacted criminal syndicalism laws to combat anarchy and advocation of the violent overthrow of the government at various times in history. Included in many of these laws were prohibitions against the written or spoken word that advocated the violent overthrow of the government, rebellion against the government, or anarchy. Prior to 1969, the courts generally upheld such provisions, particularly in the case *Gitlow v. New York*. However, this precedent was reversed in *Brandenburg v. Ohio*.

Alien and Sedition Acts of 1798

These acts, especially the Sedition Act, also called the Act for the Punishment of Certain Crimes, greatly restricted freedom of speech and freedom of the press in the first major attempt to control political dissent in the new nation of the United States. A series of four acts passed by the Federalist-controlled Congress during President John Adams's term of office, these laws were directed at curbing subversive activities by possible foreign agents. The infamous XYZ affair greatly strained U.S. relations with France and war was believed to be imminent. Additionally, the Federalists were alarmed by the growing strength of the Democratic-Republican Party and angry at many of the remarks made about the Federalists in the Republican press. The other laws making up this legislation established a residency requirement for aliens before they could apply for citizenship, allowed the president to deport any alien considered dangerous to the nation's safety or peace, and allowed the deportation of any enemy alien during a time of war. These last three laws were never enforced and eventually were repealed or expired on their own. The Sedition Act resulted in several prosecutions and ten convictions before it expired by statutory regulation in 1801. The unpopularity of these laws largely contributed to the Democratic-Republican victories of the era, most notably Thomas Jefferson's rise to the presidency in 1800.

Postal Act of 1865

The first postal regulation of obscene material, this law makes it illegal to send obscene material of any kind through the mails, including envelopes or postcards with "scurrilous epithets" written or printed on them. This piece of legislation, as amended and codified by the Comstock Act, has remained the device for most of the federal prosecutions of obscenity. It allows for a maximum fine of $5,000 or up to five years in jail, or both.

Regina v. Hicklin
L.R. 3 Q.B. 360 (1868)

The *Hicklin* test, the original standard for defining obscenity, required proof that the item in question had the tendency to deprave and corrupt the minds of individuals open to immoral influences. This 1868 case was an English court decision, but the test it set down was used by the U.S. courts until it was rejected by the *Roth* decision in 1957. The original English case involved the publication of an anti-Catholic pamphlet that was declared obscene because it included specific statements contained in confessionals. The two most important elements of the *Hicklin* test were that the item did not have to be shown to offend the "average person" but only had to be shown to have a bad effect on any susceptible group and that only a single passage within the work had to be determined as obscene for the entire work to be declared illegal. Prominent books ruled as obscene under *Hicklin* included *Casanova's Homecoming* by Arthur Schnitzler, *The Well of Loneliness* by Radclyffe Hall, *An American Tragedy* by Theodore Dreiser, *Lady Chatterley's Lover* by D. H. Lawrence, and *Tropic of Cancer* and *Tropic of Capricorn,* both by Henry Miller.

Comstock Act

Also known as the Federal Anti-Obscenity Act of 1873, this law has been responsible for nearly all of the convictions within the federal courts for obscenity. It reenacted the Postal Act of 1865 and placed the regulations against sending obscene materials through the mails into the U.S. Code (Title 18 U.S.C. Sec. 1461). Named for Anthony Comstock, the leading nineteenth-century anti-obscenity crusader, the Comstock Act does not make obscenity a crime but instead makes it illegal to send obscene literature through the mail. This law added the descriptive words *lewd* and *lascivious* to the wording of the Postal Act as a further prohibition within the statutory definition. In 1909, the Comstock Act was amended to include the phrase "and every filthy" as well as the word *vile* to the definition of what could be banned from the mails.

United States v. Kennerly
209 F. 119 (S.D.N.Y., 1913)

Kennerly is often cited because of the well-respected opinion of the noted jurist Learned Hand, and it is a prime example of the dissent against the *Hicklin* test, despite its dominance in the courts for much of the first half of the twentieth century. Judge Hand espoused the concept of community standards in this decision, acknowledging that society changes its tolerance regarding sexual matters over time.

Espionage Act of 1917 and Sedition Act of 1918

These two laws were enacted during World War I to protect U.S. interests from suspected subversives in the country during the war and were most often used to prosecute antiwar dissenters. The text of the law made it illegal to "willfully utter, print, write or publish any disloyal, profane, scurrilous or abusive language about the form of government of the United States or the Constitution." Provisions were also made against acts of espionage, including making false statements with the intent to damage the war effort, making statements causing disloyalty or insubordination within military ranks, and the obstruction of recruiting efforts. Among many war dissenters prosecuted under these acts was the Socialist Eugene Debs, who ran for the presidency in 1920 from prison while serving his sentence. The laws inspired the so-called Red Scare, or the anti-Communist Palmer raids, led by Attorney General A. Mitchell Palmer. These laws also were the subject of many landmark cases of the era including *Schenck v. United States, Frohwerk v. United States, Abrams v. United States,* and *Debs v. United States.*

Schenck v. United States
39 S.Ct. 247 (1919)

Schenck v. United States established the "clear and present danger" test for protection of dissenting speech. When the United States entered World War I in 1917, the Selective Service Act was enacted to build up the military forces. The Espionage Act was also passed to protect the nation from sabotage, and this act made it illegal to use false statements to interfere with the war effort, to promote the success of the enemy, or to obstruct recruiting efforts. Charles Schenck was head of the Socialist Party and had published leaflets criticizing the draft and urging draftees to resist. The Supreme Court, in a decision written by Chief Justice Oliver Wendell Holmes, upheld the Espionage Act conviction on the grounds that Schenck's call for resistance presented a "clear and present danger" during a time of war. Holmes acknowledged that Schenck expressed ideas that would have been within his constitutional rights during peacetime but held that the conditions of the time dictated that Schenck's act was a threat to security.

Frohwerk v. United States
39 S.Ct. 249 (1919)

The *Frohwerk* case was the first case to affirm the *Schenck* test of a "clear and present danger." Under the Espionage Act of 1917, many antiwar dissenters were convicted of interfering with the war, including Jacob Frohwerk. Two other celebrated cases of the time prosecuted under this law were *Debs v. United States* 39 S.Ct. 252 (1919) and *Abrams v. United States* 40 S.Ct. 17 (1919). In *Debs,* the great Socialist Party leader Eugene Debs was convicted and sentenced to ten years in prison. He ran for the presidency from his cell and was only released by a pardon from President Warren G. Harding.

Meyer v. Nebraska
43 S.Ct. 625 (1923)

In this school administrative rights case, it was ruled that the state may not ban the teaching of subjects that are not harmful to the health or morals of children. Robert Meyer was convicted of teaching his Zion Parochial School students their subjects in German. A Nebraska law prohibiting the use of any foreign language for elementary school instruction was stricken on the grounds that it violated the teacher's right to instruct.

Gitlow v. New York
45 S.Ct. 625 (1925)

Gitlow established the "bad tendency" test regarding protected speech. In 1902, the State of New York had passed the Anarchy Act in the wake of that assassination of President William McKinley by the anarchist Leon Czolgosz. This law made it illegal to advocate the overthrow of the government by force or violence. Benjamin Gitlow, a member of the radical wing of the Socialist Party, published a pamphlet in 1925 attacking the moderate wing of the Socialists. This manifesto entitled "The Revolutionary Age" also predicted victory in the struggle by the proletariat and called for mass strikes. The Supreme Court upheld Gitlow's conviction but suspended the test of a "clear and present danger" established in the earlier *Schenck* case. Clear and present danger went out of favor during the Court's use of bad tendency. In a sense, clear and present danger was rejected by the Court but not specifically. The same is true about the bad tendency doctrine now. Theoretically, the Court could still invoke it. Justice Edward Sanford argued, in the written opinion, that speech of such nature can be punished even though there is no imminent danger because the speech is of a "bad tendency" that threatens breaches of the peace. Though the "bad tendency" doctrine was invoked in cases for several years, most notably *Whitney v. California,* the Court rejected this restriction in 1937 in the case *Dejonge v. Oregon.*

Scopes v. State
154 Tenn. 105 (1927)

This very famous case is known as the "Scopes monkey trial" and was immortalized in the book and later the movie *Inherit the Wind.* John Scopes was charged with teaching evolution in his classroom, which was against Tennessee state law. His trial became an international event with the prosecution conducted by three-time presidential candidate William Jennings Bryan and the defense by the noted attorney Clarence Darrow. Scopes was convicted and fined $100. The law was never overturned in this case, but Scopes's conviction was reversed on a technicality by the Tennessee Supreme Court.

Whitney v. California
47 S.Ct. 641 (1927)

Whitney upheld the California Syndicalism Act, which prohibited advocacy of the violent overthrow of the government and affirmed the

Gitlow "bad tendency" test. Anita Whitney was a 60-year-old woman who joined the Communist Labor Party and was convicted of violating the California Syndicalism Act based solely on her membership in that party.

Tariff Act of 1930

This regulation of international commerce enables the U.S. Customs Service to confiscate any material it deems obscene. It is the primary piece of legislation used to block the entry of obscene materials produced in other countries. Upon a court order ruling an item obscene, the Customs Service can destroy any copies of that item. The actions of the service represent a form of national censorship. Such noted works as Henry Miller's *Tropic of Cancer* and *Tropic of Capricorn* have fallen victim to this act. The law also permits the confiscation of items that are not considered obscene if they are shipped in the same container with materials ruled obscene, unless the owner of the container can show that the obscene materials were shipped without his or her knowledge or consent.

United States v. One Book Called "Ulysses"
72 F.2d 705 (1934)

The *Ulysses* case is an example of a major literary masterpiece that survived a challenge under the *Hicklin* test. In a New York district court decision, the court found that the language used, though considered obscene by the standards of the day, was necessary to the purpose of the work and natural for the type of characters portrayed. The opinion rejected the usual practice of citing excerpts to prove obscenity and instead viewed the book for its literary value as a whole. This test became known as the *Ulysses* standard because it was the first case in which a work was judged as a whole.

Dejonge v. Oregon
57 S.Ct. 255 (1937)

Dejonge effectively reversed the "bad tendency" doctrine set down in *Gitlow*. Dirk Dejonge was convicted under the Oregon Criminal Syndicalism Act for his membership in the Communist Party. The Supreme Court ruled that mere bad tendency was not enough to show criminal action. Though the "bad tendency" doctrine has never been ruled unconstitutional, the *Dejonge* case places it into doubt.

Foreign Agents Registration Act of 1938

This law had one provision relevant to free speech issues. It defined "communist political propaganda" as any item or form of communication or expression (1) that attempted to convert or indoctrinate anyone or any section of the general public to a political viewpoint contrary to that of the United States or (2) that promoted racial or religious dissension or advocated violence or the violent overthrow of the U.S. government. This definition was used by subsequent acts, particularly the Postal Service and Federal Employees Salary Act of 1962, in determining what could or could not be sent through the mail.

Hatch Act of 1939

Also known as the Hatch Political Activities Act, the Hatch Act governs the political activities of federal employees including limitations on their right to speak or act in political campaigns or causes. The law was named for its sponsor, Carl Hatch, a Democratic senator from New Mexico. The original intent of the law was to protect employees from supervisors who might pressure subordinates into campaigning for a candidate or providing some other support. Except for voting, all federal employees, with the exception of the top political appointees, are barred from all forms of partisan political activities including campaigning or making speeches. These provisions have been challenged in recent years as a violation of First Amendment rights, but the law has been upheld by the Supreme Court in such cases as *Civil Service Commission v. Letter Carriers* (1973) and *Oklahoma v. United States Civil Service Commission* (1947). Many states have passed their own Hatch acts governing state employees as well.

Smith Act of 1940

Also known as the Alien Registration Act of 1940, the Smith Act is the primary U.S. law regulating political dissent for the purpose of ensuring national loyalty. Named for one of its sponsors, Howard W. Smith, a Democratic congressman from Virginia, the Smith Act was the first peacetime sedition law in the United States since the Alien and Sedition Acts of 1798. To date, it remains the federal sedition law. In 1948 it was amended, and it was slightly revised again in 1957. The statute makes it a crime to advocate the overthrow of the U.S. government by violence or force, to publish any form of communication that advocates the violent overthrow of the government, or to establish an organization for this purpose. The Supreme Court has ruled that the Smith Act is constitutional. The two most relevant cases are *Dennis v. United States* (1951) and *Yates v. United States* (1957).

Bridges v. California
62 S.Ct. 190 (1941)

This landmark Supreme Court case reversed the *Gitlow* bad tendency doctrine by reaffirming the clear and present danger test. Harry Bridges was a labor leader of a union involved in a trial. After he threatened the secretary of labor with a strike if the secretary enforced the trial judge's ruling against his union, Bridges was convicted of contempt of court. The Supreme Court not only reversed the contempt charge, which was based on the bad tendency test, but also permitted fair comments on pending cases and judges similar to Bridges's criticisms of the trial judge in his case.

Chaplinsky v. New Hampshire
62 S.Ct. 766 (1942)

The *Chaplinsky* decision established the famous "fighting words" doctrine in which works or utterances that stir anger in others and that have little social value are not protected by the First Amendment. Walter Chaplinsky, a Jehovah's Witness, was distributing literature in Rochester, New Hampshire. Town citizens complained to the chief of police that Chaplinsky had denounced all religions as a "racket." When the chief warned Chaplinsky that he was angering the crowd, Chaplinsky called the chief a "God-damned racketeer" and "a damn Fascist and the whole government of Rochester are Fascists or agents of Fascists." Chaplinsky was convicted of violating a statute prohibiting offensive, derisive, or annoying words said to others in a public place. The Supreme Court upheld the conviction on the grounds that the words were "fighting words" that could provoke the average person to retaliation, thereby causing a breach of the peace. This decision has remained a test of permissible speech, though two cases challenging the rule, *Gooding v. Wilson* (1972) and *Lewis v. New Orleans* (1974), were dismissed on the grounds that the laws under which they were prosecuted were "vague" and "overbroad."

Valentine v. Chrestensen
62 S.Ct. 920 (1942)

This was the first major commercial speech case of the Supreme Court. Under *Valentine* the concept of "commercial speech" was created, and the Court ruled that such commercial speech did not enjoy the same protection as noncommercial speech. Several subsequent cases, however, have drastically modified this doctrine and allowed more protection in certain circumstances.

Terminiello v. Chicago
69 S.Ct. 894 (1949)

The *Terminiello* decision ruled that when an audience provokes public disorder, the speaker's words are protected by the First Amendment. Father Arthur Terminiello was a defrocked Catholic priest. In 1949, he delivered a speech entitled "Christian Nationalism or World Communism—Which?" to a crowd of 8,000 in a Chicago auditorium. An ugly mob that developed outside the auditorium blocked access to the doors; tossed bottles, stink bombs, and bricks inside; and shouted "Hitlers," "Nazis," and "God-damned Fascists" at Terminiello and his followers. Terminiello, recognizing that some of the mob had entered the hall, called them "slimy scum" and went on to predict a destruction of the society by "communist, Zionist Jews." He was arrested for breach of the peace. The Supreme Court reversed Terminiello's conviction on the grounds that one purpose of free speech is to invite dispute and that this may, on occasion, cause disorder. The deciding factor was that when a crowd creates disorder, an individual's right to speak must be protected.

Internal Security Act of 1950

The Internal Security Act placed severe limitations on political dissent branded "communist" as well as on the right to association. During the cold war era of the 1950s, this act was passed to curtail what were seen as subversive activities by Communist organizations. Also called the McCarran Act, its chief sponsor was Patrick McCarran, a Democratic senator from Nevada, and it was enacted over President Harry Truman's veto. The provisions of the law created a Subversives Activities Control Board that could order any organization it found to be Communist to register with the Justice Department and submit its membership list. The act also made it illegal to conduct any activities that might establish a totalitarian dictatorship in the United States. Court rulings in the 1960s upheld the provisions for registering organizations but struck down requirements for revealing member-ship. Since 1968, the board has only compiled a public list of organizations and a list of groups and individuals it considers to be Communist, and it no longer requires registration with the Justice Department.

Dennis v. United States
71 S.Ct. 857 (1951)

The *Dennis* case established the concept that "advocacy of abstract ideas" is constitutionally acceptable but "advocacy of action" is not. Eugene Dennis was the secretary of the Communist Party in the United States. He was convicted under the Alien Registration Act of 1940, also known as the Smith Act, for advocating the violent overthrow of the U.S. government. Dennis argued that he advocated force only because the ruling classes would never allow a peaceful transformation to a Communist government. Chief Justice Fred Vinson, writing for the majority, upheld the conviction on the "clear and present danger" test in that Dennis's advocacy of action threatened peace and stability. Vinson noted that the Smith Act was not directed at mere discussion or ideas. The Court saw conspiracy to overthrow the government as sufficient grounds for suppression of speech. The concept that advocacy of action was punishable but advocacy of ideas was protected was further supported by the 1957 case of *Yates v. United States.*

Feiner v. New York
71 S.Ct. 303 (1951)

In *Feiner,* the Supreme Court ruled that when a speaker, not a crowd, provokes disorder, his or her speech is not protected. Irving Feiner was a college student in Syracuse, New York, who was using a loudspeaker to encourage attendance at a Young Progressives rally in the Hotel Syracuse. After Feiner made derogatory remarks about President Truman and the local authorities, the crowd became restless. Feiner also urged blacks in the audience to "rise up in arms and fight for their rights." At this point, a white person in the crowd demanded that the police arrest Feiner and threatened to punch out the speaker. Because the police feared a riot, Feiner was arrested for disorderly conduct. Chief Justice Fred Vinson's majority opinion found that the content of Feiner's message was not the cause of the arrest but instead that the arrest had resulted from the reaction that the message provoked. Vinson cautioned against handing police authorities complete discretion to stop lawful public meetings but said that incitement to riot was a breach of the peace and was not protected by the First Amendment.

Beauharnais v. Illinois
72 S.Ct. 725 (1952)

This seminal case was the first Supreme Court decision to apply the notion of group libel, which suggests that classes of individuals can be harmed in the same manner as one person. Joseph Beauharnais was the president of the White Circle League, a racist organization in Chicago. He and his supporters were arrested for distributing leaflets on street corners that called for excluding blacks from white neighborhoods and that claimed blacks would increase crime levels if they were allowed to establish homes in white neighborhoods. The Court upheld the Illinois law prohibiting any publication that defamed any race, color, creed, or religion and stated that the legislature had acted within reason to curb statements made to flare the emotional debate about racial issues. Justices Hugo Black and William Douglas dissented, arguing that the Illinois law created a state censorship system.

Burstyn v. Wilson
72 S.Ct. 777 (1952)

The *Burstyn* case established the film medium as a legitimate form of expression protected by the First Amendment and reversed several earlier decisions, most notably *Mutual Film Corporation v. Industrial Commission of Ohio* (35 S.Ct. 387 [1915]), which had declared film to be a medium subject to censorship. Roberto Rossellini's film *The Miracle* was banned in New York State on the grounds that it was sacrilegious. The Court ruled that films are not different from books, even when they entertain as well as inform.

Neiman-Marcus v. Lait
107 F.Supp. 96 (1952)

This was the first federal case that permitted corporations to sue for libel. Neiman-Marcus sued publishers of a book that claimed its models and sales personnel were call girls. A federal court supported the argument of "corporate libel" and determined that corporations as well as individuals can suffer such damage.

Roth v. United States
77 S.Ct. 1304 (1957)

The *Roth* test is the second landmark obscenity standard, and it greatly liberalized the test for obscenity and reversed the *Hicklin* test. Samuel Roth was a publisher of books and magazines that were considered obscene by some authorities. Roth was convicted under federal obscenity statutes when he mailed advertisements in an attempt to boost sales. The *Roth* test is one of the most significant tests for obscenity because it set broad criteria for courts to use in defining what was to be considered obscene. In addition, it had a wide-ranging impact on, first, the publishing of classic literature ruled obscene under the *Hicklin* test and, second, the production and distribution of pornography after 1957. The *Roth* test has four components. First, the mere portrayal of sexual acts is insufficient grounds to declare a work obscene. Instead, it must be shown that a work appeals to the "prurient interest." Second, the test must not be applied only to one susceptible group but to the average person. Third, "contemporary community standards," though ways of determining such standards are not set forth, must be violated before a work can be judged obscene. Last, a work must be considered in its entirety. If only one passage in the work is considered obscene, the work cannot be censored or banned on the basis of that passage alone.

Sweezy v. New Hampshire
77 S.Ct. 1203 (1957)

In *Sweezy*, the Supreme Court defended academic freedom and reinstated a professor who had been fired for expressing views as a "classic Marxist" and "Socialist." Paul Sweezy, a visiting lecturer at the University of New Hampshire, was dismissed for admitting that he held Marxist and Socialist views. The 1951 New Hampshire Subversive Activities Act had made it unlawful to employ "subversive persons." The Court reversed Sweezy's dismissal on the grounds that the questions Sweezy refused to answer during a dismissal hearing had not been authorized by the New Hampshire legislature. Chief Justice Earl Warren also wrote an eloquent defense of academic freedom, stating that "to impose any strait-jacket upon the intellectual leaders in our colleges and universities would impel the future of our Nation."

Yates v. United States
77 S.Ct. 1064 (1957)

The *Dennis* test of "advocacy of action" was clarified in *Yates*. Oleta Yates was convicted of conspiracy to overthrow the government by organizing Communist Party activities. The Supreme Court reversed her conviction on the grounds that mere discussion was not "advocacy of action" but instead "advocacy of abstract ideas" and, as such, was protected speech.

Farmers Educational and Cooperative Union of America
v. WDAY, Inc.
79 S.Ct. 1302 (1959)

The Supreme Court ruled in this case that broadcast stations cannot be held accountable for libelous statements made by individuals who have been given equal time under Federal Communications Commission guidelines. The case involved a candidate for the U.S. Senate who suggested that the Farmers Union was Communist-controlled during an equal-time debate.

Smith v. California
80 S.Ct. 215 (1959)

In cases regarding obscenity, the concept of "scienter" is the level of awareness needed to prove that an individual is legally responsible. In *Smith*, the Court ruled that an accused party must be aware that obscenity existed in a work before he or she could be convicted of possessing or selling obscene materials. Eleazar Smith was a bookstore owner charged with selling an obscene book. No proof that Smith knew the contents of the book was shown. The Court feared that without this protection, a chilling effect would occur on what could legally be sold.

Noto v. United States
81 S.Ct. 1517 (1961)

This case is notable because it ended prosecutions under the membership clause of the Smith Act. John Noto was able to show that there was a lack of evidence in the Communist Party literature to prove that "advocacy of action" existed as a result of membership in the party. Consequently, his conviction based on his membership in the Communist Party was overturned by the Supreme Court.

Times Film Corporation v. Chicago
81 S.Ct. 391 (1961)

The *Times Film Corporation* case permitted prior restraint in the public showing of films. The case involved an attempt to show the film *Don Juan* in Chicago. Denied a permit to show the film, the corporation sued. Relying on both the *Roth* and the *Near* decisions, the Court recognized the difficulties caused by prior restraint but ruled that exceptional cases existed and that film showings were considered exceptional.

Manual Enterprises v. Day
82 S.Ct. 1432 (1962)

In *Manual Enterprises,* the Court broadened the *Roth* test concerning "prurient interest appeal" to also include "patent offensiveness." Postmaster General J. Edward Day had ruled that certain magazines of male nudes appealed to homosexuals and therefore were obscene. Justice John Harlan reversed Day's ban on these magazines, arguing that both "prurient interest appeal" and "patent offensiveness" had to be shown for material to be declared obscene.

Garrison v. Louisiana
85 S.Ct. 209 (1964)

An important clarification of the "actual malice" doctrine was made in this case involving Jim Garrison, one of the individuals closely involved with President John Kennedy's assassination. Garrison was the New Orleans district attorney who believed the Mafia killed President Kennedy. Garrison's angry confrontations with Louisiana justices ended when the Supreme Court ruled that they, and any other public official, must show more than a "reasonable belief" with a libel charge. This test requiring more than a "reasonable belief" means that it is not enough to show that it seems obvious to most people that a statement was libelous (a reasonable belief) but that it must be proven that the person who made the statement meant to hurt someone (actual malice).

Jacobellis v. Ohio
84 S.Ct. 1676 (1964)

In another test of the *Roth* standard, the Supreme Court added two concepts: first, that a work must be determined to be "utterly without redeeming social importance" and, second, that community standards were "national" in scope. Nico Jacobellis was a motion-picture theater manager who had shown a film that contained an explicit love scene. Justice William Brennan argued, in the majority opinion, that to be considered obscene, a work had to be completely without redeeming social value. Brennan also made it clear that *Roth* never meant "community" standards to allow a case-by-case challenge in every community but rather viewed such "community" standards as one national standard.

New York Times v. Sullivan
84 S.Ct. 710 (1964)

The *New York Times* case established the doctrine of "actual malice," also known as the *New York Times* rule, in the Supreme Court. L. B. Sullivan was a commissioner of the City of Montgomery, Alabama, who was responsible for public affairs, including the police department. On March 29, 1960, the *New York Times* carried a full-page, paid advertisement condemning the Montgomery police for actions taken against students in a civil rights demonstration. Some of the statements, made by black clergy who commissioned the ad, were later proven to be false. Sullivan was awarded $500,000 in damages by the Alabama courts, but this award was reversed by the Supreme Court. The *New York Times* rule now requires all public officials to prove "actual malice" on the part of the defendant in libel cases. "Actual malice" is the publication of a falsehood with prior knowledge that it is not true or with reckless disregard for the truth.

Freedman v. Maryland
85 S.Ct. 734 (1965)

Freedman provided better and more specific criteria for establishing prior restraint. Ronald Freedman challenged the Maryland Board of Censors by showing the film *Revenge at Daybreak* without submitting it for prior approval. The Court overturned the Maryland statutes concerning approval of films and established three criteria for prior restraint. First, the censoring agency has the burden of proof to show that obscenity exists. Second, only a brief period of prior restraint is allowed for judicial review. Last, there must be an assurance of prompt judicial review.

Bond v. Floyd
87 S.Ct. 339 (1966)

The *Bond* case established the concept that, in a democracy, the representatives of government must have the "widest latitude" to express their views on policy issues. In 1966, Julian Bond was the only Black American representative in the Georgia House of

Representatives. In a speech, Bond praised the Student Non-violent Coordination Committee's (SNCC) call for resistance against the draft and the Vietnam War, though he pointed out that he still had his draft card and had not counseled anyone else to burn theirs. On the grounds that these remarks indicated a lack of support for the Constitution, the Georgia House refused to seat Bond or to allow him to take the oath of office. The Court, in a unanimous decision, reversed the expulsion and stated that government legislators and policy makers needed the "widest latitude" possible in the development of policy in order to preserve the principles of democracy.

Ginzburg v. United States
86 S.Ct. 969 (1966)

In this case, the Supreme Court considered materials with a sexual theme to be obscene if they are commercially exploited, even if their actual content would not be judged obscene under constitutional tests. Ralph Ginzburg, a publisher of sex-oriented books, tried to operate an advertising campaign through the Intercourse and Blue Ball, Pennsylvania, post offices. Ginzburg was convicted of violating federal obscenity statutes when he mailed large numbers of circulars through the Middlesex, New Jersey, post office. The Court believed the deliberate attempt to appeal to the reader's sexual interests met the test of "prurient interest."

Associated Press v. Walker
87 S.Ct. 1975 (1967)

This famous case established the concept of "hot news," which is news that needs to be disseminated immediately before it becomes irrelevant, as a defense in libel cases. General Edwin Walker charged a newspaper with libel for reports on his actions during the court-ordered entry of James Meredith, the first black American enrolled at the University of Mississippi. The Court ruled that in cases involving public figures, no libel could be charged for the publication of "hot news."

A Book Named "John Cleland's Memoirs of a Woman of Pleasure" v. Attorney General of Massachusetts
86 S.Ct. 975 (1967)

In *Memoirs,* Justice William Brennan clarified the previous concepts of "prurient interest," "patent offensiveness," and "utterly without social redeeming value" by requiring that each test be applied independently. Though *Fanny Hill,* as the Cleland book was also known, was considered to have little social value, it could not be judged obscene because it was not "utterly worthless." This became the final revision of the *Roth* test and is known as the *Memoirs* standard.

Curtis Publishing Company v. Butts; Associated Press v. Walker
87 S.Ct. 1975 (1967)

In the *Butts* case, the Supreme Court defined "reckless disregard" and introduced the concept of "hot news" in libel cases. When a reporter has time to investigate a story that is not "hot news" (news that needs to be disseminated immediately), it is a "reckless disregard for the truth" if an investigation is not made and falsehoods are reported as a result. The *Butts* case involved the alleged fixing of a football game between the University of Georgia coach Wally Butts and the University of Alabama coach Paul "Bear" Bryant.

Redrup v. New York
87 S.Ct. 1414 (1967)

Redrup is most notable as marking a period in the Supreme Court of minimum regulation of obscenity. The *Redrup* decision detailed the differences of opinion within the Court, which were then used for issuing summary reversals, without opinions. From 1967 to 1973, the Court decided 31 cases as a result of *Redrup* without hearing actual arguments.

Ginsberg v. New York
88 S.Ct. 1274 (1968)

In *Ginsberg,* the Supreme Court made it clear that the sale of obscene literature to youths is illegal. Sam Ginsberg was convicted of selling obscene magazines to a youth without determining the youth's age. The Court ruled that the state has an interest in protecting the welfare of children and that this interest permits the state to enforce broader standards regarding children than those for adults.

Oestereich v. Selective Service Board No. 11
89 S.Ct. 414 (1968)

This case clarified the O'Brien draft card–burning decision and ruled that an agency cannot switch a person's status or exemption as punishment for actions unrelated to the merits of that status. James Oestereich, a divinity student in the Boston area, deposited his draft card in the collection plate at church in protest of the Vietnam War. The Selective Service Board reclassified his draft status as a seminarian to I-A, or eligible for military duty, when it learned of his action. Justice William O. Douglas, writing for the majority, stated, "Once a person registers and qualifies for a statutory exemption we find no legislative authority to deprive him of that exemption because of conduct of activities unrelated to the merits of granting or continuing that exemption." Oestereich's conviction was overturned.

Pickering v. Board of Education
88 S.Ct. 731 (1968)

In this landmark academic freedom case, the Supreme Court strengthened the legal concept of academic freedom in overruling the dismissal of a teacher for writing a letter to the local newspaper. Marvin Pickering was an Illinois high school teacher who wrote a highly critical letter to the local paper. The letter criticized the school board and the superintendent for the way proposals to raise educational funding were conducted and for the manner of funding athletic programs. The school board charged Pickering with failure to comply with the faculty handbook, which required that all letters to local media be submitted for approval. The board also charged that Pickering had made factual errors regarding the athletic budget and that his letter could create too much controversy that might hurt the efforts of the school system to maintain funding. Pickering was dismissed after a hearing, but the Supreme Court, in a unanimous decision, reversed the dismissal. The Court's logic relied on the "actual malice" principle established in *New York Yimes v. Sullivan* and also, more important, found that a contribution to the public debate was to be equally protected whether it came from a member of the general public or a school employee.

United States v. O'Brien
88 S.Ct. 1673 (1968)

The *O'Brien* decision indicated that the Supreme Court is willing to protect "pure speech" more than "symbolic speech." On March 31, 1966, David O'Brien and three friends burned their draft cards on the steps of the South Boston Courthouse as a protest of the Vietnam War and conscription. O'Brien was convicted of violating a 1965 federal law prohibiting destruction or alteration of the card. The Supreme Court rejected O'Brien's argument that, as symbolic speech, his act was protected by the First Amendment. The Court recognized the legitimate need to raise manpower for the military and argued that in a situation where both speech and nonspeech elements existed, the government was justified in regulating the nonspeech activities. With this case, the Supreme Court ruled that the draft system was constitutional and that the government could demand compliance with the law.

Brandenburg v. Ohio
89 S.Ct. 1827 (1969)

In *Brandenburg,* the Supreme Court redefined the *Dennis* principle of "advocacy of action." Clarence Brandenburg was a leader of the Ohio Ku Klux Klan. In a rally televised on Cincinnati TV, Brandenburg, wearing the Klan white robe, stated that "revenge" might be necessary if the president and the Congress continued to suppress the white race. In a second broadcast, he also said, "Personally, I believe the nigger should be returned to Africa, the Jew returned to Israel." Brandenburg was convicted under the Ohio Criminal Syndicalism Act and sentenced to one to ten years in prison for these remarks. The Supreme Court declared the Ohio statute unconstitutional and reversed Brandenburg's conviction on the grounds that any advocacy of action that does not call for illegal action is protected by the First Amendment.

Keefe v. Geanakos
418 F.2d 359 (1969)

In an appeals court faculty rights decision, the use of a "dirty" word in classroom instruction was upheld. Robert Keefe, a high-school English teacher, assigned an article that had the word "mother-fucker" in its text. Both the article and the word's significance were discussed in class. When he was suspended from his job after a committee hearing was held, Keefe sued in federal court. The court of appeals noted that other forms of instruction and materials included obscene words and that students were well aware of the word in question and ruled in favor of Keefe's use in this situation. Two other federal cases, *Parducci v. Rutland* (316 F.Supp. 352 [1970]) and *Mailloux v. Kiley* (323 F.Supp. 1387 [1971]) dealt with similar words in the classroom and supported the Keefe decision on much the same grounds.

Stanley v. Georgia
89 S.Ct. 1243 (1969)

The *Stanley* decision "prohibits making mere private possession of obscene materials a crime" and is the major privacy guideline in obscenity cases. Robert Stanley was suspected of running a bookmaking operation out of his home. A police raid failed to discover any gambling evidence, but several pornographic films were found. Stanley was convicted of the possession of obscene materials. The Court agreed with Stanley that the right to privacy protected his choice of reading and viewing materials within the confines of his own home.

Street v. New York
89 S.Ct. 1354 (1969)

The *Street* decision declared the act of flag burning to be protected symbolic speech. Sidney Street heard the news that a sniper had killed James Meredith, the first black to be admitted to the University of Mississippi, on June 6, 1966. In his anger, he burned a U.S. flag on a street corner in New York City, saying, "We don't need no damn flag." Street was convicted of violating a New York State statute that prohibited defiling the flag. The Supreme Court overturned his conviction. They found that Street had not incited anyone else to commit an illegal act and that he had not uttered any unprotected words or speech, such as "fighting words." Furthermore, Justice John Harlan, writing for the majority, argued that the speech in this case was within the constitutional guarantees to disagree with the existing order. The dissenting justices, however, believed Street had not been punished for expressing his ideas, a constitutionally protected right, but for destroying the property of the flag, even though it was his own flag.

Tinker v. Des Moines Independent Community School District
89 S.Ct. 733 (1969)

The *Tinker* case demonstrated that the Supreme Court was more willing to protect symbolic speech if it could be considered "display" rather than "desecration." *Tinker* also became a landmark student rights case. Several public school students in Des Moines, Iowa, decided to wear black armbands to school as a protest against the Vietnam War. When school administrators demanded the removal of the armbands, members of the Tinker and Eckhardt families refused and were suspended from school. The fathers of the students brought the case to the Supreme Court. Justice Abe Fortas wrote the majority opinion and found wearing armbands as a protest akin to "pure speech." Fortas noted that the school authorities had not banned any other symbol and that the armband was not connected to any disruptive behavior. The Court ruled in this case that such displays of symbolic speech are permissible under the Constitution.

Watts v. United States
89 S.Ct. 1399 (1969)

The *Watts* case established the concept that "threatening words" are not protected, at least in certain cases. During an antiwar rally at the Washington Monument in the nation's capital on August 17, 1966, Robert Watts was a participant in a small-group discussion about the draft. He loudly complained about having just received his notice to report for his military physical and said that "if they ever make me carry a rifle the first man I want to get in my sights is L.B.J. [President Lyndon Johnson]." Watts thereupon was arrested for threatening the president. The Supreme Court noted that these were "threatening words" but that in context they were said in the heat of political debate, with considerable evidence presented that no willfulness to carry out the threat existed. Such words in this case were called "political hyperbole" and, though they were threatening, were judged under these circumstances to be pro-tected by the First Amendment. In the case *Kelner v. United States,* the Court found an actual intent to harm in the threatening words and affirmed the conviction of Russell Kelner for planning the assassination of Yasir Arafat, leader of the Palestinian Liberation Organization. These two cases make the doctrine of threatening words ambiguous.

Greenbelt Publishing Association v. Bresler
90 S.Ct. 1527 (1970)

The doctrine of "robust debate" was established in the *Greenbelt* libel case. The Court ruled that society's interest during discussions of substantial concern required a "robust debate" and that this debate was more important than an individual's need to maintain a good reputation. The case involved a news report on a city council debate about housing zone ordinances where some people in attendance accused a real-estate developer of using blackmail tactics.

Guzick v. Drebus
431 F.2d 594 (1970);
cert. denied 91 S.Ct. 941 (1971)

In refusing to hear the *Guzick* case, which involved a student rights issue, the Supreme Court affirmed an appeals court decision denying a student the right to distribute pamphlets. Thomas Guzick, a student at Shaw High School in Chicago, asked the principal for permission to distribute pamphlets for an antiwar rally. When denied the permission, Guzick sued in federal court. The appeals court compared *Guzick* to *Tinker* and found that Shaw High had a long-standing rule prohibiting all items such as buttons, banners, and pamphlets unrelated to education matters, whereas in *Tinker* a similar general prohibition was lacking. The Court also saw that racial polarization in the school was a problem and that political symbols contributed to that situation. The justices believed that the school had a legitimate need to maintain order under these circumstances.

Cohen v. California
91 S.Ct. 1780 (1971)

The *Cohen* case, a major dissenting speech decision, ruled that "offensive" words that did not fall into any unprotected class of speech, such as fighting words or threatening words, were permissible under the First Amendment. During the Vietnam War, there were many forms of protest. Paul Cohen wore a jacket into the Los Angeles County Courthouse that had "Fuck the Draft" inscribed on the back. Upon his arrest, he told the police he wore the jacket only to let others know of his feelings about the war and the draft. The Supreme Court reversed Cohen's conviction for disturbing the peace. Justice John Harlan wrote that offended persons could easily turn their eyes aside and that vulgarity varies in definition from one person to the next. Harlan stated that forbidding a particular word would run the risk of suppressing ideas.

United States v. Thirty-Seven (37) Photographs
91 S.Ct. 1400 (1971)

Thirty-Seven Photographs was the first of several cases that limited the *Stanley* decision regarding privacy. Milton Luros, a publisher of books with sexual themes, was stopped upon entering the United States from a European trip and convicted of possessing pornographic photos. The Court rejected his claim of private possession because a port of entry was not Luros's home. The effect of *Stanley*, *Thirty-Seven Photographs*, and such cases as *United States v. Reidel* (91 S.Ct. 1410 [1971]) and *United States v. Orito* (93 S.Ct. 2674 [1973]) was to limit the protection for private possession of obscene materials to the narrow definition of one's own home.

Board of Regents v. Roth
92 S.Ct. 2701 (1972)

This academic freedom case established that nontenured faculty have fewer rights than tenured faculty. David Roth was given a one-year contract to teach political science at the Wisconsin State University at Oshkosh. His contract was not renewed at the end of the year and no reason was given for not rehiring him. Roth claimed the decision was made to punish him for criticizing the school's administrators for suspending an entire group of black students without determining individual guilt. The Supreme Court upheld Roth's contract denial on the grounds that he did not have a substantial "property" interest in such a decision because he was a nontenure-track faculty member. The Court also reasoned that, although it may be appropriate to give reasons for not rehiring someone, Roth was not constitutionally entitled to such reasons.

Perry v. Sindermann
92 S.Ct. 2717 (1972)

In another important academic freedom case, the Supreme Court recognized that an informal system of tenure exists that provides procedural safeguards to faculty members with many years of service. Robert Sindermann had held several nontenured positions within the state college system of Texas. While he was teaching government and social science at Odessa Junior College, Sindermann had a disagreement with the school's administration. The board of regents did not offer Sindermann a new contract at the end of the 1969 academic year and issued a press release claiming insubordination as the reason. Sindermann was not given a hearing or an official reason for the contract denial. The Supreme Court sided with the professor and ruled that the lack of a hearing before the nonrenewal was a violation of his rights. Using *Board of Regents v. Roth,* the Court reminded the Texas state college system that nontenured faculty did not have such rights unless they had a substantial property interest in continued employment or if nonrenewal would deprive the faculty member of an interest in "liberty" (based entirely on his right to free expression).

The Court accepted Sindermann's argument that his many years of service had produced an informal tenure understanding and that as a result he was entitled to due process.

President's Council District 25 v. Community School Board No. 25
cert. denied, 93 S.Ct. 308 (1972)

President's Council, a school book censorship case, permitted a school authority to restrict the borrowing of a book or other work considered questionable by any one group. The school library in a Queens, New York, school district ordered a copy of *Down These Mean Streets* by Piri Thomas to familiarize the white, middle-class youth of the school with life in nearby Harlem. After objections arose, the school board wrote a policy permitting the book to remain in the library but restricted borrowing privileges to adults. The appeals court argued that no denial of First Amendment rights existed because the book could be discussed in class or checked out by any parent or teacher. The Supreme Court denied certiorari, a court order calling the records of a case up from a lower court, making the appeals court decision final.

Meinhold v. Taylor
cert. denied, 94 S.Ct. 247 (1973)

In refusing to hear this case, the Supreme Court affirmed a lower court ruling permitting school authorities to punish a teacher for expressing his opinion on school matters. Alvin Meinhold was a Nevada public school teacher. After he told his own children he did not believe in compulsory school attendance, he was dismissed for unprofessional conduct. The Nevada Supreme Court held that a teacher's behavior outside the classroom was as important as that inside the classroom. The Supreme Court refused to hear the case, letting the Nevada decision stand. This precedent was reversed in *Givhan v. Western Line Consolidated School District.*

Miller v. California
93 S.Ct. 2607 (1973)

The *Miller* case, a landmark obscenity ruling, is the current standard for defining obscenity. This test is of extreme significance because it reversed the *Roth* test and created much more strict standards by which works can be considered acceptable. Marvin Miller was convicted for distributing advertisements depicting sexual acts, including photos of sexual organs, through the mails to unwilling persons. The *Miller* test has three components. First, the Court defined "community" as not needing to meet a "national" standard. Under *Roth,* community standards remained undefined, and prosecutions were often unable to show that the work in question was unacceptable in any community. With *Miller,* the Court recognized that there were differences in acceptable conduct in each of the states. Second, the concept of "patent offensiveness" was declared the main standard for declaring a work unacceptable, and the Court provided several specific examples of what it considered to be patently offensive. Last, the *Roth* standard of "utterly without social redeeming value" was replaced with a new criterium of "the work, taken as whole, [must lack] serious literary, artistic, political, or scientific value."

Hamling v. United States
97 S.Ct. 2085 (1974)

The *Hamling* case reversed the "national" standard set down in *Jacobellis* as part of the test for obscenity. Justice William Rehnquist argued that the *Miller* test is a "state-wide standard" which must take into account the contemporary moral values of the citizens of only that state, not the entire U.S. as with the *Roth* test. Rehnquist also wrote that the contemporary values of one geographical region as opposed to another region in the same state could be used to judge the offensive nature of the work, such as the more conservative southern region of California rather than the more liberal San Francisco Bay area. In the *Hamling* case, a pornographic novel publisher, William Hamling, failed in his attempt to argue that the jurors in the case, drawn from the conservative Southern District of California, did not represent the entire state for judging "contemporary community standards." However, the Court also determined that juries could use evidence of standards existing in other locales when attempting to determine whether a work is obscene.

Gertz v. Robert Welch, Inc.
94 S.Ct. 2997 (1974)

The Supreme Court ruled in the *Gertz* case that private citizens have more protection against libel than public officials. The case involved an attorney representing a family suing a police officer for the death of one of the family members. Elmer Gertz, the attorney, was accused by the John Birch Society publication *American Opinion* of being a communist. Gertz was ruled a private citizen and it was determined

that negligence, not actual malice, was the test for libel in this
situation. Gertz was free to sue for libel in this instance.

Jenkins v. Georgia
94 S.Ct. 2750 (1974)

In a major test of the *Miller* obscenity standard, the Court determined
in *Jenkins* that a legally constituted jury did not have a full license to
decide what was "patently offensive" and that nudity alone, even
within a sexual context, was not obscene under the *Miller* test. In a
unanimous decision, the Court ruled in favor of the film *Carnal
Knowledge,* ruling that the sexual behavior in the film was only
intimated and that nothing in the film could be construed as patently
offensive using the *Miller* standard.

Smith v. Goguen
94 S.Ct. 1242 (1974)

In another symbolic speech case over use of the flag, a Massachusetts
statute banning misuse of the flag was struck down as vague. Valorie
Goguen had a small U.S. flag sewn to the posterior of his blue jeans
and was convicted of violating the Massachusetts statute. The Supreme
Court declared the law unconstitutional on the grounds that it failed
to define the difference between unceremonial treatments of the flag
that are criminal and those that are not, such as casual clothing styles.

Spence v. Washington
94 S.Ct. 2727 (1974)

Also a flag case, the *Spence* ruling declared that a peace symbol sewn
on the flag and displayed on private property was protected "symbolic
speech." Harold Spence displayed his altered flag from his apartment
window in protest of the invasion of Cambodia and the killing of four
students at Kent State University by Ohio National Guardsmen. He
was convicted of violating a Washington state law prohibiting im-
proper display of the flag. The Supreme Court noted that not only
did Spence's protest take place on personal property and on private
land, but also the symbol was flown without breach of the peace. The
Court considered this act the expression of an idea and therefore
protected by the First Amendment. In both *Spence* and *Goguen,* Justice
William Rehnquist, who is now chief justice, wrote a dissenting
opinion that argued that the preservation of a "unique national

symbol" outweighed any "abstract, scholastic interpretations" of the First Amendment.

Kelner v. United States
534 F.2d 1020 (1976)

As mentioned in the annotation of the *Watts* case (1969), Russell Kelner, a member of the Jewish Defense League, announced that his organization planned to assassinate Yasir Arafat, the leader of the Palestinian Liberation Organization (PLO). Though Kelner argued that this speech was "political hyperbole," the Supreme Court disagreed and found that when intent to harm was present, "threatening words" were not protected speech.

Minarcini v. Strongsville City School District
541 F.2d 577 (1977)

The *Strongsville* case, a school book censorship case, is often cited for its argument against removal of books from a school library. From a list of recommended readings, three books—Kurt Vonnegut's *Cat's Cradle, God Bless You, Mr. Rosewater* and Joseph Heller's *Catch-22*— were considered objectionable by the school board and were removed both from the curriculum and from the school library. The appeals court upheld a district court decision recognizing the authority of the school board to establish the curriculum but reversed the district court's sanction of the removal of the books from the library. The appeals court argued that although a school board has the power to establish a library and set rules for it, the board cannot remove a properly selected book on grounds of personal objections to its contents. Furthermore, the court found that the library provides a useful and necessary adjunct to classroom discussion and that the removal of titles included in classroom discussion or lessons could not be permitted.

Mt. Healthy City School District Board of Education v. Doyle
97 S.Ct. 568 (1977)

In an important faculty rights case, the Supreme Court established the concept that lawful speech activities cannot be used for dismissal on conduct charges if those activities play a substantial role in the dismissal decision and it cannot be shown that the dismissal decision would have been made without such conduct being considered. Fred

Doyle, a nontenured teacher in the Mt. Healthy schools, was involved in several troubling incidents. He got into a slapping match with another teacher, called students "sons-of-bitches," made an obscene gesture to two students who disobeyed him, and argued with the cafeteria staff over the portion of food served him. Doyle also complained about the dress code for teachers in a call to the local radio station. His contract was not renewed for a "notable lack of tact in handling professional matters." The Supreme Court reversed this decision on the grounds that the call to the radio station played a substantial role in Doyle's contract denial and that the school district could not prove Doyle would not have been rehired if such a call had not been made.

Smith v. United States
97 S.Ct. 1756 (1977)

In another challenge to the *Miller* obscenity test, the Supreme Court ruled that state legislatures cannot write community standards into law but that juries must determine such standards on their own. The Court recognized the right of a state to regulate obscenity but not to establish "community standards" in judicial proceedings. *Smith* reduced the effects of *Hamling v. United States* (1977) and *Jenkins v. Georgia* (1974) by placing the power of declaring items obscene squarely with juries, not with states.

Ward v. Illinois
97 S.Ct. 2750 (1977)

Also a challenge to *Miller,* the *Ward* decision made it clear that the examples included in the *Miller* opinion were not meant to be the only situations considered obscene. Wesley Ward argued that sadomasochistic materials were not illegal because *Miller* examples did not include any specific reference to them. Justice Byron White, referring to *Mishkin v. New York* (1966) under the *Roth* test, argued that the examples were not intended to be exhaustive.

Wooley v. Maynard
97 S.Ct. 1428 (1977)

In the context of dissenting speech, the right to refrain from speaking at all is affirmed in *Maynard.* George Maynard covered up the motto on his New Hampshire license plate, "Live Free or Die," which he found objectionable to his Jehovah's Witness beliefs. Writing for the majority, Chief Justice Warren Burger argued that our system of government also includes the right to decline to foster concepts of religious, political, or ideological causes. The Court also answered New Hampshire's claim that the motto promoted an appreciation of history and state pride. Chief Justice Burger's reasoning demonstrated that a state's desire to promote an ideology could not take precedent over the First Amendment rights of an individual.

Pinkus v. United States
98 S.Ct. 1808 (1978)

The *Pinkus* decision prohibited the inclusion of children in the definition of the "average person" in a community in cases to determine the obscenity of a work. Chief Justice Warren Burger wrote that including children as part of the "average person" criteria would reduce what would be legally protected to only those books appropriate for children.

Givhan v. Western Line Consolidated School District
99 S.Ct. 693 (1979)

A landmark academic freedom case, *Givhan* acknowledged the right of teachers to express their point of view in both public and private contexts. Bessie Givhan was refused a new contract for her junior high school teaching position. The school principal claimed that in a privately held series of conversations, Givhan had made "petty and unreasonable demands" and acted in a loud, rude, and insulting manner. In a unanimous decision, the Court, in an opinion written by Justice William Rehnquist, argued that once a private communication is made with an employer instead of in a public forum, forfieture of the freedom of speech is not permissible. This effectively overturned the decision made earlier in *Meinhold v. Taylor*. Also, Justice Rehnquist wrote that once a lawful act is shown to play a substantial role in the employer's decision to dismiss, the employer must show that the decision to dismiss would have been made even if the lawful conduct, such as complaining in private, had not taken place. This logic reaffirmed the reasoning in *Mt. Healthy City School District Board of Education v. Doyle (1977)*.

Bicknell v. Vergennes Union High School Board
638 F.2d 438 (1980)

This school book censorship case upholds a school board's authority to remove books considered vulgar and obscene. This case was initially decided before the same appeals court that ruled in favor of students' rights in *Board of Education, Island Trees Union Free School District No. 25 v. Pico* (1982). The court found that in this case, the school authorities had followed duly assembled policies and procedures and had acted, not on their own personal tastes, but as a result of complaints from parents and citizens. The appeals court also dismissed the school librarian's claim of a violation of due process, arguing that school authorities had the right to change the duties of employees so long as no adverse action, such as dismissal or reprimand, was conducted without a hearing.

Zykan v. Warsaw Community School Corporation
621 F.2d 1300 (1980)

In another appeals court school censorship case, it was decided that school authorities can remove books from the library and classrooms but not in a manner that singles out materials offensive to a single way of viewing ideas. A student, Brooke Zykan, in the Warsaw, Indiana, schools, objected to the removal of certain books from the library. The removal was part of the school board's action in objecting to the *Values Clarification* textbook series. The opinion of the court recognized the duty of the school board to monitor the content of the school library but counseled school authorities that building a library collection must be based on broad intellectual needs, as should official decisions to remove works.

Widmar v. Vincent
102 S.Ct. 269 (1981)

The *Widmar* case extended the rights of free speech and association to university campuses. A student religious group was denied meeting space on the campus of the University of Missouri at Kansas City. The Supreme Court ruled that the university's policy governing the assignment of meeting rooms was a content-based exclusion and, as such, was a violation of the First Amendment guarantee of free speech.

Board of Education, Island Trees Union Free School
District No. 25 v. Pico
102 S.Ct. 2799 (1982)

In a major school censorship decision, the Supreme Court revised the *President's Council District 25 v. Community School Board No. 25* (1972) case by establishing that students have First Amendment rights as well. The school board of the Island Trees School District attended a conference sponsored by a conservative, political group and returned with a list of books considered unacceptable for students by this organization. Eleven titles on the list were owned by the libraries of the district. The board appointed a review committee, which recommended retention of five books, removal of two, and no decision on the remaining four. The board rejected the recommendation and retained only one title out of the eleven. The Court recognized that, as in *President's Council,* school authorities have significant discretion in establishing what can be owned by the school's libraries. But Justice William Brennan, writing for the majority, also established that students have the right to the freedoms enjoyed by others. The *Pico* ruling is generally regarded as lacking a clear-cut decision on the acceptability of school censorship. However, because the board in this case acted upon information from an organization with one ideological viewpoint, the Court did make it clear that decisions to remove a book cannot be based on partisan or political ideas.

New York v. Ferber
102 S.Ct. 3348 (1982)

The production or sale of child pornography was prohibited by the Supreme Court in the *Ferber* case. Paul Ferber was convicted under an anti–child pornography statute for selling films of young boys masturbating. Justice Byron White, writing for the majority, established that the question was not one of obscenity but the harm brought to children in the production of such works. The *Miller* test could not be applied in these cases because the state has a greater interest in protecting children.

Dworkin-McKinnon Bills (1983)

Local anti-obscenity ordinances, these bills successfully defined obscenity in terms of discrimination and exploitation against women in at least one major U.S. city. The Minneapolis Neighborhood Pornography Task Force asked Andrea Dworkin, a feminist writer, to help write a new, more effective law regulating a zoned area for pornography. Dworkin redefined pornography as a form of sex discrimination and exploitation and designed the law to ban pornography on those grounds. The law was passed by the Minneapolis City Council but vetoed by the mayor. Indianapolis Mayor William Hudnut learned of the Minneapolis effort and successfully implemented a similar city ordinance in Indianapolis. Both bills characterized pornography as "the sexually explicit subordination of women, graphically depicted whether in pictures or words." Offenders can be charged with a number of offenses in selling, producing, or trafficking in pornography, or the city can file an Equal Opportunity Commission suit.

Child Protection and Obscenity Enforcement Act of 1988

The Child Protection Act, and its amended form, the Child Protection Restoration and Penalty Enforcement Act of 1990, makes it a crime to produce or possess child pornography and also broadens general obscenity enforcement by defining an illegal obscenity business as one that sells or transfers two obscene items. With the growing concern over the proliferation of child pornography and other indecent influences on children, a number of legislative mandates were attempted in the late 1980s. The Congress tried, but failed, to pass a law eliminating the so-called dial-a-porn pay telephone lines. However, Congress was able to pass this child pornography act as a rider to an antidrug crime bill in 1988. Introduced by Republican Senator Strom Thurmond of South Carolina and heavily supported by the Moral Majority and other conservative groups, the act addresses two obscenity issues. First, it makes it illegal for a parent or guardian to permit a child to be engaged in any production of child pornography. It also requires producers of any kind of media, including books, films, videos, commercial art, or photographs, to maintain records of the ages of any models or actors and actresses used in production of these materials. Second, the law defines an illegal obscenity business as any business that sells or transfers at least two obscene items, whether they are child pornography or not, with the intent of making a profit, regardless of whether any profit is made. The legislation also toughens enforcement of its provisions by placing certain burdens of proof on the business and its owners. Failure to keep records is deemed an assumption of guilt and the business is required to prove its innocence. Attempts were made to insert language that permitted the confiscation of all property owned by anyone convicted under the law, regardless of whether or not that property was obtained with profits from pornography, but these attempts were defeated. After objections were raised by civil liberties groups about some of the record-keeping provisions, the 1990 re-authorization of the law attempted to address a variety of concerns of various groups. As a result of *American Library Association v. Thornburg,* the enforcement of this act and its re-authorization were delayed until regulations could be written by the Justice Department.

Texas v. Johnson
109 S.Ct. 2522 (1990)

Flag burning as a form of symbolic speech was again affirmed in this recent political speech case. Despite the conservative majority in the Court, the *Street* case was validated in this flag-burning case. The *Johnson* case sparked much political debate between conservative Republicans and liberal Democrats, and Congress has attempted to pass several flag desecration acts as a result of this ruling.

University of Pennsylvania v. EEOC
110 S.Ct. 577 (1990)

This academic freedom case raises serious questions about privacy of communications in tenure and promotion decisions. The Equal Employment Opportunity Commission (EEOC) had sued the University of Pennsylvania for the release of confidential peer review letters as part of a sex discrimination investigation. The Supreme Court supported the EEOC and ruled that in such cases, review letters must be part of the public record when requested.

Barnes v. Glen Theatre
59 USLW 4745 (1991)

In a continuing trend toward a more conservative stance on obscenity, the Supreme Court reversed its earlier decisions that nude dancing is a form of expression. The Glen Theatre challenged an Indiana law that prohibited nude dancing in any public establishment. Previous decisions had ruled such exhibitions a permissible form of expression, though it was also ruled that states could deny a liquor license to bars with nude dancers.

Osbourne v. Ohio
110 S.Ct. 1691 (1991)

The allowable private possession of child pornography was denied in this landmark Supreme Court case. The Court had earlier prohibited the sale of child pornography in *New York v. Ferber;* however, the *Osbourne* case also bucked the *Stanley v. Georgia* decision that permitted private possession of such material, which was considered an issue of privacy, as well. This case is another example of conservative obscenity decisions under the Rehnquist Court.

Rust v. Sullivan
111 S.Ct. 1759 (1991)

Though this was ostensibly an abortion case, the Supreme Court permitted a gag rule on health clinic workers and doctors against dispensing abortion information or giving abortion counseling. The defendants argued that the Bush administration rule prohibiting abortion counseling in federally funded clinics violated the free speech clause of the First Amendment and especially the doctrine of absolute privilege, which grants immunity from libel prosecutions to certain groups of individuals, especially to a doctor and his or her patient and to a husband and wife. Justice Rehnquist argued that it was not a matter of free speech but sponsorship instead. Accordingly, the government can set such rules where it sponsors programs through funding, though Rehnquist indicated exceptions for university teaching would probably be made.

Laws and Cases Involving Freedom of the Press

In a very broad sense, freedom of the press is the protection of speech in print. As with speech, the right to hold ideas brings the accompanying right to express those ideas. To put that expression in print can be afforded no less protection than in speech, and for this reason, freedom of the press is a fundamental right of U.S. society.

However, as the concept of freedom of the press has developed in this nation, it has been applied principally to the news media, first as publishers of newspapers and then later as broadcast news media. In a lesser sense, freedom of the press applies to publishers of books, primarily, and also other forms of literature, but much of this material can be more appropriately considered under freedom of speech concerns. This section details the cases relevant to news media, broadcast journalism, and student journalism.

Lewis Publishing Company v. Morgan;
Journal of Commerce and Commercial Bulletin v. Burleson
33 S.Ct. 867 (1913)

Though not considered a prior restraint case at the time, the *Lewis Publishing* case was the first primary post-office control decision with prior restraint implications. The 1912 Newspaper Publicity Law required that all newspapers and magazines file a statement listing the names of the editors, publishers, and stockholders twice a year and also required that all advertising be clearly labeled as such. The publishers believed such information could be used against the paper, but the Court affirmed the provisions of the act and held that the requirements were not a burden on the free press but merely proper regulations for the second-class mail privilege.

Milwaukee Social Democrat Publishing Company v. Burleson
41 S.Ct. 352 (1921)

The *Milwaukee Leader* case was argued by the newspaper as a prior restraint of free press because the paper was required to publish more patriotically loyal editorials before regaining mail privileges. As the United States entered its first year of involvement in World War I, the *Milwaukee Leader*, published by Milwaukee Social Democrat Publishing Company, stepped up its antiwar editorials, denouncing the draft and claiming the war was capitalistic and benefitted only the wealthy. The Supreme Court upheld the revocation of the paper's second-class mail privilege, reasoning that the editorials encouraged violations of the law, especially the National Defense Act. Justices Louis Brandeis and Oliver Wendell Holmes dissented, agreeing that this was an instance of prior restraint, and their opinion contributed to the landmark *Near* decision that later overturned this ruling.

Near v. Minnesota
51 S.Ct. 625 (1931)

The *Near* case established the judicial doctrine of immunity from prior restraint. In 1927, the *Saturday Press* printed several articles highly critical of the police and many other public figures in Minneapolis. The articles charged the chief of police with having connections with gangsters and participating in graft, the county attorney with failing to act to correct this problem, and the city's mayor with dereliction of duty. The formation of a special grand jury to investigate the problem was also demanded in the articles. The county attorney, acting under a state ordinance banning publications of a malicious, scandalous, and defamatory nature, obtained a restraining order against the publisher, J. M. Near, that prevented further publication of the magazine. In a decision written by Chief Justice Charles Evans Hughes, the Supreme Court noted that historically the treatment of the conduct of public officials in the press had to that point always been a free and open discussion without prior restraint. Libel prosecutions were available as a remedy for false accusations as well. Hughes laid down the principle that the First Amendment does not permit any authority to ban a publication before the publication is produced.

Federal Communications Act of 1934

This statute established the limitations of expression in the conduct of radio and television broadcasting. Several important sections of the law pertain to free speech. The "equal time" section (313[a]) requires that any broadcasting station that allows one qualified candidate for public office to use the station for a broadcast must extend the same opportunity to all qualified candidates. Stations are permitted to deny broadcast time to candidates as long as *all* candidates are refused use. Furthermore, Section 315(a) prohibits the censorship of any broadcast granted under the equal time provisions. The FCC's "fairness doctrine" is similar to the equal time provisions but also establishes the rule that all sides of a discussion on a public issue must be afforded fair coverage. Prior to 1954, the act prohibited the broadcasting of giveaway programs or advertisements that used prizes as inducements to purchase a product. This section was struck down by the Supreme Court in *Federal Communications Commission v. American Braodcasting Company.* Lotteries were also banned on the airways, but Congress made an exception for state government operated lotteries in 1975. The primary rules regulating what forms of speech can be broadcast are in the indecency and censorship provisions. Title 18 of the United States Code (U.S.C.), Section 1464, makes it a crime to broadcast or say over the airwaves any obscene, indecent, or profane language. This section was affirmed in *Federal Communications Commission v. Pacifica,* the so-called dirty words case. However, censorship of the content of broadcasts is not permitted under Title 47 U.S.C., Section 326.

United States v. Gregg
286 F.Supp. 848 (1934)

In the first federal action to validate the right of the federal government to regulate broadcasting, the *Gregg* case increased the authority of licensing agencies by permitting the regulation of nonlicensed, intrastate broadcasting stations. The *Gregg* case took place in the early days of radio when station broadcasting within a state's boundaries did not require a license. This district court case was the basis for the landmark case *National Broadcasting Company v. United States,* which established the regulatory authority of the FCC.

Grosjean v. American Publishing Company
56 S.Ct. 444 (1936)

The validity of taxation as a form of prior restraint of the press was decided in the *Grosjean* case. Governor Huey Long of Louisiana had a law passed requiring all newspapers with a weekly circulation over 20,000 to pay a tax of 2 percent on its total receipts. Only 13 state newspapers met the criteria, but 12 of the 13 were highly critical of Long during his career. Nine of the publishers sued against the tax, and the Supreme Court agreed with their position. The justices saw this as a prior restraint of the press in two ways. First, it limited the amount of receipts from advertising. Second, it restricted circulation. The tax was viewed as unfair and hence as a prior restraint of the press because it was clearly designed to limit the profits of only those newspapers critical of Governor Long.

National Broadcasting Company v. United States;
Columbia Broadcasting System v. United States
63 S.Ct. 997 (1943)

The *National Broadcasting Company* case was the first major challenge to the Federal Communications Commission's (FCC) regulations and established broadcasting as a separate medium with more regulation allowable than print media. Although there were several lower court challenges to radio regulation beginning in 1927, the Supreme Court first dealt with regulation of broadcasting in this case concerning the Federal Communications Act of 1934. Under the provisions of this law, the FCC adopted several regulations to end "chain broadcasting," which was the simultaneous broadcasting of an identical program by two or more connected stations. The FCC's data showed that most of the radio broadcasts were controlled by three networks, NBC, CBS, and the Mutual Broadcasting System, so the regulations were implemented in an attempt to create more competition. Though the networks sued to prevent the regulations, the Supreme Court held that broadcasting was a limited access medium and as such was not entitled to the same protections of intellectual freedom as other media.

Hannegan v. Esquire
66 S.Ct. 456 (1946)

This important case confirms the right of publishers to send material through the mail and restricts post office controls. The United States

Post Office provides a second-class mailing privilege to periodicals. *Esquire* magazine had its second-class privilege revoked after the postal department ruled that some of the issues were offensive and not suitable for the public good. Upon appeal to the Supreme Court, it was decided that Congress did not intend every publisher to prove to the postmaster general how the publication contributed to the public good. Justice William Douglas, writing for the majority, argued that only the public could make that decision after choosing from the full range of publications available.

Farmers Educational and Cooperative Union of America, North Dakota Division v. WDAY
79 S.Ct. 1302 (1959)

Immunity from libel suits for broadcasters was granted when the Supreme Court affirmed the equal-time rule in this case concerning political candidates. Radio station WDAY in North Dakota broadcast the remarks of a 1956 senatorial candidate without censoring any part of the speech. The candidate accused the other candidates and the Farmers Union of establishing a communist farming system. Section 315 of the Federal Communications Act protects stations from liability caused by the comments of political candidates. The Supreme Court upheld the provisions of Section 315 and argued that if broadcasters were denied immunity it would have a serious chilling effect on remarks made.

In re Palmetto Broadcasting Company
33 FCC 250 (1962)

This administrative court ruling recognized the dangers of censorship but allowed the FCC to deny license renewal to a radio station with excessive indecent programming. Station WDKD devoted 25 percent of its programming to off-color, vulgar jokes. The FCC ruling also showed concern that the station was the only broadcasting facility in its community and that the programming was not balanced.

Lamont v. Postmaster General
85 S.Ct. 1491 (1965)

The *Lamont* case confirmed the right of every person to receive information without post office interference or infringement. Dr.

Corliss Lamont, a publisher and distributor of pamphlets, ordered a copy of the *Peking Review*. Under the Postal Service and Federal Employees Salary Act of 1962, the postal authorities could detain any material considered to be Communist political propaganda. Regulations required a notification to be sent to the recipient of the items informing him or her that a request card had to be returned to secure the materials or they would be destroyed, with only 20 days allowed for a reply. Lamont refused to reply via the postcard and filed suit instead. The Post Office considered the suit notification to fall under the regulations and released the journal. When the case reached the Supreme Court, the justices viewed the requirement of returning the postcard as a restriction on an individual's rights. The Court prohibited enforcement of this law and affirmed a person's right to receive information without post office control.

Mills v. Alabama
86 S.Ct. 1434 (1966)

In this case, information on elections was determined to be necessary for a free and democratic society. James E. Mills had published an editorial in favor of a city government ordinance proposal. He was charged with violating an Alabama law prohibiting the publishing of politically oriented articles and comments prior to an election. The Court reversed Mills's conviction, stating that the First Amendment was designed to protect free discussion of all governmental affairs.

United States v. Southwestern Cable Company;
Midwestern Television v. Southwestern Cable Company
88 S.Ct. 1994 (1968)

Similar to *National Broadcasting Company v. United States* in impact, in this case the Supreme Court upheld the same concept of authority for the FCC in the regulation of the cable TV industry. Though an earlier case involving the same issue, *Carter Mountain Transmission Corporation v. Federal Communications Commission,* was turned away by the Supreme Court, the *Southwestern Cable* decision was the first definitive statement by the Court on the cable TV industry. The Midwestern Television Company charged that Southwestern had transmitted signals to stations within Midwestern's franchise. The FCC took action to punish Southwestern, which filed for review of the action. The Supreme Court unanimously ruled for the FCC in order to protect the most efficient and equitable transmission of cable television programming.

New York State Broadcasters Association v. United States
414 F.2d 990 (1969)

This case was a First Amendment challenge to FCC regulations prohibiting the promotion of lotteries by the broadcast media, including giveaway programs and games. The FCC regulations prohibited the broadcast of any information concerning lotteries except as ordinary news reporting on state-operated lotteries. The New York State Broadcasters Association challenged this regulation on the grounds that such regulations denied the right of the people to receive information. The court of appeals disagreed and upheld the FCC but noted a flaw in the law. The court concluded that a literal reading of the regulation was unconstitutional but that the regulation had been applied appropriately in this case.

Red Lion Broadcasting Company
v. Federal Communications Commission;
United States v. Radio Television News Directors Association
89 S.Ct. 1794 (1969)

The "personal attack" rule and the fairness doctrine of the Federal Communications Act were upheld in the *Red Lion* case, keeping broadcasting channels open to all points of political view without regard to a party's ability to pay. The Red Lion Broadcasting Company aired a program during the 1964 presidential campaign that included an attack on Fred Cook, author of a biography of Barry Goldwater, by the Reverend Billy James Hargis. When Cook asked for equal time, Red Lion rejected the request on the grounds that the personal-attack rule required paid sponsorship. In the resulting ruling, the Supreme Court developed a doctrine of media access that guaranteed the public suitable access to social, political, aesthetic, and moral ideas.

In re WUHY-FM, Eastern Educational Radio
24 FCC 2d 408 (1970)

The *WUHY* decision is notable because it permitted a ban on specific words rather than using the *Roth* test for judging a work in its entirety. WUHY-FM broadcast an interview with Grateful Dead guitarist Jerry Garcia on January 4, 1970. Garcia's comments were interspersed with the words *fuck* and *shit*. As a result, the FCC fined the radio station $100. On appeal, the administrative court upheld the fine on the grounds that the words were obscene and had no redeeming social value in this context.

New York Times Company v. United States
91 S.Ct. 2140 (1971)

In this seminal case, the Supreme Court declared that the government has the responsibility to justify imposing prior restraint. This case has become known as the Pentagon Papers case. Daniel Ellsberg was a scholar for the Rand Corporation think tank and one of Secretary of Defense Robert McNamara's "whiz kids." Though Ellsberg supported the Vietnam War early on and contributed to the Pentagon Papers, a classified document, he later became disillusioned with the war effort. In 1971, he turned the papers over to the *New York Times* and the *Washington Post* as an antiwar act. After the papers published three installments, the U.S. government issued a restraining order preventing any further publication. Arguments were presented to the Supreme Court by the government that the restraining order was issued to prevent a threat to national security. The publishers argued that the government was attempting to prevent embarrassing disclosures. A sharply divided court ruled that the restraining order constituted a prior restraint of the press and that any legitimate prior restraint required the government to substantially prove a real need to restrict the publication.

Baker v. F&F Investment
470 F.2d 778 (1972)

This U.S. Court of Appeals case permitted Alfred Balk, a reporter for the *Saturday Evening Post,* to refuse to reveal his source on a story about "block-busting," real estate sales designed to exclude blacks and other minorities by offering properties to such groups only in certain neighborhoods. The Court recognized the deterrent effect that divulging a source would have on news gathering and noted the ambiguity in federal law regarding reporter privileges.

Brandywine-Main Line Radio
v. Federal Communications Commission
473 F.2d 16 (1972)

The *Brandywine* case is important because it is the primary decision backing the fairness doctrine. The conservative, fundamentalist preacher Carl McIntire acquired radio station WXUR in 1965 through his Faith Theological Seminary but over the objections of local citizen groups wary that McIntire would not allow the broadcasting of opposing views. McIntire agreed to abide by the fairness doctrine in the original hearing. The FCC denied renewal of the license after testimony showed anti-Semitic attacks and a failure to provide opposing viewpoints. WXUR became the first station in history to lose its license because of noncompliance with the fairness doctrine.

Branzburg v. Hayes; In the Matter of Pappas; United States v. Caldwell
92 S.Ct. 2646 (1972)

This difficult case rejected the concept of confidential privilege for a national news reporter. The *Branzburg* decision comes from three separate but similar cases heard together by the Supreme Court. In all three cases, a news reporter refused to reveal the sources for the information he or she had gathered. All the reporters claimed the sources of privileged information needed to be kept secret to protect their integrity and their ability to deal with confidential sources in the future. Paul Branzburg wrote an article for the *Louisville Courier-Journal* about drug use and the "drug scene" in Frankfort, Kentucky. To obtain his data, he spent two weeks interviewing and observing drug users. One part of the story described two youths synthesizing hashish from marijuana. Branzburg was ordered to appear before a grand jury, but he secured a court order protecting him from revealing confidential sources. When the case reached the Supreme Court, Justice Byron White, writing for the majority, noted that protection for reporters, known as shield laws, was a state matter and not provided for in the Constitution. Therefore, such issues had to be settled in state courts. In the *Pappas* and *Caldwell* cases, White also reasoned that lacking statutory protection, the reporters had no claim to privilege in their situations.

In re Bridge
295 A.2d 3 (1972); cert. denied 93 S.Ct. 1500 (1973)

The *Bridge* case showed that a reporter could waive his or her right to privileges under a shield law by disclosing the source of his or her information. Peter Bridge included the name of his source on a political bribery story, who claimed an unknown man offered her a bribe. Bridge refused to testify about any information on the case. The Supreme Court declined to hear the case, letting stand the lower court's ruling that Bridge was not protected in this case.

Lightman v. Maryland
294 A.2d 149 (1972);
cert. denied 93 S.Ct. 1922 (1973)

A federal court of appeals ruled that if a reporter is an observer of illegal activity, then he or she is not protected under the state's shield law regarding confidential sources even though he or she is protecting the identity of those committing the illegal act. David Lightman wanted to check the accuracy of a story of an Ocean City, Maryland, shopkeeper who permitted drug buyers to sample marijuana before purchasing any quantities, so Lightman became a customer himself. The Supreme Court affirmed the lower court's decision by refusing to hear the case.

Democratic National Committee v. McCord;
In re Bernstein
356 F.Supp. 1394 (1973)

In this case, a U.S. District Court recognized the chilling effect of a subpoena of documents held by Carl Bernstein, the *Washington Post* Watergate reporter. It also permitted the Nixon campaign to refuse to hand over similar documents.

Papish v. Board of Curators of the University of Missouri
93 S.Ct. 1197 (1973)

The *Papish* case provides protection to student journalists and the student press. Barbara Papish, a graduate journalism student at the University of Missouri, was expelled for distributing a campus newspaper with obscenities. The front page article included a political cartoon depicting a policeman raping the Statue of Liberty and another article was about an organization named "Up Against the Wall, Mother-Fucker." Papish was expelled after a hearing by the Student Conduct Committee that was affirmed by the chancellor. The Supreme Court reversed the expulsion and reasoned that neither the cartoon nor the epithet were constitutionally obscene. The Court afforded the same freedom of press to student journalism as to other forms of the press in this case.

Sonderling Broadcasting Corporation, WGLD-FM
27 P.&F.Rad.Regs.2d 285 (1973)

The *Sonderling* case used the *Roth* test in determining the permissible nature of radio broadcast programming. WGLD-FM in Oak Park,

Illinois, aired a regular talk show on sex-oriented topics. One such show discussed oral sex, including explicit comments by callers. The FCC fined the station $2,000. In determining the acceptability of the program on appeal, the administrative court used the *Roth* test and concluded that the program was "patently offensive." It also relied upon the *WUHY* case for its definition of "indecent"

Miami Herald Publishing Company v. Tornillo
94 S.Ct. 2831 (1974)

In *Tornillo*, the principle of a candidate's "right to reply" was upheld because of the potential chilling effect on publishing the news. Pat Tornillo was a candidate for the Florida House of Representatives and the executive director of the Classroom Teacher's Association. Under a 1913 Florida statute, all candidates for political office had a right to reply free of charge to any newspaper article that charged misconduct or attacked their character. The *Miami Herald* called Tornillo a "czar" and a law breaker for his role as a leader of an illegal teachers' strike in 1960. The paper refused to grant Tornillo his "right to reply" under the statute, and he sued in the Florida Supreme Court. When the case reached the U.S. Supreme Court, Tornillo's right to reply was sustained because fairness in a campaign entitled assailed candidates an opportunity to respond. If the right to reply did not exist, the public would be denied the chance to hear both sides. The Court also saw the right to reply law as promoting the flow of ideas without creating a prior restraint condition.

Citizens Committee to Save WEFM
v. Federal Communications Commission
506 F.2d 246 (1974)

The *WEFM* case points to the need to gauge citizen interests and concerns in decisions regarding format changes. A citizens' group objected to radio station WEFM's decision to drop a classical music format for popular music programming. The court of appeals questioned the validity of arguments made for market-place decisions governing such format changes and ruled that the FCC should have held hearings to gauge citizen concerns. The change in format was allowed to stand, and the FCC issued a new ruling that removed the commission from ever hearing such complaints about format changes.

United States v. Orsini
424 F.Supp. 229 (1976)

A U.S. District Court, using the *Branzburg* case reasoning, protected a *Newsweek* reporter's confidential source about federal tactics in capturing international drug traffickers. Dominique Orsini, an alleged narcotics dealer, sought the information to show that his arrest was a violation of due process.

Writer's Guild of America, West
v. Federal Communications Commission
423 F.Supp. 1064 (1976)

The "family viewing policy" of the FCC, which prohibits entertainment programs not suitable for family viewing during the first hour of network entertainment time except under special circumstances, was struck down as a violation of the First Amendment by the court of appeals. The Writer's Guild, including television directors, actors, and producers, argued that the policy limited artistic expression. The court agreed and reasoned that the policy violated the First Amendment because the FCC chairman issued threats of regulatory action for noncompliance.

Federal Communications Commission v. Pacifica Foundation
98 S.Ct. 3026 (1978)

In *Pacifica*, the Supreme Court upheld regulations banning obscenity and indecent words in broadcasts in what became known as the "dirty words" case. Comedian George Carlin developed a monologue on the "seven dirty words you can't say on TV." In this routine Carlin discusses and repeatedly recites variations on seven indecent words. The Carlin monologue was aired as part of a broadcast on WBAI radio in 1978, and a father complained to the FCC that his son had heard the program and was offended. The FCC ruled that such programs had to be aired during a time of day when most children would not accidentally be exposed to such words. The Court agreed that the context and time of day were important considerations in deciding whether content could be broadcast or whether it was protected by the First Amendment. Under *Pacifica*, the FCC may regulate "indecent" as well as "obscene" expression.

Zurcher v. Stanford Daily;
Bergna v. Stanford Daily
98 S.Ct. 1970 (1978)

Upholding police authority over free press interests of the First
Amendment, the *Stanford Daily* decision permitted searches of news
agency records under proper warrant for evidence in a crime. In
1971, a riot broke out at the Stanford University Hospital. In the
scuffle, several policemen were hurt but were unable to identify their
assailants. Two days later, the *Stanford Daily*, the university's student
paper, published articles and photos of the fight. The police obtained
a search warrant to collect evidence, but the newspaper staff went
to court claiming such a search violated the First Amendment's
freedom of the press and the Fourth Amendment's protection against
unreasonable searches. The Supreme Court disagreed and reasoned
that with probable cause and regarding evidence useful in solving
a crime held by a third party, even a newspaper, the interests of
the government outweighed the press's right to withhold such
information.

United States v. Progressive
467 F.Supp. 990 (1979)

The best example of a permissible use of prior restraint is shown in
the *Progressive* case. In 1979, the liberal periodical *The Progressive* was
stopped by a restraining order from publishing a story entitled "The
H-bomb Secret: How We Got It, Why We're Telling It." The publisher
attempted to lift the order in district court, arguing that it was a prior
restraint of the press and that the information the magazine had
obtained came only from public documents available to anyone. The
government claimed the article would seriously damage national
security. The district court sided with the government, using the logic
that publishing the technical data of hydrogen bombs was like
publishing troop movements in a war. This case never reached the
Supreme Court but is a well-known historical event as well as being
exemplary on the issue of prior restraint.

Snepp v. United States
100 S.Ct. 763 (1980)

Under certain circumstances, especially concerning national security,
prepublication review, normally considered an instance of prior

restraint, is permitted according to the *Snepp* case. Frank Snepp was a retired CIA agent who, when with the agency, signed a contractual agreement to submit any publication while an agent or afterward for prepublication review. The review was to ensure that any sensitive or top secret information was not revealed to the general public. Snepp published *Decent Interval,* a book highly critical of the U.S. pullout from Vietnam in 1975. Charged with violation of the contract, Snepp appealed on the grounds that prepublication review constituted a prior restraint of the free press. The Court disagreed, arguing that a "constructive trust" had been agreed to by the agency and Snepp that allowed him and the agency a fair remedy for any wrongdoing. Snepp was guaranteed protection from liability by submitting to pre-publication review and could only lose the profits of the publication if he failed to do so.

League of Women Voters v. Federal Communications Commission
731 F.2d 995 (1984)

This case provides for the right to "editorialize" by federally funded, noncommercial, educational stations. The regulations for equal time for political candidates have evolved over time. In 1975, "non-studio" debates were first allowed providing they were covered live and no favoritism was shown. To this point, it was believed that sponsorship of debates presented a potential danger of abuse by broadcasters. By 1983, this rule was dropped. The League of Women Voters challenged the rule change on the grounds that it permitted studios, including public stations, to avoid providing equal time for all candidates. The court of appeals disagreed and permitted stations to editorialize.

Hazelwood School District v. Kuhlmeier
108 S.Ct. 562 (1988)

In *Hazelwood,* the Supreme Court signaled its willingness to drop the *Tinker* logic used for protection of student rights. Student editors of the Hazelwood, Missouri, East High School newspaper *Spectrum* sued because of a decision by the school authorities to censor two pages of the May 13, 1983, issue. The deleted pages included two stories on contemporary issues, teen pregnancy and divorce. Justice Byron White, writing for the majority, rejected the *Tinker* argument made in the case, arguing that the school paper's purpose was to give students practical experience in journalism and therefore that school authorities had the right to establish the content of instruction activities.

Cases Involving the Right to Association and Assembly

The Bill of Rights guarantees the right of assembly and the right to request that problems caused by government action be solved. As the First Amendment states, "Congress shall make no law . . . abridging the freedom of speech, or the press; or the right of the people peaceably to assemble and to petition the government for a redress of grievances." With the guarantee of the right to hold a belief and to express it, the next natural step is the right to associate with other individuals who hold the same beliefs and to be able to meet and discuss these ideas. Just as important, the next progression is the right to meet and discuss these ideas with those individuals who do not hold the same beliefs in an attempt to influence and educate them on the merits of those ideas. The following cases are the most important Supreme Court decisions that define the limits to the freedom of association.

Hague v. Congress of Industrial Organizations
59 S.Ct. 954 (1939)

In the first major case on the right to assemble, the Supreme Court declared peaceable gatherings to be protected under the First Amendment. In Jersey City, New Jersey, the director of public safety was authorized to reject requests for permits to assemble publicly if he or she felt that a riot, disturbance, or other disorderly acts would occur as a result of the assembly. The Congress of Industrial Organizations (CIO), a labor group, was consistently denied such a permit because the individuals making the requests were considered Communists. The CIO and its representatives also were denied entry into the city, had their literature seized, and in some cases were arrested. In the suit brought against Mayor Frank Hague and the city, Hague argued that the city-owned parks and streets were akin to an individual's own home and therefore that the city was permitted to exclude whomever they wanted. The Supreme Court disagreed and stated that, though the right to assemble could be regulated for order and in the public interest, no authority could deny this right on the grounds of ideas held as long as the intention for a peaceable assembly was apparent.

Cantwell v. Connecticut
310 U.S. 296 (1940)

The *Cantwell* decision is a free exercise of religion case detailed in the "Cases on Freedom of Religion" section of this chapter. The Supreme Court also ruled on a freedom of association aspect. In this case, the right to solicit members to an organization was upheld, allowing the government to regulate only the time, place, and manner of such solicitations.

Thornhill v. Alabama
60 S.Ct. 736 (1940)

The Supreme Court ruled in the *Thornhill* case that picketing is protected by the First Amendment. Byron Thornhill, a union organizer, urged a group of strikebreakers to not cross a picket line. Though there was no incitement to violence and his urging was done peacefully, Thornhill was convicted of violating the Alabama anti-picketing law. The Supreme Court not only reversed the conviction but also struck down the Alabama law as unconstitutional because of vagueness and overbreadth. The law was considered overbroad because the Court viewed the dissemination of information concerning a labor dispute as important to free discussion. The statute also did not define the term "picket" and was thus vague.

Cox v. New Hampshire
61 S.Ct. 762 (1941)

In *Cox*, the Supreme Court permitted a state to regulate the use of streets and parks in the public interest. A large group of Jehovah's Witnesses participated in an informational march in Manchester, New Hampshire, on July 8, 1939. Marching in small groups, single file, they passed out literature and carried banners. The Jehovah's Witnesses were arrested for parading without a permit, and the state also argued that the march obstructed traffic. The Supreme Court agreed and affirmed the conviction on the grounds that a state has a legitimate interest in public safety and regulation of the normal use of the streets.

Korematsu v. United States
65 S.Ct. 193 (1944)

This famous case let stand the decision by President Franklin
Roosevelt to place Japanese-Americans in detention camps during
World War II. Executive Order 9066 was issued to protect the western
United States from possible sabotage. Roosevelt had accepted
arguments that Japanese-Americans living on the West Coast were
potentially loyal to Japan and capable of sabotage when he also issued
the Civilian Exclusion Order No. 34. Fred Toyosabubo Korematsu was
convicted of disobeying the order and was sentenced to five years of
probation. The Supreme Court upheld his conviction on appeal. The
Court argued, in an opinion written by Justice Hugo Black, that
Korematsu was not ordered to a camp based on his ancestry but
because of the potential military danger. In 1988, the U.S. Congress
recognized the injustice of this decision and provided reparations to
those who were sent to the camps.

Kunz v. New York
71 S.Ct. 312 (1951)

The right to meet publicly was defined further in this 1951 case. Carl
Jacob Kunz was an ordained Baptist minister who made fiery
speeches, often attacking Catholics and Jews. Although he was issued a
permit in New York City in 1946, the permit was denied afterward
because of Kunz's ridicule of these religions. In 1948, Kunz delivered
an address at Columbus Circle and was arrested for speaking without
a permit. This permit law was struck down by the Court because there
were no conditions in the law to guide the police commissioner as to
when to refuse a permit.

Niemotko v. Maryland
71 S.Ct. 325 (1951)

In *Niemotko,* the Supreme Court ruled that a permit or license could
not be denied because of the personal objections of the authorities.
Daniel Niemotko attempted to get a permit for Bible talks in the town
park of Havre de Grace, Maryland. There were no regulations
governing the permit but an unwritten rule was generally followed.
The town authorities denied the permit primarily because Niemotko
represented the Jehovah's Witnesses. He was convicted of using the
park without a permit when he spoke despite the permit denial. The
Supreme Court overturned the conviction on the grounds that the

lack of standards constituted a prior restraint and also that it was unconstitutional to deny such permits because of personal displeasure with the views held by the petitioner.

Adler v. Board of Education
72 S.Ct. 380 (1952)

In this case the Supreme Court supported a New York State law requiring that all organizations advocating the overthrow of the government be registered with the state and allowing that list to be used as evidence in dismissing teachers belonging to any of the listed groups. This statute was known as the Feinberg law. The Court argued that New York had set reasonable terms for employment and that teachers who disagreed could find employment elsewhere. This decision later was reversed in the landmark case *Keyishian v. Board of Regents*.

Poulos v. New Hampshire
73 S.Ct. 760 (1953)

In *Poulos* the Supreme Court ruled that it is illegal to disobey a valid ordinance even if the ordinance is applied in a discriminatory manner. In a case similar to the *Niemotko* case, the Court seemingly reversed itself and upheld the conviction of William Poulos, a Jehovah's Witness, for holding a meeting in a town park despite being denied a permit. Justice Stanley Reed argued for the majority that Poulos had a defense if he had challenged the ordinance, but failing that, that he had a legal obligation to obey the law.

National Association for the Advancement of Colored People v. Alabama
78 S.Ct. 1163 (1958)

In this seminal case, the Supreme Court established the right of an organization to maintain the confidentiality of its list of members. The NAACP began in 1909 as a nonprofit corporation dedicated to eliminating racial barriers. Many of its organizations and activities were in southern states and it enjoyed some successes, especially in the 1950s. In a backlash against these activities, southern authorities attempted a number of tactics to deflate the growing influence of the NAACP. The Alabama attorney general in 1956 demanded that the NAACP comply with a law requiring foreign corporations to qualify to conduct business in the state. He ordered the NAACP to produce various records, including its membership lists with names and addresses. The NAACP complied with all requests except submission of the membership list, claiming a constitutional right to keep this information confidential. The Alabama courts found the association in contempt of court and fined it $100,000. The Supreme Court reversed this fine, stating that any organization had the right to protect its membership lists in the pursuit of lawful goals. Justice John Harlan, writing for the majority, acknowledged that revealing the names could place members in jeopardy with the possible loss of jobs and safety of their persons. As a consequence, such a requirement would discourage individuals from joining the group and therefore constituted a restraint on the freedom of association.

Shelton v. Tucker
81 S.Ct. 247 (1960)

A law requiring teachers to submit a list of organizations they held membership in was declared unconstitutional in this case. B. T. Shelton had been a teacher in the Little Rock, Arkansas, schools for 25 years. When asked to submit a list of organizations he belonged to, he refused, and his contract then was not renewed. The Supreme Court found that the law went beyond determining the competency of teachers and, instead, interfered with their associational freedom.

Cramp v. Board of Instruction of Orange County, Florida
82 S.Ct. 275 (1961)

The *Cramp* decision addressed the constitutionality of loyalty oaths for instructors. David Cramp, a public school teacher for nine years, had never taken a Florida oath that required every teacher to state that he or she had not aided the Communist Party in any way. Cramp challenged the law instead of signing the oath. The Supreme Court questioned the vagueness of the terms *aid, support,* and *influence* as included in the statute and declared the act unconstitutional on these grounds.

Konigsberg v. State Bar of California
81 S.Ct. 997 (1961)

In this case, the Supreme Court declared that the right to associate is not absolute. Raphael Konigsberg was refused admittance to the

California Bar. Despite holding a law degree from the University of Southern California and qualifying for the bar, he was denied admittance because he refused to answer questions concerning his membership in the Communist Party. The Court upheld California's decision stating that the rights of speech and association were never considered absolute. In this situation, the justices viewed California's interests as outweighing Konigsberg's right to associate.

Edwards v. South Carolina
83 S.Ct. 680 (1963)

In *Edwards,* the Supreme Court recognized the right to demonstrate. In 1961, 187 black high school and college students marched on the South Carolina State Capitol from the Zion Baptist Church in Columbia. Walking in groups of 15, they reached the grounds and were granted permission by the police to enter as long as they acted peacefully. Their protest against discrimination drew a crowd, though no violence occurred or was apparent, yet the police ordered the students to disband within 15 minutes. The students refused and sang the "Star-Spangled Banner" and other patriotic songs instead. After 15 minutes, they were all arrested and fined from $10 to $100 or given 5 to 30 days in jail. The Supreme Court reversed these convictions on the grounds that the students had a valid complaint and demonstrated peacefully. The Court concluded that the expression of unpopular viewpoints could not be banned.

Adderley v. Florida
87 S.Ct. 242 (1966)

This important case declared that demonstrations directed against private property could not be permitted. Following the arrest of several protestors, over 200 Florida A&M University students demonstrated at the town jail and blocked its entrance. The Supreme Court upheld the convictions of those arrested on the grounds that the jail was private property designed for the purpose of security and traditionally closed to the public.

Keyishian v. Board of Regents
87 S.Ct. 675 (1967)

In *Keyishian,* the Supreme Court struck down loyalty oaths as a violation of academic freedom. Harry Keyishian was an English instructor at the State University of New York at Buffalo. New York State law required that all teachers sign a certificate stating they were not a Communist or if they had ever been, acknowledging that they had told the proper authority of their involvement. Keyishian refused to sign the certificate. His contract then was not renewed. Justice William Brennan, writing for the majority, found the action unconstitutional. Brennan's reasoning showed that a dismissal based solely on membership without proving any intent to commit unlawful acts was a violation of an individual's rights. Brennan also wrote, "The classroom is peculiarly the 'marketplace of ideas.' The Nation's future depends upon leaders trained through wide exposure to that robust exchange of ideas."

Healy v. James
92 S.Ct. 2338 (1972)

The *Healy* case established the right of students to associate. Students at Central Connecticut State College applied to the school for recognition of a local chapter of the Students for a Democratic Society (S.D.S.), a leftist, activist organization involved in several Vietnam War protests. Their application stressed the educational nature of the local chapter and pledged independence from the national S.D.S. organization. The school committee reviewing the application approved recognition but the president of the college, Dr. F. Don James, denied this recognition. James claimed the national organization's policies were in conflict with Central Connecticut's goals and policies. The Supreme Court ruled that the establishment of such organizations could not be denied if there was firm evidence that the laws of the campus would be followed. This also showed that organizations could be denied official recognition if they did not foreswear disobedience to campus regulations.

Police Department of Chicago v. Mosley
92 S.Ct. 2286 (1972)

The *Mosley* case is important because it declared laws restricting picketing in terms of subject matter instead of in terms of time, place, and manner to be unconstitutional. Earl Mosley frequently picketed Jones Commercial High School in Chicago, usually by himself. He carried a sign reading, "Jones High School practices black discrimination. Jones High School has a black quota" in peaceful demonstrations. An ordinance was passed during this time banning picketing within 150 feet of any public school, except as a labor dispute. The Supreme Court agreed with Mosley's suit on the grounds that the statute made a distinction between labor disputes and other peaceful reasons for picketing.

National Socialist Party of America
v. Village of Skokie
97 S.Ct. 2205 (1977)

In the famous Nazi march case, the Supreme Court ruled that regulations of a gathering must provide strict procedural safeguards including immediate legal review. Upon learning plans of a proposed march through Skokie, Illinois, by the National Socialist Party of America, or Nazi Party, the Circuit Court of Cook County prohibited the Nazis from a number of activities, including marching or parading in Nazi uniform or the uniform of the party, wearing or showing a Nazi swastika, and distributing any literature that incited or promoted hatred against members of the Jewish faith or any other ancestry or faith. These acts were particularly repugnant in Skokie, which had a large Jewish population, many of whom were survivors of the Holocaust in World War II. The Supreme Court sided with the Nazi Party and denied the injunction against the march. The reasoning of the Court showed that the party had to go through appellate review (appeals court decisions) in order to practice their right of assembly and that this process was too lengthy and therefore failed to provide procedural safeguards sufficient to protect the party's right of assembly.

PruneYard Shopping Center v. Robins
100 S.Ct. 2035 (1980)

In *PruneYard,* the Supreme Court upheld the right to petition in privately owned shopping centers. Several students set up a table in the PruneYard Shopping Center to gather signatures for a petition opposing a United Nations resolution against Zionism. A security guard told them to leave because the mall's rules prohibited such activities not related to any of the center's commercial purposes. The students complied but filed suit against the center. In the opinion written by Justice William Rehnquist, the Court held that once the shopping center opened its doors to the public, it could not prohibit lawful free speech activity.

National Association for the Advancement of Colored People
v. Claiborne Hardware Company
102 S.Ct. 3409 (1982)

In this landmark case, the Supreme Court declared that boycotts are protected by the First Amendment. The facts of the case began in 1966 when black citizens of Claiborne County, Mississippi, presented a list of demands for racial equality to white officials. After several years during which these demands were largely ignored, a boycott against local merchants was organized. The merchants filed suit in state court to regain from the NAACP losses sustained during the boycott. The Supreme Court, in a decision written by Justice John Stevens, rejected the merchants' arguments on the grounds that the boycott involved constitutionally protected activity. Stevens noted that if any losses resulted from violent conduct, then the merchants could recover such damages, but that nonviolent activity was protected by the Constitution.

Laws Regulating the Free Flow of Information

Executive Orders Concerning Classified Documents:
Executive Order 11,652 (1973), Executive Order 12,065 (1979),
and Executive Order 12,356 (1983)

There are three important executive orders that have been issued by presidents to define classification of sensitive government documents. The classification scheme determines which government documents will be withheld from public view. Immediately following World War II, the Pentagon attempted to maintain the tight censorship control it had enjoyed during the war effort. Despite some Pentagon proposals during this initial period, the classification of documents did not take shape until President Truman created four categories of documents during the Korean conflict: "top secret," "secret," "confidential," and "restricted." The restricted category was eliminated by President Dwight Eisenhower in 1953. Executive Order 11,652, issued by President Richard Nixon, was the first major presidential order after the establishment of the code. It was designed to streamline the process and eliminate the classification of nonsensitive documents within these categories, thus opening up previously held publications for research and review. This order reduced the number of agencies permitted to classify materials and promoted faster means of declassifying documents deemed no longer sensitive. The concern for the number and types of documents classified continued through the 1970s and 1980s. President Jimmy Carter issued Executive Order 12,065 in 1979 to define the types of materials that can be classified. These included military plans or operations, foreign government information, foreign relations of the United States, government programs for safeguarding nuclear facilities, and materials deemed important to national security. President Ronald Reagan expanded these definitions to include cryptology, confidential sources, and the capabilities of systems relating to national security in his Executive Order 12,356 (1983). President Reagan also attempted to establish regulations requiring government employees who classify documents to submit for prepublication review any book, article, or other publishable work that they may wish to write in their lifetimes, but this was never enacted.

Freedom of Information Act of 1966

The Freedom of Information Act (FOIA) has opened many public documents once shielded from public view. This law was the result of extensive efforts by Carl Moss, a congressman from California. Under the Administrative Procedures Act of 1946, government information was only available to those individuals who could prove a need for it. The intent of the FOIA is to provide the right to access to non-classified or nonsensitive documents. Government files kept on an individual may also be requested by that person. The implementation of this law has had a powerful impact on society. Researchers have been able to discover new evidence on many major historical events. Private citizens have also been able to hold the government account-able for misconduct in the investigation or surveillance of individuals. As the law was originally written in 1966, loopholes existed enabling many agencies to avoid compliance. After the revelations of the FBI's COINTELPRO operation of spy activities on U.S. citizens, most of these loopholes were closed. There are still nine exemptions including classified documents, individual tax records, trade secrets, interagency memoranda not available at law, personal information files unless it is the requester's own file, investigatory records of law enforcement cases, documents on the supervision of banks, and petroleum information.

Federal Advisory Committee Act of 1972

This was the first attempt by Congress to open up the meetings of federal agencies to the public. It required regulatory agencies or committees to announce their meetings in the *Federal Register* and to keep records and minutes of their proceedings. The act failed to have any substance as many exemptions existed, enabling most government bodies to keep their doors closed. This situation was vastly improved with the passage of the Sunshine Act in 1976.

Privacy Act of 1974

The Privacy Act provides protection for citizens from abuse by government agencies using information gathered on individuals by federal agents. In 1974, it was discovered that the FBI had conducted surreptitious surveillance of private citizens. The publicity generated a demand for the end of abuse concerning information gathered and kept on Americans. The Privacy Act was passed along with amendments to the Freedom of Information Act. It established the right of any citizen to inspect any file that may exist on him or her and, more important, to have corrected any misinformation contained in the file. The law also prohibits agencies from turning the files over to other agencies or generally circulating the information to government officials. For the most part, the Privacy Act has not been as effective as intended. Most suits have been filed under the Freedom of Information Act, and the courts have not been given much opportunity to legally define the provisions of the Privacy Act as yet.

Sunshine Act of 1976

This law has largely been responsible for opening meetings of regulatory agencies to the public. The Sunshine Act grew out of the failures of the Federal Advisory Committee Act. It requires all "collegial" agencies, which are those headed by a body of two or more members such as a regulatory commission, to conduct meetings open to the public if such meetings will result in decisions affecting official agency business. Though the law does provide for exemptions, most of which are the same as for the Freedom of Information Act, this act has been more effective in providing open access to federal regulatory agencies.

Whistleblowers Act of 1978

A "whistleblower" is an employee of the government who reports any wrongdoing or mismanagement within an agency by an agency official or by an agency itself. This law, also known as the Civil Service

Reform Act, protects federal employees who report wrong doings. Whistleblowers are often dismissed from their jobs as punishment for speaking out, sometimes by the very individuals they report. The Civil Service Reform Act attempts to protect federal employees willing to report violations of law or waste of funds. The Office of Special Counsel, headed by an ombudsman appointed by the president, is empowered to counteract any action taken against a whistleblower who legally reports agency abuses.

5

Directory of Organizations

Accuracy in Media (AIM)
1275 K Street, NW, Suite 1150
Washington, DC 20005
(202) 371-6740
FAX (202) 371-9054
Toll-free (800) 637-1782
Executive Secretary: Donald K. Irvine

This news media watchdog was founded in 1969 as an organization of primarily business professionals, conservatives, and Republican activists. It searches for factual errors made in news reporting, as well as substantial liberal and antibusiness bias in news coverage. *Media Monitor,* a daily three-minute radio program aired on over 200 stations throughout the nation, is also produced by AIM. Accuracy in Media is affiliated with Accuracy in Academia.

PUBLICATIONS: *AIM Report,* semimonthly, is a report of cases of inaccurate news reporting and biased news stories. *AIM Report* also reports these news stories from the conservative perspective. Also publishes *Index of AIM Report,* an annual index.

Action for Children's Television (ACT)
20 University Road
Cambridge, MA 02138
(617) 876-6620
President: Peggy Charren

This organization's purpose is to encourage and support quality television programming for children and to work to eliminate commercialism.

Founded in 1968, it has a membership of 20,000, consisting of individuals and supporting organizations concerned about the content of children's TV programs. It conducts national symposia on children and the media and commissions studies on children's television. It lobbies the networks, Congress, and the Federal Communications Commission for varied programming to meet the needs of all children.

PUBLICATIONS: ACT has published numerous monographs including *TV-Smart Books for Kids; TV, Books and Children;* and *TV News and Children.* It has also produced the films *It's as Easy as Selling Candy to a Baby* and *Kids for Sale.*

Adult Video Association
270 N. Canon Drive, Suite 1370
Beverly Hills, CA 90210
(818) 882-6323
Co-Chair: Ron Sullivan

Founded in 1987 as the Adult Film Association of America as a trade organization for the producers of adult and pornographic films and videos, this group strives to maintain the right to view adult films in the privacy of one's home and fights against laws making the production, sale, and possession of adult films illegal. Legal services are provided to members charged with possession of obscenity. Publicity and lobbying campaigns are conducted on behalf of its members.

PUBLICATIONS: *Newsletter of the Adult Video Association,* a monthly, is available to the membership and includes news of the association.

American Bar Association
Section on Individual Rights and Responsibilities
1155 E. 60th Street
Chicago, IL 60637
(312) 988-5000
Contact: Stephen Rubin

The Section on Individual Rights of the American Bar Association (ABA) educates the law profession on civil liberties and human rights issues and concerns. The section is one of several major divisions of the ABA and has a long history of promoting civil liberties and human rights.

PUBLICATIONS: *Human Rights* contains analytical law review articles and speeches that discuss human rights issues in depth.

American Civil Liberties Union (ACLU)
132 W. 43rd Street
New York, NY 10036
(212) 944-9800
FAX (212) 354-5290
Executive Director: Ira Glasser

The American Civil Liberties Union is the largest and most well-known organization combatting infractions of the Bill of Rights. The ACLU was founded in 1920 and its membership now numbers more than 375,000, with a statewide organization in each state and over 200 local boards. Membership in the ACLU and local boards is open to individuals interested in civil liberties, including scholars, legal professionals, and any concerned citizen. The ACLU will provide legal support for litigation that has a Bill of Rights issue as its main component and also operates a public education campaign through publishing and advertising. Several litigation projects are sponsored, including women's rights, gay and lesbian rights, and children's rights. The ACLU has been instrumental in most First Amendment cases since the group's inception. The ACLU Foundation is the tax-exempt fundraising arm of the ACLU.

PUBLICATIONS: *Civil Liberties* is a quarterly that provides in-depth analysis of issues and current civil liberties cases and an analysis of the Supreme Court and its trends in civil liberties rulings.

American Family Association (AFA)
P.O. Drawer 2440
Tupelo, MS 38803
(601) 844-5036
Executive Director: Donald E. Wildmon

Formerly the National Federation of Decency and founded in 1977, the American Family Association fosters a biblical ethic of decency in U.S. society, primarily by influencing the content of television and radio programs. It consists of over 560 grassroots organizations throughout the United States and is directed by Reverend Wildmon and a staff of 25. The AFA organizes local groups for letter-writing campaigns to networks, broadcasters, and sponsors to protest the amount of sex, violence, and profanity in broadcasted programs.

PUBLICATIONS: *AFA Journal* is a monthly report of issues in family television programming and the efforts of the association to influence the networks and sponsors about the content of broadcasting.

American Library Association (ALA)
Office for Intellectual Freedom
50 E. Huron Street
Chicago, IL 60611
(312) 280-4223
FAX (312) 440-9374
Toll-free (800) 545-2433
Director: Judith Krug

The Office for Intellectual Freedom (OIF) of the ALA provides assistance to libraries and librarians in the defense of intellectual freedom and support when challenged by individuals and groups demanding the censorship or removal of materials. The Office for Intellectual Freedom is a service of the largest association of libraries and librarians and has a staff of six. It compiles statistics on censorship activities and maintains a database on censorship incidents. The OIF promotes the unrestricted use of library materials through publications, workshops and public speaking engagements. It works closely with the association's Intellectual Freedom Committee to review, develop and revise association policies. It also coordinates activities with the Freedom to Read Foundation and the ALA Intellectual Freedom Round Table interest group.

PUBLICATIONS: *Newsletter on Intellectual Freedom,* a bimonthly, publishes specific instances of censorship of all forms of media, art and public speeches. Articles on current intellectual freedom issues and book reviews are also included. OIF also publishes *Memorandum,* a bimonthly newsletter to committee members and other interested librarians.

American Newspaper Publisher's Association Foundation
The Newspaper Center
Box 17407
Dulles Airport
Washington, D.C. 20041
(703) 648-1000
FAX (703) 620-1265
Vice-President & Director: Rosalind G. Stark

The foundation promotes the place of newspapers in keeping citizens informed, combats illiteracy, and educates the public on the rights guaranteed by the First Amendment. It provides assistance to local newspapers with the creation of programs that promote these aims. Founded in 1961 as the educational arm of The American Newspaper Publisher's Association, the foundation is a nonmembership organization with a staff of 12 and is supported by newspaper publishers. It sponsors projects related to the U.S. Constitution and the Bill of Rights. The foundation is affiliated with the First Amendment Congress.

PUBLICATIONS: *Minority Task Force Newsletter* is a quarterly of issues for minorities in newspapers. The foundation also publishes *Press To Read,* a quarterly newsletter of education and literacy issues, and *Update,* published eight times a year about the activities of the foundation.

Americans for Constitutional Freedom
900 Third Avenue, Suite 1600
New York, NY 10022
(212) 891-2070
FAX (212) 759-6351
Executive Director: Christopher M. Finan

Founded in 1990 after the merger of Media Coalition (founded in 1973) and Americans for Constitutional Freedom (founded in 1986), the association is made up of individuals, trade associations, and businesses from, primarily, the periodical publishing and distribution industries. The organization was formed to combat censorship and to lobby for the First Amendment rights of publishers and distributors. It also conducts opinion polls on censorship and the First Amendment.

Americans for Decency
P.O. Box 218
Staten Island, NY 10302
(718) 442-6088
Founder: Paul J. Gangemi

Americans for Decency combats what it views as numerous social problems, particularly pornography, free access to marijuana, sex education, abortion, loud and vulgar music, the ERA, and homosexuality through boycotts of products, letter-writing campaigns to government legislators and the networks, and grassroots organizing. Based primarily in New York City, it was founded in 1975 as a loosely formed group of individuals and organizations to promote its members' idea of decency in the United States.

PUBLICATIONS: *Celestial News: Past-Present-Future* and *News-Time: The Truth Is News in Our Time* are both little-known periodicals and published on varying schedules.

Americans for Religious Liberty
P.O. Box 6656
Silver Spring, MD 20916
(301) 598-2447
Executive Director: Edd Doerr

This association began as a movement to counteract the activities of the Liberty Federation (formerly the Moral Majority). It conducts research and enters into litigation where intellectual freedom and the traditional church-state relationships are being challenged. Founded in 1980 as Voice of Reason, the Americans for Religious Liberty has a membership of 6,400. It absorbed the Center for Moral Decency in 1982. Members are dedicated to the preservation of intellectual and personal freedoms and the principle of separation of church and state.

PUBLICATIONS: *Voice of Reason Newsletter,* a quarterly of the original association that includes membership news and research results. The group also has published two books, *Religious Liberty in Crisis* and *Abortion Rights and Fetal "Personhood."*

Americans United for Separation of Church and State (AUSCS)
8120 Fenton Street
Silver Spring, MD 20910
(301) 589-3707
FAX (301) 495-9173
Executive Director: Rev. Robert L. Maddox

The AUSCS was created to champion the principle of separation of church and state and to educate the public on the history and value of the First Amendment to the U.S. Constitution. Founded in 1947 as Protestants and Other Americans United for Separation of Church and State, AUSCS has a membership of 50,000 with 115 local groups. The Religious Liberty Award and the Madison/Jefferson Award are given annually by AUSCS. The group follows trends in church/state affairs and enters into court actions where actual violations of the separation principle occur.

PUBLICATIONS: *Church and State* is a monthly journal of opinion on the issue of the separation of church and state. National and international aspects are regularly discussed.

Anti-Defamation League of B'Nai B'Rith
823 United Nations Plaza
New York, NY 10017
(212) 490-2525
Director: Abraham H. Foxman

The Anti-Defamation League is dedicated to eradicating anti-Semitism and to securing justice and fairness for all citizens. Founded in 1913, it operates and maintains several institutes including the Jewish Foundation for Christian Rescuers, the International Center for Holocaust Studies, and the World of Difference Project. It promotes improved interfaith relationships and activities and works to educate citizens about Israel and the Jewish people. It works to counteract antidemocratic extremisms. The Janusz Korczak Literacy Competition for the best books about children and four annual awards are given, including the Hubert H. Humphrey First Amendment Award.

PUBLICATIONS: *The Anti-Defamation League Bulletin* is published ten times per year and reports the activities of the league. *Dimensions* is a quarterly of Holocaust studies.

Article 19: International Centre on Censorship
90 Borough High Street
London SEI ILL, England
71-4034822
FAX 71-4031943
Electronic mail Gelt, NGEONET:GEO2:ARTICLE19
Director: Frances D'Souza

Article 19 is the most active worldwide organization combatting censorship. Founded in 1986, it invites individuals in 32 nations to advocate freedom of expression and to eliminate censorship throughout the world. The organization lobbies governments for greater access to information and for increased freedoms of speech and press. It also works to support victims of censorship worldwide.

PUBLICATIONS: *World Report on Censorship* is a biennial review of issues and censorship incidents. Article 19 also issues *Country Reports*, a country by country report of problems, and *Censorship Reports*, which lists specific instances of censorship, on a periodic basis.

Association of American Publishers (AAP)
Freedom to Read Committee
220 E. 23rd Street
New York, NY 10010
(212) 689-8920
Chair: Richard Kleeman

The Association of American Publishers is the professional association of textbook, trade, and commercial publishers created by the merger of the American Educational Publishers Institute and the American Book Publishers Council in 1970. The AAP represents the interests of book publishers in a number of areas. Two committees, the Freedom to Read Committee and the International Freedom to Publish Committee, are primarily concerned with protecting the freedom of expression and First Amendment rights. The committees monitor trends, case law, and legislation affecting the freedom to publish in the United States (Freedom to Read Committee) and abroad (International Freedom to Publish). The AAP will enter into litigation in cases challenging books and materials as a plaintiff or friend-of-the-court.

PUBLICATIONS: Several trade publications for news and activities of publishers and their events are published and include *AAP Exhibits Directory*, an annual; *AAP Monthly Report*, with news of the association; *Green Book of College Publishing*, for textbook publishing news; and *International Fairs Calendar*, for news of book fairs around the world.

Authors League of America
234 W. 44th Street
New York, NY 10036
(212) 391-9198
Administrator: Peggy Randall

The Authors League is the professional association of authors. It was founded in 1912, and its 15,000 members are authors of books, plays, and magazine articles. The association is divided into the Authors Guild and the Dramatists Guild. Besides professional issues, the league enters into litigation where censorship is taking place. Most notably it has been involved in the *Island Trees v. Pico* (1969) case.

PUBLICATIONS: Both the *Authors Guild Bulletin* and the *Dramatists Guild Bulletin* are quarterlies of professional news.

Catholic League for Religious Freedom and Civil Rights
301 City Avenue, Suite 320
Bala Cynwyd, PA 19004
(414) 289-0170
Executive Officer: John M. Tierney

Founded in 1973, the Catholic League acts as the Catholic anti-defamation organization to combat defamation and ridicule against Catholics. It conducts publicity campaigns to promote Catholic values and will provide legal support to Catholics in cases where their religious and civil rights are threatened.

PUBLICATIONS: The bimonthly *Catholic League Publications* and the monthly *Catholic League Newsletter* discuss social, moral, and ethical issues from a Catholic perspective and provide news of the association.

Center for Constitutional Rights
666 Broadway, 7th Floor
New York, NY 10012
(212) 614-6464
FAX (212) 614-6499
Executive Director: Patricia Maher

The Center for Constitutional Rights works to maintain civil liberties for all people and combats abuses in women's rights, civil rights, freedom of the press, electronic surveillance, and affirmative action. Projects, programs, and litigation are conducted under the Ella Baker Student Program, the Movement Support Network, and, in Mississippi, the Voting Rights Project. The center also sponsors training for law students. The center began in 1966 as the Civil Rights Legal Defense Fund and was called the Law Center for Constitutional Rights until 1970.

PUBLICATIONS: Two annuals, *Docket* and the center's *Annual Report*, detail cases and program results.

Children's Legal Foundation
2845 E. Camelback Road, Suite 740
Phoenix, AZ 85016
(602) 381-1322
FAX (602) 381-1613
President: Robert J. Hubbard, Jr.

Founded in 1957 by Charles Keating as Citizens for Decent Literature, this organization changed its name to Citizens for Decency through Law in 1973 and to the current name in 1989. The foundation is dedicated to fighting pornography, obscenity, and materials harmful to children. It conducts public education activities on the harmful effects of pornography distributed through newsstands, bookstores, television, and theaters. The organization assists local groups in bringing cases against distributors and provides assistance to law enforcement agencies and legislators in enacting and enforcing laws controlling pornography and obscenity.

PUBLICATIONS: *The CLF Reporter* is a quarterly of foundation activities and research findings.

Christian Crusade
P.O. Box 977
Tulsa, OK 74102
(918) 665-2345
President: Dr. Billy James Hargis

The Christian Crusade was created as a religious foundation to promote conservative Christian ideals and to combat socialist and communist influences in U.S. life. Founded in 1948 as Christian Echoes National Ministry, the Christian Crusade has 55,000 religious followers, primarily Christian fundamentalists. It conducts interfaith evangelistic crusades and worldwide missionary activities. It opposes the concept of secular humanism in public education and has lobbied for legislation in this regard. It is affiliated with Christian Americans for Life.

PUBLICATIONS: *Billy James Hargis' Christian Crusade* is published monthly for the membership and discusses current events from a conservative perspective.

Citizens for Decency through Law. *See* Children's Legal Foundation

Citizens for Decent Literature. *See* Children's Legal Foundation

Citizens for Excellence in Education (CEE)
c/o National Association of Christian Educators
P.O. Box 3200
Costa Mesa, CA 92628
(714) 546-5931
Chief Executive Officer: Dr. Robert Simons

The CEE is a committee of the National Association of Christian Educators that promotes grassroots organizations lobbying local school districts to return traditional family values to public school instruction. Its purpose is to assist parents at the local level in support of these goals. Local branches of the Citizens for Excellence in Education have been organized in many communities around the nation. Their activities range from textbook selection and review to campaigns against library books and curriculums promoting humanism, sex education, and value-neutral instruction methods.

Civil Rights Legal Defense Fund. *See* Center for Constitutional Rights

Coalition for Better Television. *See* American Family Association

Concerned Women for America
370 L'Enfant Promenade, SW, Suite 800
Washington, DC 20024
(202) 488-7000
FAX (202) 488-0806
President: Beverly LaHaye

Concerned Women for America is an educational and legal foundation that promotes traditional U.S. family values. Founded in 1979 as an organization for wives of evangelical Christian ministers, it now numbers 600,000, primarily women of various faiths. Political action is organized through what the organization calls "kitchen table lobbyists," which are local groups using primarily letter-writing campaigns against the ERA, feminist initiatives, and public school issues such as use of materials offensive to Christians and rules prohibiting Christian activities. In 1991, the organization announced the formation of a network of legal offices, called the American Justice League, to counteract the efforts of the ACLU.

PUBLICATIONS: A monthly newsletter for the membership is published.

Constitutional Rights Foundation
601 S. Kingsley Drive
Los Angeles, CA 90005
(213) 487-5590
Executive Director: Todd Clark

Founded in 1963, this educational foundation, with a staff of 47 and a budget over $2 million, is dedicated to providing leadership in the instruction of citizenship to school students. The foundation develops activities for students, teachers, and teacher trainees on the values of the Constitution, especially the Bill of Rights. Programs include teacher and student internships in government; in-service training for teachers; student and teacher workshops; and technical assistance to public, professional, and educational agencies on citizenship education for youth.

PUBLICATIONS: *Bill of Rights in Action* is a quarterly newsletter of educational activities, readings, and questions useful for classroom instructions. The foundation also publishes curriculum material for use in courses on criminal and civil law, history, political science, and role-playing simulation games.

Council on Interracial Books for Children
1841 Broadway, Room 608
New York, NY 10023
(212) 757-5339
Executive Director: Melba Johnson Kgositsile

The council began in 1965 as a response to the existence of bias based on race, sex, age, or physical disability that seemed prevalent in children's books. The council is supported by 26 individuals, associations, and corporations. It reviews new children's books, television shows, and videos and reports any racist or sexist language. It also administers the Racism and Sexism Resource Center for Education, which develops materials promoting antiracist and antisexist teaching activities. The council absorbed the Foundation for Change in 1978.

PUBLICATIONS: *Interracial Books for Children Bulletin* is published eight times per year. It is a book-review publication specializing in multicultural materials and evaluation of racist and sexist publications.

Eagle Forum
Box 618
Alton, IL 62002
(618) 462-5415
President: Phyllis Schlafly

The Eagle Forum is an outgrowth of Phyllis Schlafly's STOP-ERA organization. It consists of over 80,000 men and women concerned with pro-family values and conservative traditions, though its local grassroots organizations are mostly made up of women. The forum organizes campaigns to promote issues of traditional morality, private enterprise, and national defense and in opposition to the ERA, the National Education Association's curriculum agenda, and the inclusion of secular humanism, multiculturalism, sex education, and globalism in the public schools. It awards the Fulltime Homemaker Award annually. Its Eagle Forum political action committee (PAC) targets support for conservative political candidates and opponents of the ERA.

PUBLICATIONS: The *Phyllis Schlafly Report* began with the STOP-ERA organization and has continued as the forum for articles and commentaries on social, political, and economic issues from the conservative perspective. It is published monthly.

Educational Research Analysts
P.O. Box 7518
Longview, TX 75607-7518
(903) 753-5993
President: Mel Gabler

Educational Research Analysts is a textbook research and review organization founded in 1961 under the direction of Mel and Norma Gabler. It is not open to membership but has a staff of eight that examines school textbooks under consideration for purchase by the Texas Education Agency. Errors in facts, important omissions, lack of academic skills, and content that is objectionable to traditional values are brought to the Texas textbook review process. The organization also reports on its findings and assists other groups desiring a review of textbooks.

PUBLICATIONS: *Mel Gabler's Newsletter* is the primary source of conservative textbook reviewing. It lists questionable portions of textbooks by page and is published twice a year. The books *Textbooks on Trial, What Are They Teaching Our Children,* and *Are Textbooks Harming Our Children?* are also available.

Fairness and Accuracy in Reporting
130 W. 25th Street
New York, NY 10001
(212) 633-6700
FAX (212) 727-7668
Executive Director: Jeff Cohen

Founded in 1986, this interest group has a staff of eight that promotes freedom of the press and free speech through publications, public presentations, and media programs. The organization encourages pluralism in the media and reports on issues of performance of the news media in news coverage.

PUBLICATIONS: Its principal journal is *Extra!* which contains articles on news coverage. It also has published the books *Are You on the Nightline Guest List, All the Usual Suspects: MacNeil-Lehrer Newshow,* and *Labor and the Media.*

First Amendment Congress
c/o Claudia Haskel
1250 14th Street, Suite 840
Denver, CO 80202
(303) 556-4522
Director: Claudia Haskel

A membership of 30 journalism and communications-related associations, the First Amendment Congress was founded in 1979 to increase awareness of the First Amendment of the U.S. Constitution by all Americans. It conducts local, state, and national "First Amendment Congresses" that provide a forum for the public to discuss media-related issues such as media credibility, fairness and accuracy in reporting, and news coverage. It also produces materials useful for classroom instruction at the K–12 levels on freedoms guaranteed by the First Amendment.

PUBLICATIONS: The quarterly *First Amendment Congress—Newsletter* is the source of the organization's activities. In addition to brochures and booklets for classroom instruction, it also produces audiovisual materials and videotapes.

Free Press Association
P.O. Box 15548
Columbus, OH 43215
(614) 236-1908
Executive Director: Michael Grossberg

Begun as an international network of members of the press in 1981, the Free Press Association is primarily an organization of freelance writers whose primary purpose is to protect individual rights and defend the First Amendment. The association opposes all government censorship of the press, follows important cases and trends in intellectual freedom, and reports on the outcome of these cases to its membership. The Mencken Award for best news story is announced annually.

PUBLICATIONS: The *Free Press Network* is a bimonthly newsletter to the members on press issues such as libel, pornography, censorship, and bans on advertising.

Freedom of Information Center
University of Missouri
20 Walter Williams Hall
Columbia, MO 65211
(314) 882-4856
Manager: Kathleen Edwards

This is a research service of the Journalism Library at the University of Missouri–Columbia, begun in 1958, that maintains a clearinghouse for materials on the flow of information. Inexpensive research services are available to students, legal professionals, reporters, and scholars on censorship, First Amendment cases and issues, libel cases and law, pornography, shield laws, and minorities in the media.

PUBLICATIONS: *The FOI Digests and Reports* used to be the main publication, but it was discontinued in 1985. Back issues are available as well as the *Freedom of Information Files Index*, a guide to resources available on the flow of information.

Freedom to Read Foundation
50 E. Huron Street
Chicago, IL 60611
(312) 280-4226
FAX (312) 440-9374
Toll-free (800) 545-2433
Executive Director: Judith F. Krug

This organization was founded in 1969 as an organization of individuals, associations, and corporations interested in the protection of freedom of speech and freedom of the press, with a special emphasis on First Amendment rights of librarians and libraries. The foundation's main purpose is to promote both the right of libraries to make available to the public any creative work legally acquired and the recognition of libraries as repositories of knowledge. The foundation provides legal counsel and support to librarians and libraries being challenged by groups or authorities for defending freedom of speech or press.

PUBLICATIONS: A newsletter, *News*, of foundation activities is published quarterly and also reports on censorship controversies and federal and state laws affecting First Amendment rights.

Fund for Free Expression
485 5th Avenue
New York, NY 10017
(212) 972-8400
FAX (212) 972-0905
Chairman: Roland Algrant

The fund was founded in 1975 as a society of journalists, writers, editors, and publishers to support freedom of expression throughout the world. Educational and public policy projects are offered to promote the rights included in Article 19 of the Universal Declaration of Human Rights. The fund sponsors *Article 19: Index on Censorship*, a report on worldwide censorship, in the United States as well as other international publications on freedom of expression.

PUBLICATIONS: The fund issues reports on human rights on a periodic basis.

The Heritage Foundation
214 Massachusetts Avenue, NE
Washington, DC 20002
(202) 546-4400
President: Edwin J. Feulner, Jr.

The Heritage Foundation, founded in 1973, is not open to membership but operates as a public policy research institute and conservative lobbying organization. The foundation's research focuses on free enterprise, limited government theories, individual liberty, a strong national defense, and traditional values. The foundation's analyses are disseminated to scholars and conservative organizations. The Heritage Foundation also provides support for conservative causes including anti-pornography and anti-obscenity campaigns.

PUBLICATIONS: *Backgrounders* discusses policy issues not related to legislation. It is issued on an irregular basis, once or more per month. The foundation also publishes the bimonthly *Heritage Today,* which provides the most in-depth view of the foundation's studies and principles, and the annual *Heritage Foundation—Issue Bulletin,* which has the primary purpose of promoting the issues of importance to the foundation.

Invisible Empire Knights of the Ku Klux Klan
c/o Empire Publishing Company
P.O. Box 700
Gulf, NC 27256
(919) 774-8972

Invisible Empire Knights of the Ku Klux Klan
P.O. Box 23
Crawfordsville, IN 47933
(317) 597-2444
Imperial Wizard: Ken Taylor

Knights of the Ku Klux Klan
P.O. Box 2222
Harrison, AL 76202
(501) 427-3414
Electronic bulletin board (214) 263-3109
Director: Rev. Thom Robb

Although these three distinct groups have separate backgrounds, members, and specific functions and are not associated with each other, they represent the traditions of the Ku Klux Klan (KKK) and collectively carry out its purpose and activities. The Ku Klux Klan is the original and most well-known white supremacist organization that advocates the separation of the races and promotes the supremacy of the white race over all other races. The Klan also supports, through protests and local organizational efforts, conservative and traditional-values campaigns such as anti-pornography and anti-obscenity campaigns, school textbook protests, and issues of patriotism in addition to mounting anti-black, anti-integration rallies and protests. The North Carolina Klan claims direct links to the original 1865 Ku Klux Klan. It publishes *The Klansman,* the most well-known KKK periodical (bimonthly, $6 annually). The Alabama Knights of the KKK publishes the *White Patriot: Worldwide Voice of the Aryan People,* a monthly promoting white supremacy ($10 annually). The Indiana Klan stresses that their purpose is not hatred against other races but the "love of the white races, Western culture, Christianity and the U.S. Constitution." Their primary publications are the pamphlets "Patriotism: A Message from the Knights of the Ku Klux Klan," "The Untold Story about the Knights of the Ku Klux Klan," and "Your Rights on the Street."

John Birch Society
P.O. Box 8040
Appleton, WI 54913
(414) 749-3780
FAX (414) 749-3785
Chairman: Allen Bubolz

Named for Captain John Birch, a Baptist missionary killed by Communist Chinese in 1945, and founded by Robert Welch in 1958, the John Birch Society is one of the original and most well known anticommunist, conservative organizations in the United States. The society has funded many national campaigns including the Impeach Earl Warren campaign, the movement to withdraw the United States from the United Nations, and several anti-pornography and school textbook protests. The Movement to Restore Decency is an operation supported by the society to combat trends in society that conflict with traditional values.

PUBLICATIONS: *The BRI Directory of Congress,* issued biennially, provides a critique of the members of Congress from the Birch Society perspective. The *JBS Bulletin* is a monthly journal of Birch Society opinions and issues. The Birch Society also produces books and videotapes on a variety of conservative issues.

Libel Defense Resource Center
404 Park Avenue South, 16th Floor
New York, NY 10016
(212) 889-2306
FAX (212) 689-3315
Secretary and General Counsel: Henry R. Kaufman

The Libel Defense Resource Center was founded in 1981 as an organization of publishers, broadcasters, journalists, and media organizations concerned about libel and privacy law. The center serves as a legal resource to its members in combatting libel charges and keeping its members and the public informed about current developments in libel cases, legal theories, privileges, and defenses. It maintains an extensive brief, pleading, and libel information bank.

PUBLICATIONS: The *Annual LDRC 50-State Survey of Current Developments in Media Libel and Invasion of Privacy Law* reports the state of libel case law throughout the nation.

The Liberty Federation
P.O. Box 190
Forest, VA 24551
(804) 528-5000
President: Jerry C. Nims

Founded in 1979 as the Moral Majority by the Reverend Jerry Falwell, the Liberty Federation has an organization in every state and a membership of over 4 million. The primary purpose of the federation is to organize conservatives and religious fundamentalists for political action to combat pornography, the legalization of abortion, and homosexual rights and to support conservative political candidates. It conducts its activities through the ministries of the Reverend Jerry Falwell and through local organizations challenging schools, libraries, and government authorities over such issues.

The Liberty Lobby
300 Independence Avenue, SE
Washington, DC 20003
(202) 546-5611
Policy Board Chair: Vincent J. Ryan

The Liberty Lobby is one of the largest and most active conservative political action groups in the nation. Founded in 1955, it has lobbied for over "102 conservative, pro-individual liberty, pro-patriotic" issues, including the free gold market, repeal of women's suffrage, separation of church and state, and withdrawal of the United States from the United Nations. The Liberty Lobby opposes federal aid to education, the Equal Rights Amendment, abortion on demand, and pornography through publicity, support for political action, and government lobbying.

PUBLICATIONS: The weekly newspaper *The Spotlight* is the primary vehicle for disseminating the lobby's viewpoints on news, issues, and political candidates. The Liberty Lobby also publishes the *Congressional Handbook and Liberty Lobby Ledger*, a report on congressional votes measured against lobby stances.

Media Alliance
Ft. Mason Center, Building D
San Francisco, CA 94123
(415) 441-2557
Executive Director: Micha Peled

Media Alliance is a support group for journalists, especially writers, photographers, broadcast workers, and public relations individuals. The alliance works to maintain a free press by developing cooperation, rather than competition, within the profession. Professional education classes, job referral services, and skill-sharing programs are the group's primary projects. The alliance also publishes progressive positions on issues affecting society and on freedom of the press.

PUBLICATIONS: *Media File* is a bimonthly review of press issues that has the look of the better underground papers of the 1970s. The alliance also publishes the quarterly liberal journal *Propaganda Review*, with features, editorials, and book reviews on propaganda, both national and international.

Media Coalition. *See* Americans for Constitutional Freedom

Meikeljohn Civil Liberties Institute
P.O. Box 673
Berkeley, CA 94701
(415) 848-0599
President: Ann Fagan Ginger

The Meikeljohn Institute was founded in 1965 to develop resources for legal action for civil rights and civil liberties cases. It collects attorney working papers and unreported rulings filed in court with these issues as a theme. The institute concentrates on a peace law and education project that contains a legal brief library for cases and research reports. It also houses the archives for the National Lawyers Guild, which holds primary documents on the civil rights movement, the free speech movement, and the Vietnam War era.

PUBLICATIONS: *The Human Rights Organizations and Periodicals Directory* is a biennial list of human rights groups and journals. *The Peace Law Docket*, formerly *Studies in Law and Social Change*, is a biennial journal of constitutional, political, and social issues. The institute's newsletter of activities is *News from MCLI*.

Moral Majority. *See* Liberty Federation

Morality in Media
475 Riverside Drive
New York, NY 10115
(212) 870-3222
President: Joseph J. Reilly, Jr.

Begun as Operation Yorkville by Father Charles Coughlin, a member of the 1970 President's Commission on Pornography and Obscenity, Morality in Media is an organization of citizens concerned about the spread of pornography and its dehumanizing effects. It is supported by the Roman Catholic Church. Its primary activities are educational in nature and it encourages individuals to lobby law enforcement agencies to enforce obscenity laws. It also operates the National Obscenity Law Center as a legal clearinghouse for the support of obscenity prosecutions.

PUBLICATIONS: *Obscenity Law Bulletin* is jointly published by Morality in Media and the National Obscenity Law Center. A bimonthly, it is a journal of legal issues, current cases of obscenity prosecutions, and trends in constitutional issues of obscenity. Morality in Media's newsletter of activities is *Morality in Media Newsletter,* also a bimonthly.

National Association of Pro-America
2101 Connecticut Avenue, NW
Washington, DC 20008
(202) 328-1244
Chairman: Joan L. Hueter

Begun in 1933 as an organization of women concerned with what they see as destructive trends threatening liberty, this organization acts as a lobbyist for state and federal legislation primarily on civil liberties issues and at the federal level on national defense initiatives.

PUBLICATIONS: *Alert* is a monthly newsletter of the association's activities and concerns.

National Center for Freedom in Information Studies
Loyola University of Chicago
820 N. Michigan Avenue
Chicago, IL 60611
(312) 670-3116
Director: Edmund J. Rooney

A research and resource center on the Freedom of Information Act, this is a professional service of the Loyola University of Chicago. It sponsors research on the First Amendment, access for journalists, libel, privacy, and trial coverage, among other topics.

PUBLICATIONS: The center publishes a newsletter of activities on a periodic basis.

National Coalition against Censorship
2 W. 64th Street
New York, NY 10023
(212) 724-1500
Executive Director: Leanne Katz

A coalition of nonprofit public interest and professional associations, including the Association of American Publishers, the American Library Association, and the American Civil Liberties Union, the coalition was begun in 1974 to preserve freedom of expression and to combat all forms of censorship. Its primary activities are educating its members, presenting public meetings on the First Amendment, and supporting organizations and institutions that combat censorship.

PUBLICATIONS: *Censorship News* is a quarterly journal of censorship cases in schools and libraries that presents articles topics including school textbook censorship, creationism, and the free flow of information.

National Coalition against Pornography
800 Compton Road, Suite 9248
Cincinnati, OH 45231
(513) 521-6227
President: Dr. Jerry Kirk

The National Coalition against Pornography was founded by Dr. Jerry Kirk, a Presbyterian minister in Cincinnati, with the assistance of Charles Keating, founder of Citizens for Decent Literature. Kirk objected to the report of the 1970 President's Commission on Pornography and Obscenity because it did not take a strong stand against the ill effects of pornography. The coalition has been successful in organizing evangelical Christian groups and local organizations to protest pornography distribution in communities throughout the nation.

National Committee against Repressive Legislation
1313 W. 8th Street, Suite 313
Los Angeles, CA 90017
(213) 484-6661
Co-Chair: Ruth Calvin Emerson

This committee began in 1969 to work to disband the House Un-American Activities Committee of the U.S. Congress. It promotes the First Amendment and works against what it sees as repressive laws and inquisitorial government activities, especially government surveillance actions. The committee is aiming to reform federal criminal laws and to control federal intelligence-gathering agencies. It is currently circulating a petition directing the FBI to cease violations of the First Amendment.

PUBLICATIONS: The major publication of the committee is *The Right To Know and Freedom To Act,* a bimonthly of articles on the protection of First Amendment rights, with particular emphasis on violations by the FBI and the CIA. It also is currently producing *FBI Petition News,* which reports on the success of the petition it is circulating.

National Council of Teachers of English (NCTE)
1111 Kenyon Road
Urbana, IL 61801
(217) 328-3870
Executive Director: Miles Myers

The National Council of Teachers of English is the professional association of secondary school, junior college, and university English instructors. Its primary purpose is to increase the effectiveness of the teaching
of English at all levels. The association will enter litigation in support of
English teachers being challenged for the use of objectionable titles and
against censorship cases in schools and colleges.

PUBLICATIONS: NCTE publishes various professional literature that
discusses the issues of the teaching of English, most notably *English
Journal* and *College English*. Regarding issues on the protection of freedom of expression, *The SLATE Newsletter: Support for the Learning and
Teaching of English* discusses the social and political concerns in the teaching of English.

New Order

P.O. Box 27486
Milwaukee, WI 53227

Originally called the American Nazi Party and later the National Socialist
White People's Party, the New Order is a white supremacist organization.
It is affiliated with the National Socialist Movement and the World Union
of National Socialists. The New Order's activities include protests and
campaigns against Jewish groups, individuals, and businesses as well as
publication of materials glorifying Adolf Hitler.

PUBLICATIONS: Three publications are available to the membership:
the monthly *National Socialist Bulletin*, the bimonthly *NS Nationaller*, and
the biweekly *Social Justice*.

Parents' Music Resource Center (PMRC)

1500 Arlington Boulevard
Arlington, VA 22209
(703) 527-9466
FAX (703) 527-9468
Executive Director: Jennifer Norwood

This association grew out of parents' concerns about rock-and-roll music
lyrics and the lyrics' effects on children. It has successfully negotiated a
consumer information system with the Recording Industry Association
of America that encourages record companies to voluntarily include the
lyrics of songs on the record jackets or else label record sleeves with the
phrase "Explicit Lyrics-Parental Advisory." The PMRC does not believe
labeling is an infringement of First Amendment rights and it promotes
this viewpoint. The center lends its support to Media Watch, the organization that encourages parents to monitor their children's television
viewing. The PMRC is affiliated with the National PTA–National Congress of Parents and Teachers.

PUBLICATIONS: *Record* is a quarterly review of the music industry and the activities of the PMRC to promote record labeling.

PEN American Center
568 Broadway
New York, NY 10012
(212) 334-1660
FAX (212) 334-2181
Executive Director: Karen Kennerly

PEN American Center, the U.S. affiliate of PEN International, was formed to promote friendship and intellectual cooperation among writers, editors, and translators as well as to support freedom of expression. PEN members are dedicated to opposing suppression of the freedom of expression in any form. PEN is an acronym for poets, playwrights, editors, and translators, and the society is open to these qualified individuals by invitation only. It also sponsors writing competitions for prisoners in U.S. prisons.

PUBLICATIONS: *Grants and Awards Available to American Writers* is a biennial publication listing financial sources. *Prisoner Writing Information Bulletin* publishes works from the prisoner writing project on a periodic basis. PEN American Center also publishes a quarterly *Newsletter*. The center has published the monographs *Liberty Denied,* a study of current problems in censorship in the United States; *The World in Translation,* which is a compilation of 39 papers on various topics; and *PEN American Center: A History of the First Fifty Years.*

People for the American Way
2000 M Street, NW, Suite 400
Washington, DC 20036
(202) 467-4999
FAX (202) 293-2672
President: Arthur J. Kropp

Formed by the noted television producer Norman Lear to counter the Moral Majority, the People for the American Way is a public interest organization that promotes pluralism, freedom of expression, and religious diversity as traditional U.S. values. The group utilizes mass media campaigns in direct contention with similar efforts by conservative and religious fundamentalist organizations. People for the American Way provides support to groups and individuals combatting challenges to their First Amendment rights and produces educational materials and seminars on these issues.

PUBLICATIONS: The primary publication is the *PFAW Forum,* a quarterly newsletter of the organization's activities and viewpoints. The organization also publishes the annual *Attacks on the Freedom To Learn.*

Project Censored
Sonoma State University
Department of Communications Studies
Rohnert Park, CA 94928
(707) 664-2500
Director: Carl Jensen

Founded in 1976 by Professor Jensen, Project Censored researches the major news stories of each year and compiles a list of the "most censored news stories," which are articles that should have received major attention but did not. Jensen believes the media practice self-censorship because of their lack of perception, their drive for profit, their shared interests with business, or their commitment to the status quo. The list of the ten most censored stories is published each year.

PUBLICATIONS: "The 10 Best Censored Stories," a pamphlet, is available from the offices of Professor Jensen at Sonoma State University.

Religious Alliance against Pornography. *See* National Coalition against Pornography

Reporters Committee for Freedom of the Press
1735 I Street, NW, Suite 504
Washington, DC 20006
(202) 466-6312
Freedom of Information hotline (800) 336-4243
Executive Director: Jane E. Kirtley

The Reporters Committee was begun in 1970 to protect the First Amendment rights of reporters for all media. It has been either the plaintiff or a friend-of-the-court in every major case affecting the First Amendment rights of reporters and editors since 1972. It conducts research on how the subpoenaing of the notes of reporters affects their subsequent ability to gather confidential sources. The committee provides free legal advice to members of the press whenever freedom of the press is being challenged.

PUBLICATIONS: *News Media and the Law* reports on cases and legislation affecting the rights of reporters, editors, and news broadcasters. A quarterly, it also provides information on the activities of the committee. *News Media Update* is a biweekly of current events.

Student Press Law Center
1735 I Street, NW, Suite 504
Washington, DC 20006
(202) 466-5242
Executive Director: Mark Goodman

The Student Press Law Center is the primary support group for high school and college journalists. Begun in 1974, it is supported by journalism educators and student journalists. Its main purpose is to protect the First Amendment rights of student journalists through free legal advice, amicus curiae briefs in major cases, and research in the field of student journalism, especially regarding freedom of the press issues. It awards the Scholastic Press Freedom Award annually to the high school or college student journalist or publication that embodies the highest standards for student journalists' rights.

PUBLICATIONS: The quarterly *Student Press Law Center—Report* is a newsletter of the issues affecting student journalists, including censorship, libel, and freedom of information. The center has also published the book *Law of the Student Press,* a handbook for student journalists.

Voice of Reason. *See* Americans for Religious Liberty

Women against Pornography (WAP)
321 W. 47th Street
New York, NY 10036
(212) 307-5055
Executive Officer: Mark Rose

WAP was founded in 1979 by Susan Brownmiller, author of *Against Our Will,* and other feminists. Its primary purpose is to educate the public about the degrading effects of pornography and how it brutalizes women. WAP offers tours of the New York Times Square district to demonstrate firsthand the essence of pornography and its brutalizing effects. Multimedia materials and programs showing how pornography permeates popular culture are also available for high schools and colleges. In addition, WAP offers referral services to victims of pornography and sexual abuse.

PUBLICATIONS: The newsletter *Women against Pornography—Newsreport* is issued two to four times per year and provides information on the feminist anti-pornography movement and its activities. It discusses current trends and legislation in the struggle against pornography, sexual violence, and sex-role stereotyping.

World Press Freedom Committee
c/o The Newspaper Center
Box 17407
Washington, DC 20041
(703) 648-1000
FAX (703) 620-4557
Executive Director: Dana Bullen

The World Press Freedom Committee is an association of journalist organizations promoting freedom of the press in the world, especially the Third World, and combatting state control of the media. It promotes high standards of news reporting among Third World journalists and offers assistance to journalists who have difficulties in reporting news in their own country.

PUBLICATIONS: A newsletter is published four to eight times per year on the activities of the committee.

6

Selected Print Resources

Reference Works

THE FOLLOWING REFERENCE MATERIALS ARE relevant tools for research on intellectual freedom, including all four freedoms of the First Amendment. The indexes and abstracts are the best starting points for locating materials, especially current sources. The bibliographies are most helpful in searching for more retrospective sources.

Bibliographies and Guides

Bennett, James R. **Control of Information in the United States: An Annotated Bibliography.** Westport, CT: Meckler, 1987.

This compilation on materials about information control is intended to make the point that this phenomenon is a dangerous and frequent event. Over 2,900 entries are organized into sections such as "Anti-Communism and Anti-Sovietism," "The Complex" (such as the military-industrial complex), "Corporations," "Government," "The Pentagon," "Intelligence Agencies," and "Global."

Byerly, Greg, and Rick Rubin. **Pornography: The Conflict over Sexually Explicit Materials in the United States: An Annotated Bibliography.** New York: Garland Publishing, 1980.

A very good annotated bibliography of 444 books, dissertations, articles, and court cases. Chapters focus on books, psychological articles, sociological articles, philosophical and religious articles, popular articles, government documents, legal articles, and court cases.

Harvey, James A. **Librarians, Censorship, and Intellectual Freedom: An Annual Annotated Bibliography, 1968–69.** Chicago: American Library Association, 1970.

Though dated, this is a good annotated bibliography of pre-1970 materials on intellectual freedom, primarily those materials against censorship. Sections include works on the principles of intellectual freedom, case histories, support for the Library Bill of Rights, censorship and obscenity law, and intellectual freedom in fields other than librarianship.

Hoffman, Frank. **Intellectual Freedom and Censorship: An Annotated Bibliography.** Metuchen, NJ: Scarecrow Press, 1989.

An annotated bibliography of significant books and articles on censorship and intellectual freedom, this work contains 900 entries from a wide variety of sources and on a broad range of intellectual freedom topics. Materials on intellectual freedom in different professions, not just librarianship, are included. There is a significant discussion and coverage of court cases. This is a substantial collection of materials, though the annotations are often brief with few evaluative comments.

McCoy, Ralph E. **Freedom of the Press: An Annotated Bibliography.** Foreword by Robert B. Downs. Carbondale: Southern Illinois University Press, 1968.

An extremely comprehensive collection of books, articles, film, and other media on freedom of the press. Both the print and broadcast news industries are covered. Despite its age, this is a very useful bibliography because of the extensive subject coverage, including materials on libel, privacy, obscenity, sedition, and reporters' privileges.

———. **Freedom of the Press: A Bibliocyclopedia. Ten-Year Supplement (1967–77).** Foreword by Robert B. Downs. Carbondale: Southern Illinois University Press, 1979.

This is a useful update to McCoy's 1968 bibliography. The same format and subject coverage make this a worthwhile companion to his earlier work.

Sellen, Betty-Carol, and Patricia Young. **Feminists, Pornography and the Law: An Annotated Bibliography of Conflict, 1970–1986.** Hamden, CT: Library Professional Publications, 1987.

An excellent bibliography of sources on the feminist anti-pornography debate, this work includes books, periodical articles, newspaper articles, nonprint materials, unpublished works, and a list of organizations. Many of the entries are current, circa 1980s, materials.

Indexes and Abstracts

Alternative Press Index. Baltimore, MD: Alternative Press Center, 1969–.

This is the index for sources not found in *Reader's Guide* or other standard indexes. Over 200 alternative and radical presses and publications are indexed by subject in a broad range similar to *Reader's Guide*. A majority of the titles are published in the United States, but some foreign journals, especially titles from Great Britain, are included. The editorial policy is decidedly left of center and this is reflected in the citations.

Current Law Index. Belmont, CA: Information Access Company, 1980–.

Sponsored by the American Association of Law Libraries, this legal index has a greater coverage than the industry standard *Index to Periodical Literature*, with 700 titles indexed, 200 more than *Index to Periodical Literature*. This and the other law indexes (see *Legal Resources Index*) are extremely useful for research in First Amendment law and for following current cases in the courts. Interdisciplinary journals are indexed here as well.

Historical Abstracts: Bibliography of the World's Periodical Literature. Santa Barbara, CA: ABC-CLIO, 1955–.

This excellent source for historical and international materials on intellectual freedom includes over 20,000 articles in each volume. Articles are arranged by topic and subtopic and by country in two sections. Part A indexes modern history (1450–1914), and Part B is a compilation of post–World War I materials.

Human Rights Internet Reporter. Cambridge, MA: Human Rights Internet, Harvard Law School, 1976–.

More than just an index, it nonetheless contains an impressive and thorough annotated bibliography of books and articles on human rights around the world, including civil liberties and expressive rights. This is another important source for materials not indexed in standard sources, especially international materials. Coverage of U.S. issues is quite strong as well. The *Reporter* also includes articles and editorials, a calendar of events, and recent human rights developments.

Humanities Index. Bronx, NY: H. W. Wilson Company, 1974–.

Primarily for research in philosophy, religion, literature, and other humanities subjects, this Wilson index is one of the best for materials on freedom of religion and church-state relationships. It indexes almost 300 titles, mostly scholarly journals. Prior to 1974, it was combined with *Social Sciences Index*.

Index to Legal Periodicals. Bronx, NY: H. W. Wilson Company, 1908–.

The oldest of the legal indexes, this product has the look of all the familiar Wilson indexes. It provides access to 500 legal and interdisciplinary titles and is especially useful for historical research, with indexing going as far back as 1908. Publications from the United States, Canada, Great Britain, Ireland, Australia, and New Zealand are included. Because intellectual freedom issues are intertwined with case law, this is a very important source. It is one of the few indexes with sources on the freedom of association. Available online on Wilsonline.

Legal Resources Index. Belmont, CA: Information Access Company (IAC), 1980–.

This is the online version of *Current Law Index* with the additional coverage of six law newspapers and selected legal monographs. As of 1987, it contained 277,000 records. It is available on DIALOG, BRS, Mead Data Central, and IAC's Infotrac CD-ROM.

Library Literature. Bronx, NY: H. W. Wilson Company, 1933–.

Though a specialized index, it covers the *Newsletter on Intellectual Freedom,* one of the best sources for censorship news. Intellectual freedom challenges significantly affect libraries, and many of the library periodicals indexed include intellectual freedom articles, primarily focusing on library responses but also providing useful insight into censorship and similar topics. Available online on Wilsonline.

PAIS Bulletin. New York: Public Affairs Information Service (PAIS), 1915–.

A social sciences index, this is one of the best indexes for sources on government information and for legislation. The *Bulletin*'s monthly indexes are by subject only, with an author index included in the annual cumulation. This is very useful for research on public policy affecting intellectual freedom.

Social Sciences Citation Index. Philadelphia: Institute for Scientific Information, 1969–.

This is a worthwhile index on social and behavioral sciences as well as an important tool for scholarly research in the tracking of citations. It covers a multidisciplinary range for social science periodicals, but more importantly it includes a Citation Index to consult cited works in particular articles. The general reader will want to use *Social Sciences Index* and other indexes mentioned first.

Social Sciences Index. Bronx, NY: H. W. Wilson Company, 1974–.

Originally compiled with *Humanities Index, Social Sciences Index* has been a separate work since 1974. It is a multidisciplinary source of materials but primarily indexes sociology, political science, economics, and psychology. This is an excellent source for scholarly studies on intellectual freedom.

Directories

Christiano, David, and Lisa Young, eds. **Human Rights Organization and Periodicals Directory,** 6th ed. Berkeley, CA: Meiklejohn Civil Liberties Institute, 1990.

Though the coverage is on human rights issues, this work is produced by the venerable Meiklejohn Civil Liberties Institute, a leading resource center for intellectual freedom publications. Civil liberties groups concerned about censorship, religious freedom, and free speech rights are included. The directory also includes a federal agencies guide, a subject index, a periodicals index, and a geographic index.

Directory of Religious Organizations in the United States, 3d ed. Detroit, MI: Gale Research Company, 1992.

This directory lists a broad range of religious organizations under nine topical headings, including "Special Ministries," "Spiritual Life," "Teaching and Nursing Orders," "Academic and Educational," "Social Justice," "Foreign Missions," "Evangelical," "Media," and "Professional and Ecumenical." Each entry includes basic directory information, including membership figures and publications, plus a brief description of purpose. The "Social Justice" section includes a significant number of organizations concerned with religious freedom and civil liberties. An index of group names is also included.

Geisendorfer, James V. **A Directory of Religious and Parareligious Bodies and Organizations in the United States.** Lewiston, NY: Edwin Mellen Press, 1989.

Geisendorfer was the editorial consultant for the first edition of the *Directory of Religious Organizations in the United States* (see above). He provides a relatively up-to-date directory of over 5,700 organizations, many with a social justice and civil liberties purpose, as well as conservative and fundamentalist groups. Entries are alphabetically arranged, but there are no indexes. For this source to be very useful, the reader needs to already know the organization's correct name, though there are cross-references for name changes.

Kruzas, Anthony T., comp. and ed. **Social Service Organizations and Agencies Directory.** Detroit, MI: Gale Research Company, 1982.

In this general directory of social service agencies, advocacy groups, voluntary associations, and professional organizations, one complete chapter is devoted to civil rights and civil liberties groups. Each entry includes basic directory information and a brief description of the purpose and activities of the organization. Though this is not a complete source, it offers excellent coverage of various anti-defamation groups for the different ethnic populations in the United States as well as peace, justice, and civil liberties advocacy groups.

Naifeh, Steven W. **The Best Lawyers in America: 1991–1992.** Aiken, SC: Woodward/White, 1991.

This is a current directory of lawyers and law firms who have distinguished themselves in a specialty in legal practice. The directory is arranged by state and then by specialty, and a First Amendment section is included in most states' coverage. Name and address of the attorney and affiliated law firm constitute each entry.

Wiseberg, Laurie S., and Hazel Sirett, eds. **North American Human Rights Directory,** 3d ed. Washington, DC: Human Rights Internet, 1984.

Produced by the Human Rights Internet of Harvard University, this directory contains over 700 entries describing U.S. and Canadian organizations advocating human rights, social justice, and civil liberties. The main index is alphabetical, and acronym, geographic, and subject indexes are included to aid in cross-referencing.

Yearbooks, Dictionaries, and Encyclopedias

Black, Henry Campbell. **Black's Law Dictionary: Definitions of the Terms and Phrases of American and English Jurisprudence, Ancient and Modern,** 6th ed. St. Paul, MN: West Publishing Company, 1991.

This is the best and most prestigious legal dictionary. It should be consulted first when defining any legal term or concept. A copy is owned by almost all libraries in the United States, including public libraries and those serving academic institutions. It is most useful when reading cases of any kind to determine the meaning of legal terminology and the significance of various terms to the case itself.

The Bowker Annual: Library and Book Trade Almanac. New Providence, NJ: R. R. Bowker, 1955–.

This specialized annual for the library profession reports annual events, activities, and trends on a wide variety of topics. Each edition includes a substantial article reviewing the state of intellectual freedom in libraries and significant national affairs that have directly impacted censorship and intellectual freedom.

Chandler, Ralph C., Richard Enslen, and Peter G. Renstrom. **The Constitutional Law Dictionary.** Santa Barbara, CA: ABC-CLIO, 1985.

Volume 1 of this set concentrates on the concepts, words and phrases, and major U.S. court cases concerning individual rights, including the four freedoms of the First Amendment. There is a chapter-by-chapter approach to the Bill of Rights, with Chapter 2 covering the First Amendment in depth.

Free Speech Yearbook. Published for the Speech Communication Association. Carbondale: Southern Illinois University Press, 1962–.

The *Free Speech Yearbook* is devoted entirely to the compilation of significant commentary and analysis of free speech issues before the Supreme Court in the preceding year and the trends leading up to that term of the Court. Each article is written by a noted scholar; Franklyn Haiman, Nadine Strossen, and William Van Alstyne each contributed to the 1991 edition. Several book reviews are also included. The most current edition contains articles on corporate campaign expenditures and First Amendment implications, the Rehnquist Court's record on free speech, the flag desecration cases of 1990, and the religious freedom cases during the Court's judicial year, for example.

Green, Jonathan. **The Encyclopedia of Censorship.** New York: Facts on File, 1990.

As the title suggests, this is an encyclopedic approach to the incidents of censorship. It is international in scope but leans heavily toward British and U.S. circumstances. Green's style is readable; this work provides the general reader with a very useful reference tool.

The Guide to American Law: Everyone's Legal Encyclopedia. St. Paul, MN: West Publishing Company, 1983.

Twelve volumes, including an index and an appendix volume, this nontechnical encyclopedia covers all aspects of U.S. law. Each aspect of the Bill of Rights and all four freedoms of the First Amendment are well defined. Several insightful essays on freedom of speech, press, and religion, among others, provide a more interesting and in-depth view of these concepts by relating them to specific instances.

Hurwitz, Leon. **Historical Dictionary of Censorship in the United States.** Westport, CT: Greenwood Press, 1985.

In this detailed and thorough encyclopedic approach to censorship incidents in the United States, Hurwitz provides coverage in each entry. Judicial decisions, acts of censorship, and governmental regulations are the primary ingredients in this alphabetical arrangement.

Supreme Court Review. Chicago: University of Chicago Press, 1960–.

This annual compiles significant commentary and analysis of major Supreme Court decisions and affairs of the year. Reviews are written by noted scholars and commentators on the Supreme Court. An overview of the term is also provided by the editor. First Amendment case law occupies a significant role in Supreme Court affairs, and this annual always includes substantial commentary on the Court's treatment of First Amendment rights.

Witt, Elder. **Congressional Quarterly's Guide to the U.S. Supreme Court,** 2d ed. Washington, DC: Congressional Quarterly, 1990.

This guide to the Supreme Court and its decisions is another superior publication from Congressional Quarterly, Inc. Updated periodically, this work is a complete source of major issues facing the Court, with historical review and background information provided. First Amendment law and incidents constitute a significant portion of the work.

Special Issues of Periodicals

Academe. 76 (July–August 1990). Washington, DC: American Association of University Professors.

With the controversy over funding of the arts and the introduction of the Helms amendment denying funding by the National Endowment of Arts for any "obscene" creation, a tremendous impact on grants for higher education was foreseen. The articles in this issue discuss censorship of the arts, recent events resulting from the Helms amendment, and ethical issues, particularly the pledge requirement to receive funding.

Columbia Journalism Review. 30 (November–December 1991). New York: Columbia University, Graduate School of Journalism.

The special 30th anniversary issue is the occasion for an in-depth discussion of the First Amendment and journalism. Seven major articles on free speech and free press feature views from a variety of journalists and commentators on what they see as the greatest threat to freedom of the press. Authors include Ben Bradlee of the *Washington Post*, Jesse Jackson (now a talk show host), and columnist Molly Ivins. In addition to the main articles, a news section, "Chronicle," reports ten international incidents of press suppression, and there are three major book reviews on books about freedom of the press.

Library Trends. 19 (July 1970).Urbana: University of Illinois at Urbana-Champaign, Graduate School of Library and Information Science.

In the 18 articles on censorship, intellectual freedom, and the administration of library intellectual freedom policies, both national and international perspectives are represented. Several articles are written by well-known intellectual freedom advocates within the library profession, including Everett T. Moore, Robert Downs, David Berninghausen, and Eli Oboler. Stanley Fleishman, a well-known First Amendment attorney, also discusses legal aspects of intellectual freedom. Reports on Western Europe, Australia, New Zealand, and South Africa are rendered as well.

Library Trends. 39 (Summer/Fall 1990). Urbana: University of Illinois at Urbana-Champaign, Graduate School of Library and Information Science.

Twelve articles by librarians, scholars, and attorneys discuss and analyze recent trends in censorship and intellectual freedom. The articles review school textbook controversies, copyright issues, ethics of privacy, censorship in libraries, philosophical issues in free speech, access to information, the dilemma between ownership and intellectual freedom, national security controls on information, peer review and intellectual freedom, and collection management practices in relation to intellectual freedom. This is an excellent review of more current concerns, though skewed to the interests of libraries.

Social Education. 54 (October 1990). Washington, DC: National Council for the Social Studies.

A special section of this journal for social studies teachers features 11 articles of commentary and analysis on the First Amendment. Some of the articles discuss academic freedom and the problems of First Amendment rights in the schools, but most focus on assisting teachers in bringing these concepts into the instruction of social studies and civics classes. There is an excellent article on Justice William Brennan and one on the basic concepts of the First Amendment. In addition to the special section, the National Council for the Social Studies' position on academic freedom is provided, with editorial commentary, along with an annotated bibliography of ERIC documents on the First Amendment.

Society. 24 (July–August 1987). New Brunswick, NJ: Transaction Publishers.

Though the entire issue is not devoted to the theme, this publication includes seven articles on the problems of pornography and free speech. Each article is written by a scholar, publisher, or academician. The occasion of this issue is the Meese Commission report, and the report's conclusions are the subject of these articles. The opinions expressed are highly critical of the commission's report, either for its content, its research methods, or its direction in public policy.

Monographs

General

This is a selected list of monographs on general aspects of intellectual freedom or the freedom of information or that discuss more than one of the four freedoms of the First Amendment. The emphasis is on current publications but important retrospective titles are also listed.

Alderman, Ellen, and Caroline Kennedy. **In Our Defense: The Bill of Rights in Action.** New York: William Morrow and Company, 1991.

Each of the rights and freedoms in the Bill of Rights is illustrated with a modern incident that shows the troubling conflict that can be brought about between constitutional law and the practice of freedom. The authors present some thought-provoking arguments both about political repression of rights and about the exploitation of rights and freedoms by unscrupulous individuals. The co-author is the daughter of President John F. Kennedy.

Archer, Jules. **Who's Running Your Life? A Look at Young People's Rights.** New York: Harcourt Brace Jovanovich, 1979.

Written primarily for the use of junior high and senior high school students, this is an excellent book on the rights of students. Archer designed the book to enlighten all students on their own constitutional rights, including free speech and free press activities.

Article 19. **Information, Freedom and Censorship: World Report 1988.** London: Longman, 1988.

This is an analysis of freedom of speech and freedom of the press in every country. Arranged alphabetically by nation, it lists specific incidents of the early to mid-1980s and analyzes the climate for intellectual freedom in each country. For the United States the analysis finds a strong theoretical commitment to freedom of expression but intolerance of dissent and unorthodox views. The work asserts that in the 1980s, freedom of expression did not fare very well under President Ronald Reagan.

Barron, Jerome A., and C. Thomas Dienes. **Handbook of Free Speech and Free Press.** Boston: Little, Brown, 1979.

Compartmentalized so that the reader can check on one aspect without substantial sequential reading, this handbook details the major legal concepts of the freedoms of speech and press. The doctrines of "clear and present danger" and "prior restraint" are well covered. Commercial speech, symbolic speech, libel, privacy, news gathering, public trial and free press, and obscenity are the remaining major sections.

Bartlett, Jonathan E. **The First Amendment in a Free Society.** New York: H. W. Wilson Company, 1979.

Bartlett provides another viewpoint on the First Amendment and analyzes the protections it affords. This makes interesting reading for a review of the need for keeping the First Amendment strong.

Beman, Lamar T., comp. **Selected Articles on Censorship of Speech and the Press.** New York: H. W. Wilson Company, 1930.

Though dated, this volume compiles a significant body of early twentieth-century opinion on the freedoms of speech and press and on censorship. Articles for and against censorship are included.

Berninghausen, David K. **The Flight from Reason: Essays on Intellectual Freedom in the Academy, the Press, and the Library.** Chicago: American Library Association, 1975.

An indefatigable defender of intellectual freedom and a stalwart in the library profession, Berninghausen argues compassionately for a free and open society supported by a commitment to intellectual freedom. This is one of the greatest intellectual freedom texts, certainly within the library profession. Both press and speech issues are covered.

Berns, Walter. **The First Amendment and the Future of American Democracy.** New York: Basic Books, 1970.

This work provides a strong philosophical argument for some limitations to free speech. Berns criticizes the Supreme Court, especially under Chief Justice Earl Warren, for ignoring what he believes was the original intent of the founding fathers. He argues that some forms of censorship are necessary and believes that a free, democratic government requires religious faith promoted by freedom of religion but not separated by a wall between church and state.

———. **Freedom, Virtue and the First Amendment.** Westport, CT: Greenwood Press, 1969.

In this work originally written in 1957, Berns provides one of the more reasoned arguments against a liberal approach to the First Amendment. To Berns, censorship is needed to promote virtue. He analyzes the limitations of free speech to support his case and asserts that "the complete absence of all forms of censorship . . . is theoretically untenable and practically indefensible."

Black, Hugo. **One Man's Stand for Freedom: Mr. Justice Black and the Bill of Rights.** Irving Dilliard, ed. New York: Alfred A. Knopf, 1973.

This book provides 76 of Justice Black's Supreme Court decisions, including the landmark cases of *West Virginia Board of Education v. Barnet, Everson v. Board of Education, Korematsu v. United States, Dennis v. United States,* and many more. Irving Dilliard also pens a glowing tribute to Black.

Brant, Irving. **The Bill of Rights: Its Origin and Meaning.** Indianapolis, IN: Bobbs-Merrill, 1965.

In this important text on the history of the First Amendment, Brant shows how the amendment has evolved over time to its current state. He provides an in-depth discussion of the various interpretations of First Amendment freedoms throughout the Court's history.

Busha, Charles. **An Intellectual Freedom Primer.** Littleton, CO: Libraries Unlimited, 1977.

A book of essays on intellectual freedom, Busha's text has been a mainstay of viewpoint by and for librarians. Each essay is an incisive analysis of a major aspect of intellectual freedom including the current state of censorship and intellectual freedom (circa 1970s), privacy and computer files, censorship of the visual arts, and collections of erotica.

Cahn, Edmond. **The Great Rights.** New York: Macmillan, 1963.

This is a compilation of six essays on individual rights by Edmond Cahn, Irving Brant, Hugo Black, William Brennan, Earl Warren, and William Douglas. All are unbridled affirmations of the Bill of Rights.

Canavan, Francis. **Freedom of Expression: Purpose As Limit.** Durham, NC: Carolina Academic Press and the Claremont Institute for the Study of Statesmanship and Political Philosophy, 1984.

This reasoned approach to the major theories of freedom of expression demonstrates that there must be some limits to free speech and free press. Canavan analyzes the works of such writers and philosophers as Milton, Locke, Spinoza, and Mill and concludes that limitations to expression were a central theme of each work. This is an excellent source for research studies on the topic of intellectual freedom.

Chafee, Zechariah, Jr. **Free Speech in the United States.** Cambridge, MA: Harvard University Press, 1967.

This is the first great exposition of one of the major theories of freedom of expression, that of social utility. Chafee argues that there are two types of expression. The first pertains to individual interests, such as commercial speech, and the other serves the public interest, such as debates on issues. The first is not protected, but the second can only be limited when the need for public order outweighs the value of the exercise of expression, or when the point of social utility is reached.

Cohen, Jeremy. **Congress Shall Make No Law: Oliver Wendell Holmes, the First Amendment and Judicial Decision Making.** Ames: Iowa State University Press, 1989.

This title analyzes and discusses the judicial logic and impact of the First Amendment decisions of the great Supreme Court Justice Oliver Wendell Holmes. An in-depth analysis of Holmes's "clear and present danger" doctrine plays a central role in the work.

Demac, Donna A. **Keeping America Uninformed: Government Secrecy in the 1980s.** New York: Pilgrim Press, 1984.

Demac argues that the Reagan administration drastically tightened the standards of classification of government documents and also set far-reaching controls on public employees who deal with the news media. A well-documented report, this work shows that the free flow of information has been drastically reduced to a point where the constrictions threaten our basic democratic way of life. An excellent discussion of the role of the Office of Management and Budget (OMB) is a high point of the book.

Dennis, Everette E., Donald M. Gillmor, and David L. Grey, eds. **Justice Hugo Black and the First Amendment.** Des Moines: Iowa State University Press, 1978.

The editors of this book have collected an impressive set of essays that analyze and interpret Justice Hugo Black's opinions on the First Amendment. A scholarly approach is used, and opinion ranges from those who support Black's absolutist position to those who criticize it.

Dorsen, Norman, Paul Bender, and Burt Neuborne. **Political and Civil Rights in the United States,** 4th ed. Boston: Little, Brown, 1976.

This is the legal equivalent of Commager's *Documents of American History* in both weight and impact. The two-volume set compiles a significant number of laws, cases, and related materials on individual freedoms and civil rights.

Douglas, William O. **The Douglas Opinions.** Vern Countryman, ed. New York: Random House, 1977. Paper: Berkley-Windhover, 1978.

Contains at least significant portions of 94 opinions written by Justice William O. Douglas on topics ranging from the right to vote, citizenship, and governance issues to First Amendment rights, privacy, and due process of law.

Downs, Robert B., and Ralph E. McCoy, eds. **The First Freedom Today: Critical Issues Relating to Censorship and to Intellectual Freedom.** Chicago: American Library Association, 1984.

Over 67 articles on censorship and other intellectual freedom issues provide an in-depth view of the current climate for individual rights of expression. The articles include scholarly treatises on the First Amendment, accounts of major censorship incidents such as the West Virginia textbook controversy and soul-searching articles on the administration of intellectual freedom in libraries.

Emerson, Thomas I. **The System of Freedom of Expression.** New York: Random House, 1970.

This is the first major text of one of the great theories on the freedom of expression, known as the expression-versus-action dichotomy. Emerson views the limitations on speech as a dilemma between expression and action. He sees no instance where limiting expression is justified, even when that expression comes into conflict with the need for order. Instead, he would have actions restricted or punished.

Emord, Jonathan W. **Freedom, Technology and the First Amendment.** San Francisco: Pacific Research Institute for Public Policy, 1991.

Intellectual property rights take on a new meaning as technology changes at a rapid pace. Emord addresses this phenomenon by reminding us of our First Amendment roots; describing the evaluation of technology and intellectual property rights through the broadcasting media, and beyond; and developing a "property rights alternative."

Gordon, Andrew C., and John P. Heinz, eds. **Public Access to Information.** New Brunswick, NJ: Transaction Books, 1979.

One of the more relevant corollaries on the topic of intellectual freedom is the right to know and to receive information. This series of excellent essays on this subject is recommended for all libraries and for readers interested in issues concerning access to government information.

Haiman, Franklyn S. **Speech and Law in a Free Society.** Chicago: University of Chicago Press, 1981.

This is the first text of one of the great theories of freedom of expression, that of the communication context. Haiman argues that expression operates within four basic contexts: communication about other people, communication to other people, communication within a social order or marketplace of ideas, and communication as government involvement in that marketplace.

Helm, Lewis M., et al., eds. **Informing the Public: A Public Affairs Handbook.** White Plains, NY: Longman Publishing Group, 1981.

A retrospective analysis of issues in public information, this collection of articles makes a worthwhile tool for research on the free flow of information. Articles include discussion on the Freedom of Information Act, privacy, public service advertising, social marketing, and other topics, with a case study approach.

Hemmer, Joseph J., Jr. **The Supreme Court and the First Amendment.** New York: Praeger, 1986.

A comprehensive and thorough examination of the judicial record on the First Amendment, Hemmer's commentary is incisive and useful to even the unschooled individual interested in intellectual freedom. He presents every significant Supreme Court case and many other relevant cases in a topical approach. His discussion on major doctrines and on theories of freedom of expression is particularly illuminating.

Hickock, Eugene W., Jr., ed. **The Bill of Rights: Original Meaning and Current Understanding.** Charlottesville: University Press of Virginia, 1991.

Thirty-three essays from distinguished constitutional scholars, political scientists, and government officials describe what they see as the original intent of the framers of the Bill of Rights and whether or not current judicial rulings have strayed, rightfully or not, from this position. Conservative and liberal positions are presented.

Hudon, Edward G. **Freedom of Speech and Press in America.** Washington, DC: Public Affairs Press, 1963.

A distinguished legal scholar argues that the history and application of the First Amendment have been very volatile since its inception. Hudon argues in the manner of Zechariah Chafee that this volatility is evidence that limitations on freedom of speech and press are correct given the time and circumstances.

Irons, Peter. **The Courage of Their Convictions.** New York: Free Press, 1988.

In these 16 accounts of personal courage in the exercise of individual liberties, Irons deftly illustrates that the Bill of Rights is alive and well. Some accounts are well known, such as the Gobitis pledge of allegiance case and the Tinker student rights case, whereas others are not. All are enlightening and a rousing testimony to our civil liberties.

Kalven, Harry, Jr. **The Negro and the First Amendment.** Chicago: University of Chicago Press, 1965.

In this work adapted from a series of lectures given at Ohio State University, Professor Kalven discusses the impact of cases against Black Americans regarding the First Amendment. Major cases involving a Black American with regard to libel, privacy and freedom of association, trespass, and dissenting opinion in a public forum are described and analyzed.

Katz, Steven L. **Government Secrecy: Decisions without Democracy.** Washington, DC: People for the American Way, 1988.

A good review of recent government attempts to control the flow of information, this is an account and analysis of issues of national security and a free press. The use of the classification system and prior review are described as the primary means for controlling government employees. The use of restrictions in federal grants are discussed as a threat to academic freedom, and the press blackout of the Grenada invasion is reviewed. In closing, the author provides advice to presidential candidates.

Kauper, Paul G. **Civil Liberties and the Constitution.** Ann Arbor: University of Michigan Press, 1962.

Professor Kauper presents an insightful analysis of major Supreme Court decisions of the late 1950s and early 1960s, particularly government aid to parochial schools, obscenity cases, restrictive measures against the Communist Party, and cases involving the compulsory disclosure of membership lists. Kauper criticizes Congress, primarily, for failure to uphold a high standard for individual rights.

Koch, Adrienne, and William Peden, eds. **The Life and Selected Writings of Thomas Jefferson.** New York: Modern Library, 1944.

This is a complete compilation of Jefferson's writings, including his autobiography. Two major sections include his public papers, such as the religious freedom documents "Reply to Danbury Baptist Association" laying out his "wall of separation" logic and the Virginia Act of Religious Freedom. His letters are also reproduced, including many to his friend and confidant James Madison, author of the Bill of Rights.

Konvitz, Milton. **Bill of Rights Reader,** 4th ed. Ithaca, NY: Cornell University Press, 1968.

This is a comprehensive collection of significant and relevant cases on the Bill of Rights. First Amendment issues comprise nearly half the book. Related rights, such as the prohibition against a bill of attainder, are also included.

———. **Expanding Liberties: Freedom's Gains in Postwar America.** New York: Viking, 1966.

This very scholarly work provides an excellent analysis about the development of four aspects of intellectual freedom since World War II: religious freedom, freedom of association, academic freedom, and obscenity concerns. Konvitz, a well-known constitutional scholar, has written a reasoned analysis that is recommended reading for all interested students.

———. **First Amendment Freedoms.** Ithaca, NY: Cornell University Press, 1963.

Similar to Konvitz's *Bill of Rights Reader,* this is a thorough compilation of First Amendment cases only. Majority and dissenting opinions are included.

Ladenson, Robert F. **A Philosophy of Free Expression and Its Constitutional Applications.** Lanham, MD: Rowman & Littlefield, 1983.

In this new addition to the body of philosophy on freedom of expression, Ladenson presents a theory that combines elements of Rawls's *A Theory of Justice* with John Stuart Mill's philosophy. This is a very readable text for undergraduate students.

Levin, Murray. **Political Hysteria in America: The Democratic Capacity for Repression.** New York: Basic Books, 1971.

A study of political repression, this work analyzes several major dissenting speech incidents for their impact on the process of guaranteeing individual rights. The author concludes with an analysis of Alexis de Tocqueville's *Democracy in America* and finds that the rule of the majority permits repression too readily.

Levy, Leonard. **Jefferson and Civil Liberties: The Darker Side.** New York: Quadrangle Books, 1973.

The author attempts to debunk the notion that Thomas Jefferson was a committed champion of individual liberty. Evidence that Jefferson permitted political repression is described and analyzed.

————. **Legacy of Suppression: Freedom of Speech and Press in Early American History.** Cambridge, MA: Belknap Press, 1960.

A record of American dissent in colonial and revolutionary times indicates that political repression was rife despite the founding fathers' devotion to individual liberty. The Zenger free press case is covered at length. The author argues for a libertarian view of freedom.

Linfield, Michael. **Freedom under Fire: U.S. Civil Liberties in Times of War.** Boston: South End Press, 1990.

A radical attorney argues that during wartime, the United States takes more liberties with the First Amendment than is necessary. Linfield uses historical accounts to illustrate that wartime use of the "national security" rationale jeopardizes free speech and the rights of prisoners and the accused.

Meiklejohn, Alexander. **Free Speech and Its Relation to Self-Government.** New York: Harper & Brothers, 1948.

This is the first great work by Meiklejohn on his theory of self-government for freedom of expression. Meiklejohn stresses that expression that contributes in any way to self-government must be protected. He classifies this type of speech into four categories: education, literature and the arts, philosophy and science, and discussions on public issues.

————. **Political Freedom: The Constitutional Powers of the People.** New York: Harper & Brothers, 1960.

This contains Meiklejohn's theory of self-government as one of the philosophical approaches to freedom of expression. Meiklejohn postulates that expression that improved self-government was of the highest order and should be protected. He feels that private expression, on the other hand, is not protected by the First Amendment. This work also includes several papers on political liberty, including a strong argument for academic freedom.

Murphy, Paul L., ed. **The Historic Background of the Bill of Rights.** New York: Garland Publishing, 1990.

Twenty essays by such noted constitutional scholars as Thomas Emerson and Leonard Levy provide a reasoned analysis of the origins and meaning of the specific aspects of the Bill of Rights.

Oboler, Eli M. **Defending Intellectual Freedom: The Library and the Censor.** Westport, CT: Greenwood Press, 1980.

Oboler, an indefatigable defender of intellectual freedom in his time, presents several issues that illustrate the need to keep expression free.

Many relate to libraries and book censorship, but the message in support of general intellectual freedom is strong.

O'Brien, David M. **The Public Right To Know: The Supreme Court and the First Amendment.** New York: Praeger, 1981.

This work is a philosophical treatise on the First Amendment's provisions guaranteeing the right to know. The First Amendment does not state in explicit terms a "right to know," but O'Brien builds a credible case that this right springs from the freedoms of speech and of the press and that it is essential to maintaining an informed citizenry. This is an important text on the issue of dissemination of government information.

Rembar, Charles. **Perspective.** New York: Arbor House, 1975.

Rembar is a prolific scholar of the Constitution. In this book, he provides his own view of the role of the First Amendment in protecting civil liberties.

Richards, David A. J. **Toleration and the Constitution.** New York: Oxford University Press, 1986.

A hallmark of democracy, toleration, is examined in depth. The author delves into the theories of constitutional law and interpretation, especially as they pertain to democratic principles. The three major forms of toleration—religious liberty, free speech, and privacy—are analyzed in depth. This is a very important text for all libraries and students of the Constitution.

Robotham, John, and Gerald Shields. **Freedom of Access to Library Materials.** New York: Neal-Schuman, 1982.

In this practical guide to intellectual freedom for librarians, the authors have both compiled philosophical treatises and suggested strategies for dealing with censorship challenges. Gerald Shields is one of the more prolific writers in the field of intellectual freedom and libraries.

Rutland, Robert Allen. **The Birth of the Bill of Rights, 1776–1791.** Boston: Northeastern University Press, 1991.

A thorough history of the creation of the Bill of Rights, this is an excellent historical source for gaining insight into the intent of the authors of the first ten amendments. The English roots begin the story, and the debates over ratification of the Constitution form a large body of the text.

Schimmel, David, and Louis Fischer. **The Civil Rights of Students.** New York: Harper & Row, 1975.

One of the volumes in the ACLU series of handbooks on individual rights, this answers the most commonly asked questions on student rights regarding speech, press, and criminal investigations.

Schwartz, Bernard. **The Great Rights of Mankind: A History of the American Bill of Rights.** New York: Oxford University Press, 1956.

This work delineates the history of the adoption of the Bill of Rights. It describes the English beginnings, colonial constitutions and charters, the Articles of Confederation, the Constitutional Convention, and state ratifying conventions in historical detail.

Shiffrin, Steven H. **The First Amendment, Democracy and Romance.** Cambridge, MA: Harvard University Press, 1990.

In this unique treatise on the relevance of romance to democracy and dissent, Shiffrin also discusses the First Amendment in relation to Kantian theory. Specifically, an argument is made that constitutional review is too mechanical and does not deal sufficiently with the complexity of human lives. This is must reading for all students of the Constitution and civil liberties.

Shumate, T. Daniel, ed. **The First Amendment: The Legacy of George Mason.** Fairfax, VA: George Mason University Press, 1987.

This work includes four essays on human and civil rights and liberties, with a focus on the teachings of George Mason. Freedom of religion, free speech, and U.S. foreign policy are specific topics addressed. The Virginia Declaration of Rights is reproduced in an appendix.

Stevens, John D. **Shaping the First Amendment: The Development of Free Expression.** Beverly Hills, CA: Sage, 1982.

Providing the thoughts and impressions of law professor John Stevens on the development of First Amendment law and theory, this book offers important insights into dissenting speech, particularly. Stevens admires publishers and editors who have been at the forefront of many freedom of expression episodes. A detailed look at the *Progressive* magazine case is also rendered.

Van Alstyne, William W. **Interpretations of the First Amendment.** Durham, NC: Duke University Press, 1984.

Van Alstyne, a law professor at Duke University, describes the First Amendment using an analogy to a Mobius strip. He is a staunch defender of intellectual freedom. This book discusses freedom of speech, freedom of the press, and public policy.

Wagman, Robert J. **The First Amendment Book.** New York: World Almanac, 1991.

An encapsulation of the meaning, forces, and trends behind the First Amendment. Attention is paid to all four freedoms with substantial coverage of the freedoms of speech and of the press. Each chapter is a dialogue that weaves incidents and court cases to build an understanding of specific aspects of the four freedoms. This very readable book is recommended for all audiences.

Weiss, Ann E. **Who's To Know! Information, the Media and Public Awareness.** New York: Houghton Mifflin, 1990.

Designed for young adult readers, this is one of the best texts for young people on censorship and the free flow of information. Weiss describes the problems inherent with censorship and explains how freedom of information suffered under the Reagan administration. Highly recommended for all high school libraries.

Witt, Elder. **The Supreme Court and Individual Rights.** 2d ed. Washington, DC: Congressional Quarterly, 1988.

Produced in the style of the *Congressional Quarterly* reports, this is a useful compilation of all our individual rights. Part I describes and discusses the most salient circumstances and Court decisions on freedom of speech, press, and religion. Other sections cover political participation, due process, and equal rights.

Yarbrough, Tinsley E. **Mr. Justice Black and His Critics.** Durham, NC: Duke University Press, 1988.

A thorough analysis of Hugo Black as a justice and his judicial philosophies. Yarbrough deflects Black's major critics, as well, saying, "Black's absolutist philosophy . . . narrowed the range of judicial discretion to a greater degree than did competing constructions."

Freedom of Religion

Arnold, O. Carroll. **Religious Freedom on Trial.** Valley Forge, PA: Judson Press, 1978.

Judge Joseph Story's view that the authors of the First Amendment's freedom of religion intended to promote Christianity through equalizing sectarian control is strongly supported. Story, a Supreme Court justice and contemporary of Chief Justice John Marshall, has been viewed by legal scholars as offering an opposing view of Jefferson's "wall of separation." Thomas Jefferson's "wall of separation" and its current interpretations are systematically and rationally attacked. Arnold also provides an annotated list of the major freedom of religion cases.

Borden, Morton. **Jews, Turks and Infidels.** Chapel Hill: University of North Carolina Press, 1984.

In this enlightening study of the struggle of U.S. Jewry to realize the religious freedom promised under the Bill of Rights, Borden chronicles the history of Jewish persecution in this nation with strong Christian values but lofty constitutional pronouncements of toleration. The religious tests for public office once used to discriminate against Jews are a little-known and very disturbing aspect of U.S. history.

Bradley, Gerald V. **Church-State Relationships in America.** Westport, CT: Greenwod Press, 1987.

A recent, scholarly voice against the concept of a wall of separation between church and state, law professor Gerald Bradley makes a rational but impassioned case for government interaction with religion, with sect neutrality as the by-word.

Buzzard, Lynn R., and Samuel Ericsson. **The Battle for Religious Liberty.** Elgin, IL: David C. Cook Publishing Company, 1982.

This topical approach to current church-state relations and activities provides a vehicle for the argument that the original intent of the First Amendment's freedom of religion clauses was to create a sect-neutral nation, not a wall of separation between church and state as argued by Thomas Jefferson. Current issues such as state aid to parochial schools, Christmas displays on government property, and home instruction are discussed.

Cogley, John, ed. **Religion in America.** Cleveland, OH: World Publishing Company, 1958.

Contains a series of essays on religious freedom by noted theologians such as Reinhold Niebuhr and constitutional scholars such as Leo Pfeffer. Sections include commentary on the separation of church and state, religion in the schools, and religion in a free society.

Cord, Robert L. **Separation of Church and State: Historical Fact and Current Fiction.** New York: Lambeth Press, 1982.

In this well-written polemic advocating government aid to religious groups and education, Cord presents a scholarly attack on the concept of a wall of separation between church and state. He details many historical incidents that show that U.S. heritage is to promote religion.

Curry, Thomas J. **The First Freedoms: Church and State in America to the Passage of the First Amendment.** New York: Oxford University Press, 1986.

A historical analysis of church-state relations in colonial and revolutionary America. Curry provides the philosophical background born out of these experiences and on which were built the freedom of religion clauses of the First Amendment.

Davis, Derek. **Original Intent: Chief Justice Rehnquist and the Course of American Church/State Relations.** Buffalo, NY: Prometheus Books, 1991.

A definitive study of the religious freedom opinions of Chief Justice William Rehnquist. The concept of "original intent" is discussed as pivotal logic framing the direction of past and future Supreme Court decisions. Davis sees disturbing changes in church-state relations under the current Court.

Evans, J. Edward. **Freedom of Religion.** Minneapolis, MN: Lerner Publications Company, 1990.

In this book for young readers, the history of toleration of religion in the United States provides a good introduction to the topic. The remainder of the text describes and discusses specific challenges to freedom of religion that have occurred over time.

Hunter, James Davidson, and Os Guinness, eds. **Articles of Faith, Articles of Peace: The Religious Liberty Clauses and the American Public Philosophy.** Washington, DC: Brookings Institute, 1990.

This work by the liberal think tank Brookings Institute features seven essays presented at the Williamsburg Charter Foundation symposium. Church-state relations, particularly from a public policy viewpoint, are the focus of the opinions.

Hutcheson, Richard G. **God in the White House: How Religion Has Changed the Modern Presidency.** New York: Macmillan, 1988.

In this study of the Nixon, Ford, Carter, and Reagan presidencies, Hutcheson argues that religion has become far too enmeshed with the conduct of presidential, and subsequently public, affairs. He makes a strong case for a wall of separation. This is one of the more useful politically themed books of recent years.

Kauper, Paul G. **Religion and the Constitution.** Baton Rouge: Louisiana State University Press, 1964.

Kauper argues that any attempt to interject religion in the public schools, no matter how watered down, does a disservice to religion in the United States. He asserts that though the Court has a "permissible accommodation" approach to establishment cases, caution must be exercised to avoid entanglement.

LaHaye, Tim. **The Battle for the Mind.** Old Tappan, NJ: Fleming H. Revell, 1980.

A primary text in the war between fundamentalist Christians and secular humanists, this work delineates Tim LaHaye's crusade against humanism. Though not everyone will agree with his decidedly one-sided opinion, this is an important book to examine for an understanding of one of the current censorship movements in the country.

Lee, Francis G. **Wall of Controversy: Church-State Conflict in America, the Justices and Their Opinions.** Malabar, FL: Robert E. Krieger Publishing Company, 1986.

Reprints the opinions written by well-known Supreme Court justices in several major freedom of religion cases. Opinions of Felix Frankfurter, Hugo Black, William Douglas, Potter Stewart, William Brennan, Lewis Powell, Warren Burger, and William Rehnquist are included.

Levy, Leonard. **The Establishment Clause: Religion and the First Amendment.** New York: Macmillan Publishing Company, 1986.

Levy is one of the leading constitutional scholars. This is one of his latest works, and in it he deftly argues for a high wall of separation between church and state. He traces the sources of disestablishment from the colonial experience, particularly, and describes the debates at the Constitutional Convention and during ratification with thorough and spritely writing. This is an important text for any college library.

McBrien, Richard P. **Caesar's Coin: Religion and Politics in America.** New York: Macmillan Publishing Company, 1987.

A Catholic theologian, McBrien argues that political decisions can be made without creating a conflict between morality and the principles of religious freedom. He uses a belief that natural law is a universal ground of morality that can help define the correct position on such issues as prayer in the schools, censorship, and abortion.

Miller, William L. **The First Liberty: Religion and the American Republic.** New York: Alfred A. Knopf, 1986.

In this unabashed advocacy of the wall of separation between church and state, Miller praises the fortitude of George Mason, Thomas Jefferson, and James Madison for the staunch support and development of our principles of freedom of religion. In addition to a thorough history of the Jeffersonian period, he discusses relevant cases since 1947 and makes a very credible argument against Supreme Court Justice Felix Frankfurter's opinions on religious freedom.

Morgan, Richard E. **The Supreme Court and Religion.** New York: Free Press, 1972.

This is a significant dissenting voice on the Supreme Court's "wall of separation" decisions, especially of the 1960s and 1970s. Morgan views the lack of support for parochial schools as bad social policy and argues that this will eventually be reversed. He uses a historical approach to analyze the treatment of freedom of religion.

Noonan, James T., Jr. **The Believer and the Powers That Are: Cases, History and Other Data Bearing on the Relation of Religion and Government.** New York: Macmillan Publishing Company, 1987.

Noonan, a judge on the Ninth Circuit Court of Appeals, wrote this for practitioners of faith to show the difficulties as well as the rich heritage of freedom of religion. This is one of the most thorough historical and judicial coverages on this topic.

Oaks, Dallin H., ed. **The Wall between Church and State.** Chicago: University of Chicago Press, 1963.

A collection of scholarly opinions on the concept of separation of church and state, this work includes some powerful voices for and against the wall of separation. A Protestant view for the concept and a Catholic view against it begin the discussion. The major themes in freedom of religion cases constitute the remainder of the text. For example, the Rev. Robert Drinan, a former congressman and a Catholic priest, supports some government aid to parochial schools.

Peterson, Merrill D., and Robert C. Vaughan, eds. **The Virginia Statute for Religious Freedom: Its Evolution and Consequences in American History.** New York: Cambridge University Press, 1988.

A collection of essays on the Jeffersonian concept of freedom of religion, this is a very scholarly approach to the historical and philosophical background of the "wall of separation" between church and state.

Pfeffer, Leo. **God, Caesar, and the Constitution: The Court as Referee of Church-State Confrontation.** Boston: Beacon Press, 1975.

Traces the judicial history of church-state relations from the constitutional period to the 1970s. Pfeffer offers criticism of the various Supreme

Court decisions on the impact on religious practices. He predicts church-state relations on topics such as the family, wars, and the schools and raises serious questions for men and women of faith.

————. **Religious Freedom.** Skokie, IL: National Textbook Company, 1977.

This is one of the best and most thorough examinations of the freedom of religion. Pfeffer is a leading constitutional scholar on religious liberty. He analyzes the historical roots and legal decisions in a concise and readable style. His conclusion is the ten theses of his 1953 work *Church, State and Freedom,* a strong argument for a high wall of separation.

Smith, Rodney K. **Public Prayer and the Constitution: A Case Study in Constitutional Interpretation.** Wilmington, DE: Scholarly Resources, 1987.

Smith frames this debate on public prayer as a dichotomy between "original intent" proponents, such as Attorney General Edwin Meese, and those, such as Justice William Brennan, who see original intent analysis as unworkable. A case is made that original intent analysis can be very useful but that some of its proponents, particularly Meese, misread or misapply it to support an ideological viewpoint.

Whitehead, John W. **The Second American Revolution.** Westchester, IL: Crossway Books, 1982.

A strong argument for a Christian approach to law and social problems is made from a constitutional, social, and religious perspective. Whitehead accuses humanists of attempting to control a Christian society through censorship of the news, literature, and television in order to maintain a society without values.

Freedom of Speech

American Civil Liberties Union. **The Censorship Debate: Summary and Critique of the Attorney General's Commission on Pornography.** Washington, DC: ACLU, 1986.

This is the best of the liberal criticism of the Meese Commission report. Both the methodology and the conclusion are attacked. The lack of any empirical data and the loading of testimony, especially the credence given to anonymous works from individuals who did not appear before the commission, form the most serious of the charges. The claim of a causal link between violent pornography and antisocial behavior is seen as a result of the overreliance on violent pornography in the evidence.

American Library Association, Office for Intellectual Freedom. **Intellectual Freedom Manual.** Chicago: American Library Association, 1974.

The *Intellectual Freedom Manual* is the Bible on intellectual freedom for librarians. It includes the Library Bill of Rights and the approved interpretations of this document. The Freedom to Read statement and strategies for combatting censorship are also listed.

Anderson, Arthur J. **Problems in Intellectual Freedom and Censorship.** New York: R. R. Bowker & Company, 1974.

One of the Problem-Centered Approaches to Librarianship series, this monumental work is a strategy for libraries and other institutions in recognizing and countering censorship challenges. The book takes a case study approach to intellectual freedom issues.

Attacks on the Freedom To Learn, 1990–1991 Report. Washington, DC: People for the American Way, 1991.

This annual report of the People for the American Way is intended to lobby against censorship. It records a substantial body of censorship of school textbooks and library books, arranged by state. Each entry includes a description of the incident, the objector, and the resolution.

Baker, C. Edwin. **Human Liberty and Freedom of Speech.** New York: Oxford University Press, 1989.

Baker supports John Stuart Mill's theory of social exchange and argues that the freedoms of speech and press are fundamental to a democratic society. He discusses Mill's theory at length and describes its application in U.S. jurisprudence.

Belknap, Michael R. **Cold War Political Justice: The Smith Act, the Communist Party, and American Civil Liberties.** Westport, CT: Greenwood Press, 1977.

An excellent, scholarly approach to the problems of sedition since 1940, this book examines the persecution of the Communist Party in the United States and the ACLU as it defended the party's members. The Smith Act is described and analyzed.

Berger, Melvin. **Censorship.** New York: Franklin Watts, 1982.

In this excellent introduction to the topic of censorship for students and individuals who know little about the topic, Berger describes a history of this phenomenon in objective terms and discusses more recent trends and issues.

Blanshard, Paul. **The Right To Read: The Battle against Censorship.** Boston: Beacon Press, 1955.

An uncompromising treatise against censorship, Blanshard's classic text is a call for vigilance in the defense of intellectual freedom. His coverage is of the full range of content restrictions. He lays the groundwork for a direction of the conduct of censorship law and prosecution.

Bollinger, Lee C. **The Tolerant Society: Freedom of Speech and Extremist Speech in America.** New York: Oxford University Press, 1986.

Bollinger develops a general theory of tolerance through the analysis of dissenting speech in the United States. He discusses the possibility that a commitment to free speech may bring on excessive intolerance. He cautions instead against the "obedient mind" because a tolerant mind is open to ideas.

Bosmajian, Haig. **Academic Freedom.** New York: Neal-Schuman, 1988.

Number four in The First Amendment in the Classroom series, this is another compilation of all the relevant cases on the topic of academic freedom. The introduction is a very worthwhile explanation of the problem.

————. **Freedom of Expression.** New York: Neal-Schuman, 1988.

In this third volume of The First Amendment in the Classroom series, Bosmajian has compiled all of the federal court decisions on freedom of speech and symbolic speech. His introductions help student readers to understand the impact of each case.

————. **The Freedom To Read: Books, Films and Plays.** New York: Neal-Schuman, 1987.

This is another in the First Amendment in the Classroom series that is intended to bring to student readers the body of law on the freedom to read. It compiles 25 federal cases that deal with book censorship in the schools. As with the others in this series, each case has a brief introduction followed by the opinion of the court.

————, comp. **Censorship, Libraries and the Law.** New York: Neal-Schuman, 1983.

Though similar to the publisher's The First Amendment in the Classroom series, this is not one of the titles in that series. It does include all relevant federal district, appeals, and Supreme Court decisions involving censorship of school library books. As with other similar books, an introductory paragraph provides background to the case, and majority and minority opinions, where appropriate, are included.

————, comp. and ed. **Obscenity and Freedom of Expression.** New York: Burt Franklin Publishing, 1976.

Covering obscenity concerns from the *Hicklin* case to the mid-1970s, this work is a compilation of over 100 legal decisions with an obscenity theme or that have impacted obscenity prosecutions. This is a good source for a quick reference to cases on this subject.

————, ed. **The Principles and Practices of Freedom of Speech.** Boston: Houghton Mifflin, 1971.

One of the more prolific authors on intellectual freedom, Bosmajian provides a substantial collection of philosophical works, such as Milton's *Areopagitica;* legislation, such as the Smith Act; and court decisions on the topic of freedom of expression. This is a good source of material for quick reference.

Broderick, Dorothy, ed. **The VOYA Reader.** Metuchen, NJ: Scarecrow Press, 1991.

Reprints 47 selections from *VOYA: Voice of Youth Advocates,* a library periodical on books, reading interests, and issues of young adult readers. Grouped under five headings, censorship articles constitute a substantial portion of the book. This is an excellent source of information for children's and young adult librarians.

Broun, Heywood, and Margaret Leech. **Anthony Comstock: Roundsman of the Lord.** New York: Literary Guild of America, 1927.

A definitive biography of America's greatest pornography crusader, Anthony Comstock. Broun also presents his views on censorship, saying, "Nobody but fools and censors believe so devoutly in the power of pornography."

Bryson, Joseph E., and Elizabeth W. Detty. **The Legal Aspects of Censorship of Public School Library and Instructional Materials.** Charlottesville, VA: Michie Company, 1982.

Designed for school media specialists and librarians, this is a practical guide to the administration of a selection policy. Suggestions for preparing a policy and set of procedures are included. The book stresses the appropriateness of selection and strategies for dealing with challenges.

Buckley, William F., Jr. **God and Man at Yale: The Superstitions of "Academic Freedom."** Chicago: Henry Regnery Company, 1951.

In his first great book, Buckley argues that academic freedom should not be either a slavish devotion to allowing any idea to remain unchallenged or the belief that the university must protect all forms of speech. Buckley believes the university's role is to teach one set of values and that this permits academe to close off other forms of speech.

Burress, Lee. **The Battle of the Books: Literary Censorship in the Public Schools, 1950–1985.** Metuchen, NJ: Scarecrow Press, 1989.

Burress examines 900 titles that have been censored in the public schools for the sources and frequency of censorship. The role publishers play and suppression by both the Left and the Right are discussed. He addresses several important questions such as the challenges against works that are critical of traditional values and U.S. society, as well as the conflict in values between the poorly educated and the better educated.

Burstyn, Varda. **Women against Censorship.** Vancouver, B.C.: Douglas & McIntyre, 1985.

Examines the conflict within the women's movement over the issues of obscenity and censorship. This collection of essays discusses the exploitation of women in pornography, attempts by feminists to deal with the proliferation of obscenity by legal and extra-legal means, and arguments made against censorship within the movement. A brief biography of each contributor is included.

Busha, Charles H. **Freedom Versus Suppression and Censorship.** Littleton, CO: Libraries Unlimited, 1972.

Originally a doctoral dissertation, this is an expanded work by one of the more well-known intellectual freedom advocates within the library profession. It reports, among other things, the results of a survey of librarians in the Midwest that shows they profess to be more liberal than they actually practice in regards to censorship.

Capaldi, Nicholas. **Clear and Present Danger: The Free Speech Controversy.** New York: Pegasus, 1969.

Freedom of speech and its conflicts in society are thoroughly analyzed from a social exchange theoretical position. An analysis of the clear and present danger doctrine is a central part of the book. Censorship, academic freedom, and political activism are also discussed.

Carmilly-Weinberger, Moshe. **Fear of Art: Censorship and Freedom of Expression in Art.** New York: R. R. Bowker & Company, 1986.

The process of art censorship is detailed with a discussion of religious objections to art, a historical background of governmental interference, and modern art movements and their trials. The author also makes a case against excessive moralizing over art and the chilling effect of censorship on artistic expression.

Censorship Litigation and the Schools. Chicago: American Library Association, Office of Intellectual Freedom, 1983.

Each of the essays included here was originally a paper presented at a 1981 colloquium on school book censorship. The overall theme is the conduct of legal sanctions and litigation regarding school library and textbooks.

Chandos, John, ed. **To Deprave and Corrupt . . . Original Studies in the Nature and Definition of Obscenity.** New York: Associated Press, 1962.

This classical review of censorship provides a significant body of scholarly opinion. One essay is by Maurice Girodias, publisher of Olympia Press, a major producer of classical pornographic novels. Other opinions are by prominent U.S. and British legal scholars.

Clapp, J. **Art Censorship: A Chronology of Proscribed and Prescribed Art.** Metuchen, NJ: Scarecrow Press, 1972.

A chronological list of censorship attempts and challenges to artistic work, from the dawn of recorded time to 1971. A thorough index provides access to specific works. A few illustrated examples, including Michelangelo's *David* and Goya's *Nude Maja,* are included.

Cline, Victor B., comp. **Where Do You Draw the Line? An Exploration into Media Violence, Pornography, and Censorship.** Provo, UT: Brigham Young University Press, 1974.

This series of essays discusses pornography and censorship and their place in society. The majority of opinion stresses that what should be acceptable should be determined by community standards or by what is seen as acceptable moral values of a majority of citizens. This is one of the more important works questioning obscenity.

Clor, Harry M. **Obscenity and Public Morality: Censorship in a Liberal Society.** Chicago: University of Chicago Press, 1969. Reprinted 1985.

In his primary treatise on obscenity, Clor argues for its control. This book is one of the more significant anti-obscenity studies. He attempts to develop a theory of free expression that also accounts for what he sees as society's need to promote morality.

————, ed. **Censorship and Freedom of Expression: Essays on Obscenity and the Law.** Chicago: Rand McNally, 1971.

This anthology is a thorough coverage of obscenity as a social ill. Legal issues are described by two prominent judges. Both liberal and conservative opinions are included that demonstrate the conflict between perceived moral values and democratic ideas.

Cornog, Martha. **Libraries, Erotica and Pornography.** New York: Oryx Press, 1991.

This collection of 17 essays on censorship and intellectual freedom concerns in libraries highlights the dilemma librarians face in reflecting current mores while promoting freedom of choice. Some issues covered include feminist issues in censorship, *Playboy* magazine in the library, vandalism of sexually oriented materials, and collections on homosexuality. This is a good source of information for libraries and librarians.

Cotham, Perry C. **Obscenity, Pornography, and Censorship.** Grand Rapids, MI: Baker Book House, 1973.

Cotham argues for a compromise between what is seen as two extreme positions: censorship of a broad range of works for obscenity by conservatives and a near absolutist view of the First Amendment by liberals. He suggests that censorship has its place but that society must be careful not to suppress literary quality, though it may be obscene.

Cowan, Geoffrey. **See No Evil: The Backstage Battle over Sex and Violence on Television.** New York: Simon and Schuster, 1979.

Describes the television industry's battle from within and without against successive waves of censorship and the changing content of TV programming. The creation of the "family hour" is also discussed.

Craig, Alec. **The Banned Books of England and Other Countries.** London: George Allen & Unwin, 1962.

Craig attempts to provide an understanding of obscenity and how it has been received by describing and analyzing several major censorship attempts. Though his examples are hardly obscene by today's standards, they provide a historical background for the theoretical approaches to obscenity prosecutions. Examples include *Ulysses*, *The Well of Loneliness*, Havelock Ellis's work, and *The Sexual Impulse* case.

————. **Suppressed Books: A History of the Conception of Literary Obscenity.** Cleveland, OH: World Publishing Company, 1963.

In this expansive discourse on literary obscenity, Craig makes a case for the great works that have been banned for their sexual themes. Works discussed include *Lady Chatterley's Lover* and *Ulysses*.

Curry, Richard O., ed. **Freedom at Risk: Secrecy, Censorship, and Repression in the 1980s.** Philadelphia: Temple University Press, 1988.

Each of these several articles describes an incident or phenomenon of concern to a free society that impacted or occurred during the presidency of Ronald Reagan. A brief biography of each contributor is also included.

Daily, Jay E. **The Anatomy of Censorship.** New York: Marcel Dekker, 1973.

Daily makes a strong argument against censorship, stating, "For with the molding of public thought we come to the essential characteristics of censorship and suppression: the maintenance of propaganda, the preservation of stereotypes, and the limitation of knowledge as a dangerous thing." Daily pulls no punches in attacking all forms of censorship and describes specific forms, both political and sexual.

Daniels, Walter M. **The Censorship of Books.** New York: H. W. Wilson Company, 1954.

This dated text provides insight into views on the topic of censorship held in the first half of this century. A reading of any article compiled in it indicates little has changed in the methods or themes surrounding censorship cases.

Davis, James E., ed. **Dealing with Censorship.** Urbana, IL: National Council of Teachers of English, 1979.

A collection of essays on censorship, this book has three main sections. The first contains reviews and surveys on the current climate of intellectual freedom, circa 1970s. The second includes articles that discuss the forces of censorship such as the textbook reviewers Mel and Norma Gabler. The third provides strategies for combatting censorship.

Day, Gary, and Clive Bloom, eds. **Perspectives on Pornography: Sexuality in Film and Literature.** New York: St. Martin's Press, 1988.

A collection of essays, the editors designed this work to bring together both male and female opinions on pornography and its impact on society. Essays included discuss violence against women, the distinction between pornography and erotica, psychoanalytic explanations of men's desire for pornography, and legal issues in defining obscenity.

DeGrazia, Edward. **Censorship Landmarks.** New York: R. R. Bowker & Company, 1969.

A total of 144 legal decisions, including historical cases as far back as 1663, that pertain to the censorship of books and other works are reproduced in this volume. Two contents-page sections provide a chronological and alphabetical guide to the cases. A thorough subject index makes this an important work for all libraries.

DeGrazia, Edward, and Roger K. Newman. **Banned Films: Movies, Censors and the First Amendment.** New York: R. R. Bowker & Company, 1982.

This is the most definitive study of film censorship and should be held by all library collections. The first half is an analysis of the history of film censorship, beginning with *Birth of a Nation.* The second half is a list of censored films, by decade, complete with credits of the film, a synopsis of the plot, and censorship activities.

Demac, Donna A. **Liberty Denied: The Current Rise of Censorship in America.** New York: PEN American Center, 1988.

Describes the most recent efforts in censorship from a topical approach. Libel, pornography, government surveillance, self-censorship, and government censorship of the media are all covered. Demac makes an impassioned plea to combat all forms of censorship in the concluding chapter. The book also provides very useful information on PEN American Center and International PEN. Arthur Miller's preface is very eloquent.

Donner, Frank. **Protectors of Privilege: Red Squads and Police Repression in Urban America.** Berkeley: University of California Press, 1990.

Author of *The Age of Surveillance,* Donner establishes a powerful indictment against police repression in the United States. Beginning with the Hay Market Riot of 1886, he chronicles major incidents of police abuse of labor demonstrators and individuals opposing industrial capitalism. He shows the increasing sophistication in police surveillance methods and concludes that the problems of police suppression keep repeating themselves.

Donnerstein, Edward, Daniel Linz, and Steve Penrod. **The Question of Pornography: Research Findings and Policy Implications.** New York: Free Press, 1987.

In this report on the findings of extensive research studies, the authors show that in works depicting aggression combined with sex, the component of violence is the cause of harm to women. The book also reviews the history of pornography regulation and discusses both individual and legal reactions to specific films and books. This is a somewhat technical, scholarly work that is useful for any study of this topic.

Downs, Donald Alexander. **The New Politics of Pornography.** Chicago: University of Chicago Press, 1989.

An excellent analysis of the feminist case against pornography, the work of Andrea Dworkin and Catherine MacKinnon forms the basis of this study. The ordinances of Minneapolis and Indianapolis based on Dworkin's work are described and analyzed. This work provides a reasoned view of a new movement toward control of pornography.

D'Souza, Dinesh. **Illiberal Education: The Politics of Race and Sex on Campus.** New York: Free Press, 1991.

This is the book that pronounced political correctness, or PC, as a scourge. D'Souza, former student editor of the conservative alternative student paper at Dartmouth University, denounces attempts by colleges and universities to enforce multiculturalism and the tendency by some liberal professors to be intolerant of conservative opinion.

Dworkin, Andrea. **Letters from a War Zone: Writings.** New York: Dutton, 1989.

This is the latest in Dworkin's anti-pornography efforts. It is a compilation of recent essays, speeches, literary criticisms, and her testimony before the Attorney General's Commission on Pornography. She is a significant, feminist voice that cannot be overlooked.

————. **Pornography: Men Possessing Women.** New York: G. P. Putnam's Sons, 1981.

Dworkin's work is one of the best feminist texts against pornography. She argues that pornography is the manifestation of men's domination over women.

Elliot, George P. **Conversions.** New York: Dutton, 1971.

This is an impassioned attack on pornography, and Elliot is one of the more significant anti-obscenity voices. He views pornography as destructive of family values, but even more so condemns literary works, such as those by Henry Miller, as more dangerous because their quality of prose makes obscenity more acceptable.

Ernst, Morris L. **Censorship.** New York: Macmillan Publishing Company, 1964.

Ernst comments on major censorship cases of history. A historical approach is followed by excerpts of each incident and Ernst's commentary on the value of its outcome. His analysis of the *Roth* standard focuses on the lack of definition of terms such as *patent offensiveness*.

Ernst, Morris L., and Alexander Lindey. **The Censor Marches On: Recent Milestones in the Administration of the Obscenity Law in the United States.** New York: Da Capo Press, 1971. Reprint of 1940 ed.

The thematic approach of this reprint edition describes the kinds of censorship attempts of the 1930s and 1940s including sex in literature, the theater and the nudist movement, birth control, and film censorship. Ernst and Lindey discuss the forces behind censorship challenges of this era, including the Legion of Decency and the Motion Picture Production Code Administration.

Ernst, Morris L., and W. Seagle. **To the Pure.** Milwood, NJ: Kraus, 1973. First published in 1928.

The preoccupation with sex by censors throughout U.S. history is described. Ernst notes the distinctions made in various arguments for censorship and provides a strong argument against them, especially the view that works must meet a test of literary criticism to be acceptable.

Evans, J. Edward. **Freedom of Speech.** Minneapolis, MN: Lerner Publications, 1990.

In this book for young readers, the historical background of the Bill of Rights is described in understandable terms. Several major issues of the conflict brought about by speech activity are then discussed. A final section offers guidelines for the reader in the exercise of speech rights.

Ferlinghetti, Lawrence. **Howl of the Censor.** Westport, CT: Greenwood Press, 1967. Reprint of 1961 ed.

Ferlinghetti's unabashed criticism of censorship and official repression is rendered in the transcripts of his trial for the publication of Allen Ginsberg's *Howl and Other Poems.*

Fiske, Marjorie. **Book Selection and Censorship: A Study of School and Public Libraries in California.** Berkeley: University of California Press, 1959.

The theory and practice of book selection is described in adept, philosophical terms. The impact of censorship charges and methods for response are given considerable attention. The unique problems of school librarianship are also addressed.

Foerstel, Herbert C. **Surveillance in the Stacks: The FBI's Library Awareness Program.** Westport, CT: Greenwood Press, 1990.

Chronicles the events and foibles of the FBI Awareness Program, which gathered surreptitious information on foreign nationals and librarians in the late 1980s. Foerstel's critical yet witty prose makes excellent reading. He demonstrates the dangers of our government's interference in the information and research process.

Forer, Lois G. **A Chilling Effect: The Mounting Threat of Libel and Invasion of Privacy Actions to the First Amendment.** New York: Norton, 1987.

Forer argues that the patchwork quilt of libel law and administration threatens free speech. She suggests a new definition of libel that rests on a "verifiably false charge that the subject committed a specific criminal or degrading act."

Fowler, Dorothy G. **Unmailable: Congress and the Post Office.** Athens: University of Georgia Press, 1977.

The definitive study of the history of censorship by the U.S. Postal Service. Every significant event and many others are described and analyzed. Fowler shows that the trend has moved from attacks being initiated by the government to being initiated by private citizens.

Frank, John P., and Robert F. Hogan. **Obscenity, the Law, and the English Teacher.** Champaign, IL: National Council of Teachers of English.

A treatise for the English teacher, this book describes the issues and trends affecting the conduct of English classroom instruction. The strategies suggested for dealing with the censor make this a very useful text.

Freedman, Warren. **Freedom of Speech on Private Property.** New York: Quorum Books, 1988.

Examines the dilemmas of the principle of free speech and its exercise on private property. This is a particularly important discussion because speech activity seeks a public forum. Public forums are often viewed in places that are actually private property such as the modern phenomena of shopping malls. This is a thorough coverage of this topic.

Fried, Richard M. **Nightmare in Red: The McCarthy Era in Retrospective.** New York: Oxford University Press, 1990.

One of the best histories of the McCarthy era, this work shows that McCarthyism was not the product of a paranoid senator but that the nation was gripped with an exaggerated fear of internal Communist threats. Fried describes many examples of both national and more localized repressions that occurred as a result of these fears.

Gardiner, Harold C., S.J. **The Catholic Viewpoint on Censorship,** revised ed. Garden City, NY: Doubleday & Company, 1961.

Gardiner presents the official church position on the use of censorship as well as commentary on censorship controversies in the United States. He discusses the role of the National Legion of Decency and the National Office for Decent Literature. The philosophy he espouses is a justification for censorship.

Gardner, Gerald C. **The Censorship Papers: Movie Censorship Letters from the Hays Office.** New York: Dodd, Mead and Company, 1987.

This is a compilation of commentary produced by the Production Code Administration, known as the Hays Office, on 60 well-known films. This is an incredible slice of history as well as fantastic remarks about some of the best pictures ever made, from *Casablanca* to *A Streetcar Named Desire.* This is worth reading as well as being kept for its value to the study of censorship.

Garrison, Dee. **Apostles of Culture: The Public Librarian and American Society, 1876–1920.** New York: Free Press, 1979.

In this excellent historical review for librarians, Garrison records the issues and materials behind censorship attempts in libraries from the founding of the American Library Association until 1920. Attention is paid to the methods used to deal with these confrontations.

Gellathy, Peter, ed. **Sex Magazines in the Library Collection: A Scholarly Study of Sex in Serials and Periodicals.** New York: Haworth Press, 1981.

A monographic supplement to the Haworth Press's *Serials Librarian,* this work compiles several essays and studies on the acquisition and maintenance of magazines with sexual content or a sexual theme. A variety of topics are included, such as the difficulties of ordering and housing such works, legal aspects, children's rights, censorship attempts, and a bibliography of gay and lesbian periodicals.

Geller, Evelyn. **Forbidden Books in American Public Libraries, 1876–1939.** Westport, CT: Greenwood Press, 1984.

This is a similar work to that by Dee Garrison but covers a longer time period until the advent of World War II. It provides a survey of censorship activity and the strategies used by librarians to confront these problems.

Gilmore, Donald H. **Sex, Censorship, and Pornography.** 2 vols. San Diego, CA: Greenleaf Classics, 1969.

A dated but useful historical survey of censorship and obscenity law, the text lacks any coverage of the *Miller* case and the subsequent conservative trend in obscenity prosecutions. Other more current books, such as Jonathon Green's *Encyclopedia of Censorship*, should be consulted first.

Glazer, Myron Perez, and Penina Migdal. **The Whistleblowers.** New York: Basic Books, 1989.

This is considered to be one of the best and most comprehensive books on "whistleblowing," the process of reporting errors or wrongdoing in the workplace. Many concerns are discussed including professionalism, religion, confidentiality, loyalty, and the role of public accountability. There are numerous interesting and instructive case studies as well.

Goodman, Michael B. **Contemporary Literary Censorship: The Case History of Burroughs' Naked Lunch.** Metuchen, NJ: Scarecrow Press, 1981.

Using extensive documentation, Goodman retells the censorship history of William Burroughs' *The Naked Lunch* from its serial publication in the *Chicago Review* through several court battles. This is a slice of history about the Beat generation as well as censorship. It is worthwhile reading.

Gorman, Carol. **Pornography.** New York: Franklin Watts, 1988.

In this book for young adult readers, Gorman transcribes a useful and credible survey of the issues and cases of pornography. She discusses the distinctions between erotic works and pornography, as well as the tests for obscenity. Reviews of anti-pornography campaigns, the Meese Commission, and social/ethical issues are also included.

Gostlin, Larry, ed. **Civil Liberties in Conflict.** London: Routledge, 1988.

A collection of articles, with editor's notes, on the conduct of civil liberties in modern times. Each article describes the difficulties that expression and the exercise of rights come to bear in society. Three main sections discuss individual liberty, free speech, and obscenity.

Graber, Mark A. **Transforming Free Speech: The Ambiguous Legacy of Civil Libertarianism.** Berkeley: University of California Press, 1991.

In this treatise formed from Zechariah Chafee's theory of social utility and springing from Michael Walzer's work *Spheres of Justice*, Graber promotes civil libertarianism in the protection of free speech. Civil libertarianism addresses issues in relation to private property. Thus, speech is protected when it is private property and not protected when the wealthier forces in society, in terms of property, use their wealth to their advantage to dominate the less fortunate.

Greenawalt, Kent. **Speech, Crime, and the Uses of Language.** New York: Oxford University Press, 1989.

A strong case is made for limiting speech linked to criminal behavior. Agreements to commit ordinary crimes (conspiracy) and extortion are two prime examples. The author argues that these limitations are neglected in most works on free speech.

Griffin, Susan. **Pornography and Silence: Culture's Revenge against Nature.** New York: Harper & Row, 1981.

A powerful argument is made against pornography, not to blatantly censor such works but to distinguish between political liberty that argues for its retention and human liberty that pornography acts against. Griffin sees eroticism in a different light than pornography and argues that pornography destroys human liberty.

Gubar, Susan, and Joan Hoff, eds. **For Adult Users Only: The Dilemma of Violent Pornography.** Bloomington: Indiana University Press, 1989.

This collection of essays on violence in pornography and the ill effects of such obscene works was inspired by recent events in the Bloomington, Indiana, area and written by, mostly, professors at the university. It has a feminist focus that sees such works as degrading to women. This is a thoughtful collection of ideas and concerns about pornography.

Haight, Anne Lyon. Updated and enlarged by Chandler B. Grannis. **Banned Books, 387 B.C. to 1978 A.D.,** 4th ed. New York: R. R. Bowker & Company, 1978.

A chronology of censorship, this is a compilation of books censored or banned throughout history. Entries are by author and listed chronologically by the first date of censorship, thereby giving a sense of the level and climate of censorship by era. Extensive appendixes include trends in censorship, statements on intellectual freedom, excerpts from major Supreme Court decisions, and excerpts from the 1970 President's Commission on Pornography and Obscenity.

Haney, Robert W. **Comstockery in America: Patterns of Censorship and Control.** New York: Da Capo Press, 1974. Reprint of 1960 ed.

An analysis of Comstock's activities demonstrates effectively the mentality of the censor. Haney challenges his readers to think about social norms in more philosophical terms and to promote a questioning mind. The book includes an extensive bibliography of materials from the 1940s and 1950s.

Hart, Harold H., ed. **Censorship: For and Against.** New York: Hart, 1971.

This collection of essays is a substantial representation of the full range of opinion on censorship. Liberal and anti-censorship remarks are by such individuals as Nat Hentoff, Eugene McCarthy, and Judith Crist. The more conservative viewpoint is provided by Charles Keating and others.

Hawkins, Gordon, and Franklin G. Zimring. **Pornography in a Free Society.** New York: Cambridge University Press, 1988.

A comparison of the makeup, methodologies, and conclusions of the three major English-language pornography commissions: the 1970 President's Commission, the 1986 Meese Commission, and the 1977 British Committee on Obscenity and Film Censorship. This is an excellent piece of scholarship and quite readable. The authors conclude that furor over pornography dies out quickly after such reports and that these actions are an adjustment to the growth in adult media.

Hendrick, Evan, Trudy Hayden, and Jack D. Novik. **Your Rights to Privacy: A Basic Guide to Legal Rights in an Information Society.** Carbondale: Southern Illinois University Press, 1990.

This is another in the American Civil Liberties Union's individual rights handbooks. Topics covered include access to government information and a person's own file under the Freedom of Information Act and the Privacy Act. Tips on correcting erroneous data in one's own file are included.

Hentoff, Nat. **American Heroes: In and Out of School.** New York: Delacorte Press, 1987.

The United States's most prolific intellectual freedom author renders another excellent book, designed for young adult readers, that promotes the ideals of the First Amendment. Hentoff recalls the exploits of ten students who stood up for the Bill of Rights despite great personal suffering. This is an important, uplifting book for all student readers.

————. **The Day They Came To Arrest the Book.** New York: Delacorte Press, 1982.

A novel for young readers, this is one of the best methods for teaching children about intellectual freedom. Hentoff brings his devotion to the First Amendment and his lucid, eloquent writing style to bear on a book censorship story involving Mark Twain's *The Adventures of Huckleberry Finn.* He portrays the school librarian as the hero of the story.

————. **The First Freedom: The Tumultuous History of Free Speech in America.** New York: Delacorte Press, 1980.

Hentoff brings his unabashed advocacy for intellectual freedom and his excellent prose to bear on the treatment of civil liberties by the United States throughout its history. Each chapter is a lively account of a success story or act of repression that illustrates the courage of those who stand up for freedom of expression. This is a must read book for everyone.

Holbrook, David, ed. **The Case against Pornography.** LaSalle, IL: Open Court, 1973.

Holbrook is a significant voice among anti-pornography scholars and writers. In this collection of articles, an attempt is made to show that obscenity may be occasionally acceptable within the content of a serious work of art. Holbrook argues that such situations, however, are rare.

Hoyt, Olga G., and Edwin P. Hoyt. **Censorship in America.** New York: Seabury, 1970.

Each decade tends to produce a major text on the trends in censorship. This is one of the best books analyzing the events of the 1960s in the areas of radio, TV, film, theater, and fine arts challenges.

Hughes, Douglas A., ed. **Perspectives on Pornography.** New York: St. Martin's Press, 1970.

This collection of essays on pornography provides a sampling of theoretical views, both for and against, regarding the value, impact, and role in society of pornography. In one piece, Anthony Burgess describes pornography as "representing social acts of sex, frequently of a perverse or wholly fantastic nature, often without consulting the limits of physical possibility."

Human (and Anti-Human) Values in Children's Books: A Content Rating Instrument for Educators and Concerned Parents. New York: Council for Interracial Books for Children, 1976.

This is the Council for Interracial Books for Children's primary work promoting selection of nonracist, nonsexist, and non-ageist materials. This work reviews over 235 titles and rates them for their content on these issues. The council does not promote outright censorship but stresses selection. Other writers and scholars have condemned this work for the labeling it contains.

Hutchison, E. R. **"Tropic of Cancer" on Trial: A Case History of Censorship.** New York: Grove Press, 1968.

One of the most important studies on the challenges to Henry Miller's *Tropic of Cancer,* this is a thorough examination of the work's literary criticism and the forces behind the censorship attempts.

Jansen, Sue Curry. **Censorship: The Knot That Binds Power and Knowledge.** New York: Oxford University Press, 1988.

Describes the use of censorship as a tool of political power. The socialist use and capitalist use of censorship are described and compared. Jansen sees the struggle against censorship as ever-continuing and one that destroys personal lives in its wake, and she asserts that constant vigilance is required to overcome these adversities.

Jenkinson, Edward B. **Censors in the Classroom: The Mind Benders.** Carbondale: Southern Illinois University Press, 1979; New York: Avon, 1982.

Reports the results of a statistical survey on censorship practices in the schools. Using a case study method, the motivations and implications of censorship are described and discussed. This is an extremely useful text for libraries and other institutions to develop strategies for dealing with censorship.

————. **The Schoolbook Protest Movement.** Bloomington, IN: Phi Delta Educational Foundation, 1986.

This in-depth study of school textbook censorship and selection examines the groups prominent in challenges to school materials, especially the Gablers' Educational Research Analysts. Methods of complaints as well as the objections made are described and discussed.

Jones, Frances M. **Defusing Censorship: The Librarian's Guide To Handling Censorship Conflicts.** Phoenix, AZ: Oryx Press, 1983.

In what probably is the best of the "advice on censorship challenges" books, Jones argues that informed planning and preparedness are far superior to kneejerk, defensive positions after a challenge is made. She also provides a step-by-step set of guidelines for librarians and school personnel.

Kalvern, Harry, Jr. **A Worthy Tradition: Freedom of Speech in America.** Jamie Kalvern, ed. New York: Harper & Row, 1988.

Taking a dual approach to the regulation of speech, content, and association, this work provides a thorough understanding of the limitations on speech. Using prime cases in constitutional history, Kalvern analyzes the basic speech issues of modern times from his scholarly background. Kalvern died before completing this book. His son, the editor, has provided a legacy on the First Amendment.

Karolides, Nicholas J., and Lee Burress. **Celebrating Censored Books.** Racine, WI: Wisconsin Council of Teachers of English, 1985.

An unabashed testimony for banned books, this collection of essays discusses classic and highly acclaimed literary works, literary criticism, and the value of literature and its themes. Of particular note, an article on self-censorship argues that fiction must be judged on its literary integrity, not its "moral rightness." This is an excellent book for English majors and teachers.

Kendrick, Walter. **The Secret Museum: Pornography in Modern Culture.** New York: Viking, 1987.

A strong argument against censorship of pornography, especially by feminist groups, is made by showing that past attempts to define and control obscenity have failed. Kendrick, a writer for the *Village Voice,* believes that further attempts to define obscenity are futile and should cease. Rather, he sees society's problems in this regard as a question of human sexuality.

Kerr, Walter. **Criticism and Censorship.** Milwaukee, WI: Bruce Publishing Company, 1956.

In an eloquent essay on art and censorship, Kerr divides the arguments on obscenity between those who defend artistic creation and those who are offended by content, regardless of the quality of the art. He decries the latter, but cautions the former that what is needed is exercise of expression in conjunction with a devotion to critically acclaimed work.

Kilpatrick, James J. **The Smut Peddlers.** Westport, CT: Greenwood Press, 1973. Reprint of 1960 ed.

One of the United States's premier conservative political commentators argues for the correctness of censorship. Kilpatrick insists that obscenity legislation is constitutional and that opponents misuse the First Amendment in defense of objectionable materials. He believes the term *obscenity* is not vague and that links between pornography and antisocial behavior do not have to be empirically proven.

Kimball, Roger. **Tenured Radicals: How Politics Has Corrupted Our Higher Education.** New York: Harper & Row, 1990.

Kimball charges that the liberal radicals of the 1960s have subverted scholarship and objectivity by mixing sociological and anthropological preaching, particularly into literature courses. This is another major text arguing that "political correctness" is rampant in academe.

Kirk, Jerry. **The Mind Polluters.** Nashville, TN: Thomas Nelson, 1985.

Kirk, the founder of the National Coalition Against Pornography, chronicles his career fighting pornography, first in his hometown of

Cincinnati and then with the coalition. He sets out to make the case against pornography as having direct harm to people and contributing to the breakdown of families and society.

Kronhausen, Eberhard, and Phyllis Kronhausen. **Pornography and the Law: The Psychology of Erotic Realism and Pornography,** 2d ed. New York: Ballantine Books, 1964.

The authors, well-known authorities on sexual mores, analyze the treatment of eroticism in literature and the psychological forces conveyed in pornography. Their intent is to bring better understanding of this genre of literature to enlighten society and reduce censorship. They analyze and criticize several famous obscenity prosecutions including those of Henry Miller's work, *Lady Chatterley's Lover,* and the use of "dirty" words in "clean" books.

Kuh, Richard H. **Foolish Figleaves? Pornography Figleaves? Pornography In and Out of Court.** New York: Macmillan Publishing Company, 1967.

In this work written during the liberal Warren Court era after *Roth* but before *Miller,* Kuh is appalled by the growth in pornography and attacks the liberal viewpoints on intellectual freedom. This is one of several standard texts with a strong argument against obscenity and should be examined along with books by Berns, Clor, Cotham, Elliott, and Kilpatrick.

Lawhorne, Clifton O. **The Supreme Court and Libel.** Carbondale: Southern Illinois University Press, 1981.

This succinct coverage packs a reasoned analysis of the law on libel in the United States. The *New York Times* rule and definition of public figures and public officials are illustrated by relevant cases.

Lawrence, D. H. **Sex, Literature and Censorship: Essays.** Harry T. Moore, ed. New York: Twayne, 1953.

Harry Moore assembled this collection of eight essays by the author of *Lady Chatterley's Lover* as a statement against censorship. He provides a look at the suppression Lawrence experienced during his lifetime in a well-written introduction. One essay, "Pornography and Obscenity," has Lawrence accusing his censors of "hole-and-corner" and "smoking-room" obscenity.

Lederor, Laura, ed. **Take Back the Night: Women on Pornography.** New York: William Morrow Company, 1980.

This is undoubtedly the first major feminist text against pornography. It includes Andrea Dworkin's first well-known essay attacking pornography as a subjugation of women. This volume belongs in any study on feminism.

Legman, G. **Love and Death: A Study in Censorship.** New York: Hacker, 1963. First published in 1949.

Legman provides a criticism of three types of literature: mysteries, comic books, and literature by and about women. His comments border on the irreverent but he makes a case against censorship.

Lewis, Felice Flanery. **Literature, Obscenity, & Law.** Carbondale: Southern Illinois University Press, 1976.

Literary criticism is used to tie together an understanding of obscenity and content objections. A comparative investigation of fictional works that have been challenged, trends in sexual content and explicit language, and court rulings provide an in-depth view of the debate between literature and censorship.

Lewis, Lionel S. **Cold War on Campus: A Study of the Politics of Organizational Control.** New Brunswick, NJ: Transaction Publications, 1988.

In this documentary study of cold war politics and the tragic outcomes of repression on college campuses, Lewis follows the cases of 126 individuals at 58 colleges and universities who were investigated and sometimes dismissed for liberal views, support of liberal candidates, or open criticism at public meetings. The lack of interviews of the participants makes this somewhat flawed, but it is a thoroughly researched study on academic freedom.

Lynn, Barry W. **Rushing to Censorship: An Interim Report on the Methods of Evidence Gathering and Evaluation by the Attorney General's Commission on Pornography.** Washington, DC: American Civil Liberties Union, 1986.

This is a major criticism of the Meese Commission's methods and conclusions. Lynn presents evidence that the testimonies and other data were skewed to violent pornography. He also criticizes the commission for giving credibility to anonymous testimony.

McCormick, John, and Mairi MacInnes, eds. **Versions of Censorship: An Anthology.** Garden City, NY: Doubleday/Anchor, 1962.

Describes several different strategies used by censors to challenge materials considered objectionable. The essays compiled here are not intended to assist or flatter the would-be censor but to help those individuals who are subject to a challenge to recognize the patterns of suppression.

The Meese Commission Exposed: Proceedings of a National Coalition against Censorship Public Information Briefing on the Attorney General's Commission on Pornography, January 16, 1986. New York: National Coalition against Censorship, 1986.

This is a definitive text criticizing the Attorney General's Commission on Pornography, its methods of data gathering, and the conclusions of its report. Scholars, celebrities, and intellectual freedom advocates are all represented in this substantial body of opinion. The data-gathering techniques sustain the greatest attacks for lack of scientific method and for reliance on biased, loaded testimony.

Merritt, Leroy C. **Book Selection and Intellectual Freedom.** New York: H. W. Wilson Company, 1970.

A longtime advocate for intellectual freedom describes the most important principles of book selection in relation to intellectual freedom. A prescription for writing selection policies, including sample policies, is a central part of the book. A seminal text for all libraries.

Mitgang, Herbert. **Dangerous Dossiers: Exposing the Secret War against America's Greatest Authors.** New York: Donald I. Fine, 1988.

Using the Freedom of Information Act, Mitgang secured the release of secret FBI and CIA files kept on many of the United States's greatest writers, including Pearl S. Buck, Thomas Mann, and E. B. White. This is shocking yet fascinating reading. It demonstrates the depth of censorship by our federal government.

Moon, Eric, ed. **Book Selection and Censorship in the Sixties.** New York: R. R. Bowker & Company, 1969.

Moon, a former president of the American Library Association, compiled 55 articles from *Library Journal* on the subject of book selection and censorship. This work records the climate of censorship during the 1960s.

Moore, Everett T. **Issues of Freedom in American Libraries.** Chicago: American Library Association, 1964.

A reprinting and compilation of intellectual freedom articles from the *ALA Bulletin*, primarily from the years 1960–1963. Specific incidents discussed include *Tropic of Cancer, Huckleberry Finn, Of Mice and Men,* and D. H. Lawrence's *Sex, Literature and Censorship.*

Moretti, Daniel S. **Obscenity and Pornography: The Law under the First Amendment.** London: Oceana, 1984.

The struggle to define obscenity is the focus of this work. Moretti describes the logic behind the definitions of each of the landmark cases on obscenity and with respect to all types of media including broadcasting and the telephone. There are several useful appendixes, such as state child pornography statutes, states that have adopted the *Miller* standard, and a model cable television pornography statute.

Murphy, Paul L. **The Meaning of Freedom of Speech: First Amendment Freedoms from Wilson to FDR.** Westport, CT: Greenwood Press, 1972.

A leading scholar records and analyzes the pressures that formed the climate for free speech activities from World War I through World War II. The history of the American Civil Liberties Union plays an integral part in this review. This is one of the more highly acclaimed historical texts.

Navasky, Victor S. **Naming Names.** New York: Penguin Books, 1980.

A poignant account of the blacklisting era, this work chronicles the history of political repression in the federal government, especially the congressional House Un-American Activities Committee. Navasky's work is an indictment of McCarthyism.

New York Public Library. **500 Years of Conflict.** New York: Oxford University Press, 1984.

This is a printed reproduction of an exhibit created by the New York Public Library in 1984. The foreword is by Vartan Gregorian. This work includes a description of the exhibit and plates of many items that constituted the displays on censorship.

Nobile, Philip, and Eric Nadler. **United States of America vs. Sex: How the Meese Commission Lied about Pornography.** New York: Minotaur Press, 1986.

A publication of *Penthouse* magazine publisher Bob Guccione, this is a critical, often satirical, attack on the Meese Commission report. It makes humorous reading and should be considered as one of the liberal voices against the commission.

Noble, William. **Bookbanning in America.** Middlebury, VT: Paul S. Eriksson, 1990.

Everything you always wanted to know about book censorship, and more, this work is an excellent review of major and lesser known incidents of censorship. Two excellent appendixes, on challenged authors and challenged books, are included.

Nordquist, Joang, comp. **Contemporary Social Issues: A Bibliographic Series. No. 7: Pornography and Censorship.** Santa Cruz, CA: Reference and Research Services, 1987.

In this pamphlet of bibliographic citations on pornography and censorship, the coverage on pornography is very good. There is a thorough list of other bibliographies, making this a useful work.

Norwich, Kenneth P. **Lobbying for Freedom: A Citizen's Guide to Fighting Censorship at the State Level.** New York: St. Martin's Press, 1975.

This is a powerful legislative handbook for the forces of intellectual freedom. A legal background on censorship is followed by a description of the legislative process and methods of lobbying state legislatures.

————. **Pornography: The Issues and the Law.** New York: Public Affairs Committee, 1972.

This pamphlet highlights the issues of the pornography debate, including the major Supreme Court tests and the report of the 1970 President's Commission on Obscenity and Pornography. Pro and con debate positions are also provided.

Oboler, Eli M. **The Fear of the Word: Censorship and Sex.** Metuchen, NJ: Scarecrow Press, 1974.

The forces of and motives for censorship are discussed and analyzed. Oboler provides a deft description of the censor mentality. An appendix includes a thorough collection of quotations on the topic as well.

O'Neil, Robert M. **Classrooms in the Crossfire: The Rights and Interests of Students, Parents, Teachers, Administrators, Librarians and the Community.** Bloomington: Indiana University Press, 1981.

A focus on legal issues and cases of school textbook and library book censorship indicates a growing concern for the struggle of control of the schools. O'Neil sees this conflict as one between legitimate citizen concern about education and violations of academic freedom. This work provides good coverage and discussion of most of the more recent relevant cases.

Osanka, Franklin Mark, and Sara Lee Johann. **Sourcebook on Pornography.** Lexington, MA: D. C. Heath, 1989.

This is a compilation of facts and sources on pornography, censorship, and the impact of pornography on society. It provides a wealth of statistics on use of pornography and its production. There are descriptions of pornography victims and perpetrators, and several scientific studies are discussed. The authors testified before the Meese Commission against pornography, and some of that testimony is reproduced here.

Pally, Marcia. **Sense and Censorship: The Vanity of Bonfires: Resource Materials on Sexually Explicit Material, Violent Material and**

Censorship: Research and Public Policy Implications. New York: Americans for Constitutional Freedom and the Freedom to Read Foundation, 1991.

This useful pocket pamphlet is loaded with a digest of reports, statistical studies, and recent events impacting on censorship activities. Rather than reproducing such works, Pally provides snippets of the resources and quotes and analysis from scholars, professionals, and other noted individuals. The Meese Commission report is criticized and materials on violence and pornography, rape, FBI data, the media and minors, and the charge of a direct link between pornography and crime are condensed and analyzed.

Paul, James C. N., and Murray L. Schwartz. **Federal Censorship: Obscenity in the Mail.** New York: Free Press of Glencoe, 1971.

A history of censorship by and through the U.S. Postal Service, this work presents the issues and trends of obscenity prosecutions under the Postal Act of 1865 and other relevant statutes. This is a useful text, though the book by Dorothy Fowler is somewhat better and more current.

Peckham, Morris. **Art and Pornography.** New York: Harper & Row, 1969.

A discussion of artistic quality and the charges against pornography from a critical viewpoint provides the framework for a case for pornographic novels. The author describes the influence of well-known pornographic literature on culture.

Pell, Eve. **The Big Chill: How the Reagan Administration, Corporate America, and Religious Conservatives Are Subverting Free Speech and the Public's Right To Know.** Boston: Beacon Press, 1984.

In this overview of censorship issues in the 1980s, Pell examines both government activities that have threatened the free flow of information and private efforts to suppress expression. The discussion on libel suits by corporations and censorship campaigns by religious conservatives is enlightening. Though flawed in some of its research, it is one of the better reviews of current issues on censorship.

People for the American Way. **Attacks on the Freedom To Learn, 1985–86.** Washington, DC: People for the American Way, 1987.

This is the fourth annual study of the climate for censorship that has been compiled by the People for the American Way. A very useful statistical guide, it shows that book and school curriculum challenges increased by 35 percent in the mid-1980s over the previous report and that obscenity was not the prime reason for complaints but rather objectionable ideas such as humanism.

Phelan, John, ed. **Communications Control: Readings in the Motives and Structures of Censorship.** New York: Sheed and Ward, 1969.

Ten essays on censorship from notable authors and writers provide a strong philosophical and balanced look at censorship. Authors included are C. S. Lewis, Zechariah Chafee, and Abraham Kaplan, and there is also an essay about Harold Innis and Marshall McLuhan.

Polenberg, Richard. **Fighting Faiths: The Abrams Case, the Supreme Court, and Free Speech.** New York: Viking Penguin, 1987.

A thorough and outstanding account of the *Abrams* dissenting speech case of 1918. Jacob Abrams was one of five Russian Jewish anarchists convicted of sedition for distributing antiwar leaflets. Their case was the occasion for Justice Oliver Wendell Holmes great "clear and present danger" doctrine. Highly recommended for all public and university libraries.

Powe, L. A., Jr. **American Broadcasting and the First Amendment.** Berkeley: University of California Press, 1988.

The future of broadcasting is predicted for both network and cable industries and is seen as an area of further regulation. Excesses of the past, particularly President Richard Nixon's "assault" on the networks and current censorship movements, are described and discussed.

Preston, William. **Aliens and Dissenters.** Cambridge, MA: Harvard University Press, 1963.

A historical coverage of radicalism and dissent from the growth of the Wobblies in 1905 through the Palmer raids of 1920. Preston describes the circumstances behind the convictions of such antiwar dissenters as Schenck, Frohwerk, and Debs, landmark dissenting speech cases.

Randall, Richard S. **Censorship of the Movies: The Social and Political Control of a Mass Medium.** Madison: University of Wisconsin Press, 1968.

In this analysis of the censorship of a major medium, film, Randall discusses the conflict between freedom of expression and a democratic society. The conduct of censorship of this medium and the legal aspects are described. There is a very practical discussion on the uniqueness of film as a medium. DeGrazia's *Banned Films* and Schumach's *The Face on the Cutting Room's Floor* are better general texts, but this work's focus on censorship definitions is useful.

————. **Freedom and Taboo: Pornography and the Politics of a Self Divided.** Berkeley: University of California Press, 1989.

A psychosexual theory of pornography forms the basis for an analysis of the pervasiveness of the obscenity debate in society. Randall rejects both a libertarian view of a marketplace as the only censor and the censor's view of suppression of content based on moral values.

Reichman, Henry. **Censorship and Selection: Issues and Answers for Schools.** Chicago: American Library Association/American Association of School Administrators, 1988.

This is an excellent guide for librarians and media specialists. The author, a former assistant director of the ALA Office for Intellectual Freedom, discusses what constitutes censorship, how to develop selection policies, and methods for dealing with complaints.

Rembar, Charles. **The End of Obscenity: The Trials of Lady Chatterley, Tropic of Cancer and Fanny Hill.** New York: Random House, 1968.

A leading scholar of intellectual freedom, Rembar discusses the history of the three most prominent censored literary works in the United States. The trials and Supreme Court decisions are described and analyzed. The anecdotes retold make this an interesting read.

Rickards, Maurice. **Banned Posters.** London: Evelyn Adams & MacKay, 1969.

A world-renowned author on poster art, Rickards presents a history of poster art censorship since 1895. All of the posters discussed are reproduced with before and after versions. This is an important text for all art history collections.

Rubin, David. **The Rights of Teachers: American Civil Liberties Union Handbook.** New York: Avon, 1972.

Another text in the American Civil Liberties Union's handbook series, *The Rights of Teachers* answers the most commonly asked questions about academic freedom. This and the other works in this series provide a useful service to average citizens in informing them of their rights.

Rushdovny, Rousas J. **The Politics of Pornography.** New Rochelle, NY: Arlington House, 1974.

No apologist for intellectual freedom, Rushdovny makes a clear stand against pornography. He takes a very moral position and argues that the growth of pornography is an attack on God and the fabric of society. This work is in the same vein as Jerry Kirk's.

Schauer, Frederick. **Free Speech: A Philosophical Enquiry.** New York: Cambridge University Press, 1982.

A legal scholar, and a member (after the publication of this text) of the Meese Commission, Schauer attempts to provide a conceptual clarification of free speech issues and succeeds in creating a useful and readable text on freedom of speech.

————. **The Law of Obscenity.** Washington, DC: Bureau of National Affairs, 1976.

A distinguished professor of law describes the historical and political underpinnings of obscenity law and case law. The major standards are described and the means for conducting a legal defense, including jury selection and expert witnesses, is discussed.

Schultz, Bud, and Ruth Schultz. **It Did Happen Here: Recollections of Political Repression in America.** Berkeley: University of California Press, 1989.

Includes a large variety of personal accounts of political and expressive repression. Pete Seeger describes the harrassment and blacklisting of the Weavers, for example. Free speech, freedom of religion, and individual liberties form the basis for most of the incidents.

Schumach, Murray. **The Face on the Cutting Room Floor: The Story of Movie and Television Censorship.** New York: Morrow, 1964.

Though dated, the thoroughness of research and coverage through film and television's major developmental periods makes this one of the best texts on censorship of these visual media. The development of film prior to the creation of the Motion Picture Code begins the discussion. Other areas covered include the blacklisting of the 1950s, television censorship, and the way Hollywood has portrayed sex and violence.

Sharp, Donald B., ed. **Commentaries on Obscenity.** Metuchen, NJ: Scarecrow Press, 1970.

A compilation of opinion on obscenity, this is an interesting historical work. Published before the *Miller* decision, this is an excellent example of the views of scholars and legal experts on obscenity and pornography under the *Roth* standard.

Smolla, Rodney A. **Jerry Falwell v. Larry Flynt: The First Amendment on Trial.** New York: St. Martin's Press, 1988.

This is a detailed account about one of the strangest events in modern free speech history. Smolla provides a humorous yet thoughtful rendition of the sequence of events surrounding the lawsuit by Jerry Falwell against *Hustler* publisher Larry Flynt for an obscene parody attacking Falwell and his mother. The case became one of the more celebrated satire–free speech cases of the twentieth century.

Sobel, Lester A., ed. **Pornography, Obscenity, and the Law.** New York: Facts on File, 1978.

Sobel has compiled a variety of material that demonstrates the concerns and problems of pornography. A beginning essay on the "age of porn" indicates that pornography is seen as a societal scourge. His review of the legal background provides some discussion on censorship of literary works as well as pornography. A discussion of organized crime's role in the production and distribution of pornography is included. There is also a reproduction of news clips on major censorship and pornography incidents of the 1960s and 1970s.

Spitzor, Matthew L. **Seven Dirty Words and Six Other Stories: Controlling the Content of Print and Broadcast.** New Haven, CT: Yale University Press, 1986.

A study of the content and movements to control such content in broadcast media compared to print media. The economic rationales for treating these two media differently form the basis of the first three "stories," and rationales about effects on viewers form the basis of the other four, including the *Pacifica* "dirty words" case. Spitzer concludes that his evidence shows no reason to treat print and broadcast media differently.

Sunderland, Land V. **Obscenity: The Court, the Congress and the President's Commission.** Washington, DC: American Enterprise Institute, 1975.

In this work prompted by the report of the 1970 President's Commission on Obscenity and Pornography, Sunderland argues that despite these findings, obscenity will be defined by the courts. The quality of the judges' work will determine the limitations that will address society's dual concern for morality and freedom of expression.

The Supreme Court Obscenity Decisions. San Diego, CA: Greenleaf Classics, 1973.

This pocket book reproduces the full text of the 1973 obscenity decisions *Miller v. California, Paris Adult Theatre v. Slaton, Kaplan v. California, U.S. v. Orito,* and *U.S. v. 12,200-ft. Reels of Super 8mm Films.* The dissenting opinions and the petitions for rehearings are also included in full. The overview is written by William Hamling, the pornography publisher who is the object of several major obscenity cases.

Swan, John, and Noel Peattie. **The Freedom To Lie: A Debate about Democracy.** Jefferson, NC: McFarland & Company, 1989.

A most incredible and lively debate on the free speech rights of an individual who espouses an abhorrent view. Originally a presentation at the American Library Association's annual conference in 1988, it was sparked by a series of incidents involving David McCalden, a purveyor of anti-Semitic tracts and books who had, among other activities, offered a $50,000 prize to anyone who could actually prove any Jews were gassed at Auschwitz. The censorship of his speaking engagements and book displays at library conferences sparked this informative and poignant debate.

Taylor, C. L. **Censorship.** Robert B. Morris, consulting ed. New York: Franklin Watts, 1986.

A book for young readers, this is an excellent and sensitive coverage of this topic for this age group. An incident of a Maryland pastor burning books and records begins the discussion. A historical overview leads the reader up to the *Miller* test. Movie and record censorship are also discussed.

Tedford, Thomas L. **Freedom of Speech in the United States.** New York: Random House, 1985.

In one of the more recent texts on the freedom of speech, Tedford surveys the historical background of the First Amendment, Supreme Court decisions, and incidents of free speech conflict. This book was designed as a textbook for colleges and universities.

Tedford, Thomas L., John J. Makay, and David L. Johnson, eds. **Perspectives on Freedom of Speech: Selected Essays from the Journals of the Speech Communication Association.** Carbondale: Southern Illinois University Press, 1987.

Commentary from the journals of the Speech Communications Association provides a scholarly review of censorship and free expression situations of the recent past. Each article describes and discusses an incident of concern to free speech such as the censorship of a photo exhibit on the birth of a baby.

Theiner, George, ed. **They Shoot Writers, Don't They?** Winchester, MA: Faber & Faber, 1984.

In this excellent collection of essays and articles from the international publication *Index on Censorship,* each entry is designed to represent a cultural response to repression. This is a very useful text, not only for learning concepts of intellectual freedom but also for gaining a sense of the problem throughout the world.

Thomas, A. H. **Censorship in Public Libraries.** Epping, Essex: R. R. Bowker & Company, 1975.

A decade by decade account of major censorship incidents in public libraries of England in the twentieth century. Two chapters discuss the P. G. Wodehouse and Enid Blyton affairs in depth.

Thomas, Cal. **Book Burning.** Wheaton, IL: Good News Publications, 1983.

Thomas, a conservative political commentator and former vice-president of the Moral Majority, accuses the liberal establishment of censoring conservative publications. He attacks publishers for failure to accept more conservative works for publication and bookstores and libraries for not stocking conservative titles that have been produced.

U.S. Commission on Obscenity and Pornography. **The Report of the Commission on Obscenity and Pornography, September 1970.** Washington, DC: U.S. Government Printing Office, 1970.

This work is the findings and conclusion of the first national commission to study pornography and obscenity. The committee found no empirical link between the use of pornography and antisocial behavior. It also recommended that pornography be decriminalized.

————. **Technical Report of the Commission on Obscenity and Pornography: Volume I: Preliminary Studies.** Washington, DC: U.S. Government Printing Office, 1970.

This supplement to the President's Commission on Obscenity and Pornography's report records the findings of the empirical research conducted for the commission, provides a literature review, and describes theoretical analyses of the topic. This is an important work to consider with the report itself.

U.S. Department of Justice, Attorney General's Commission on Pornography. **Final Report, July 1986.** 2 vols. Washington, DC: U.S. Government Printing Office, 1986.

Otherwise known as the Meese Commission report, this two-volume set consists of the findings of the second national committee to study obscenity in the past 20 years. The commission reports a causal relationship between violent pornography and antisocial behavior. In addition to a review of pornography and obscenity legislation and cases along with the sociological implications, the testimony of expert witnesses and interested individuals is reproduced.

Vitz, Paul C. **Censorship: Evidence of Bias in Our Children's Textbooks.** Ann Arbor, MI: Servant, 1986.

In this indictment of the content of textbooks used in public schools, Vitz demonstrates that the role of religion is neglected and that patriotism, business, labor, and altruism are poorly covered. He argues that the portrayal of the family is distorted and that prominent political figure profiles are usually liberal. He concludes that the best answer to this problem is tax-supported religious schools.

Widmer, Eleanor, ed. **Freedom and Culture: Literary Censorship in the '70s.** Belmont, CA: Wadsworth, 1970.

An examination of censorship during the 1970s, this compilation is designed for literature courses as a means of showing the conflict between artistic expression, literary criticism, and social norms. The novel as an object of censorship is a major aspect of the work, as well as the cultural context of U.S. censorship. This is a revision of Widmer's 1961 text *Literary Censorship: Principles, Cases, Problems.*

Woods, L. B. **A Decade of Censorship in America: The Threat to Classrooms and Libraries, 1966–1975.** Metuchen, NJ: Scarecrow Press, 1979.

Originally a doctoral dissertation, this work conveys the results of a statistical study of reported censorship incidents as published in the *Newsletter on Intellectual Freedom,* an American Library Association journal. The author found that the most censored book was J. D. Salinger's *Catcher in the Rye,* among many other quantitative data.

Woodworth, Mary L. **Intellectual Freedom, the Young Adult, and Schools: A Wisconsin Study,** revised. ed. Madison: University of Wisconsin Extension, 1976.

Reports the results of a survey of Wisconsin institutions and the censorship challenges they have experienced. Woodworth links the results together with a discussion of the forces that operate in a censorship incident and provides some interesting conclusions on how to meet such challenges.

————, ed. **The Young Adult & Intellectual Freedom: Proceedings.** Madison: University of Wisconsin School of Library Services, 1977.

Transactions of a conference held at the University of Wisconsin–Madison in 1976, this is a compilation of 19 papers delivered at the conference. Subjects include legal aspects, realistic adult novels, transitional novels, the clash between creationists and evolutionists, the treatment of ethnic groups in publications, censorship trends, and strategies for facing challenges.

Yuill, Phyllis J. **Little Black Sambo: A Closer Look.** New York: Racism and Sexism Resource Center for Educators, Council on Interracial Books for Children, 1976.

A thorough study of Helen Bannerman's *Little Black Sambo* and its history of challenges. This work also includes a discussion of Bannerman's other works and the recommendations for the book in various bibliographies.

Zurcher, Louis A., Jr., and R. George Kirkpatrick. **Citizens for Decency: Antipornography Crusades as Status Defense.** Austin: University of Texas Press, 1976.

In this in-depth study of the structure and methods of one of the country's leading anti-pornography groups, two regional anti-obscenity crusades of Citizens for Decency, one in the Midwest and one in the Southwest, are described and analyzed. Special attention is paid to the motivation of the participants, their satisfaction with the crusade, and the aftermath.

Freedom of Press

Bagdikian, Ben H. **The Effete Conspiracy and Other Crimes of the Press.** New York: Harper & Row, 1972.

Bagdikian indicts the press for being too conservative in their approach to content and vested in too many financial power concerns to report the news effectively. His book is a strong example of liberal opinion on the press.

Barron, Jerome A. **Freedom of the Press for Whom? The Right of Access to Mass Media.** Bloomington: Indiana University Press, 1973.

This book documents the self-censorship the press and broadcast industries conduct in reporting the news. It is a good study on the types of censorship within the industry.

Bosmajian, Haig, ed. **The Freedom To Publish.** New York: Neal Schuman, 1989.

This is the fifth in a series on the First Amendment for secondary school audiences. Every relevant federal case on the student right to publish a school paper, from district courts to the Supreme Court, is reproduced with majority and minority opinions. An introductory paragraph provides background to each case. Bosmajian also makes a telling argument that the Supreme Court abandoned the reasonable position under the *Tinker* decision with the ruling in the *Hazelwood* case, as part of his introductory chapter.

Campbell, Douglas S. **The Supreme Court and the Mass Media: Selected Cases, Summaries and Analyses.** New York: Praeger, 1990.

This work is arranged in three sections: cases related to libel, cases related to privacy, and cases related to First Amendment issues. This is a thorough and up-to-date compilation of press law. Each case has a background description and set of circumstances, a summary of the Court's analysis and findings, and a comment on its significance.

Charren, Peggy, and Martin W. Sandler. **Changing Channels: Living (Sensibly) with Television.** Reading, MA: Addison-Wesley Publishing Company, 1983.

A critical view of television programs, *Changing Channels* is the founder of Action for Children's Television's prescription for coping with the issues and problems of television viewing. Charren does not condemn the medium but rather argues that viewers must have a common-sense approach to what they watch. Specific criticisms of program and commercial content are detailed, however. The book is replete with photos and illustrations and is written in an easy, readable style.

Cirino, Robert. **Don't Blame the People: How the News Media Uses Bias, Distortion and Censorship to Manipulate Public Opinion.** Los Angeles: Diversity, 1971; New York: Random House, 1972.

The problem of bias in news gathering and reporting is addressed as one that denies participation to the public at large. Cirino analyzes the news coverage of the three major networks, four radio networks, the *New York Times,* the *Los Angeles Times,* and *Reader's Digest* to reach his poignant conclusion.

Devol, Kenneth S. **Mass Media and the Supreme Court: Legacy of the Warren Years,** 4th ed. Mamaroneck, NY: Hastings House, 1990.

The majority opinions of the major press cases during the Earl Warren Court are reproduced. An introductory commentary to each section provides background for understanding the direction of the Court. Both news gathering and broadcast media form the core of the book, but other sections discuss such topics as censorship and libel.

DeVolpi, A., et al. **Born Secret: The H-Bomb, the Progressive Case and National Security.** New York: Pergamon Press, 1981.

Written by several physicists who were central to the *Progressive* case, this is one of the best accounts of the government's attempt at censorship of public information. This is a treatise in support of the right to disseminate scientific and public information.

Emery, Edwin. **The Press and America: An Interpretive History of the Mass Media.** Englewood Cliffs, NJ: Prentice Hall, 1972.

A standard text and historical review of the conduct of the press in the United States. Emery discusses both the excesses of governmental repression and the excesses of the press.

Epstein, Daniel. **The Anatomy of AIM.** Columbia: University of Missouri, Freedom of Information Center, School of Journalism, 1973. Report no. 313.

This is a six-page pamphlet on the structure and activities of the media watchdog group Accuracy in Media (AIM). Epstein criticizes AIM for its ultra-conservative bias.

Estrin, Herman A., and Arthur M. Sanderson, eds. **Freedom and Censorship of the College Press.** Dubuque, IA: W. C. Brown, 1966.

This is a good collection of essays on student press issues of censorship. Though dated, the articles represent significant study and opinion on the topic through the 1960s.

Evans, J. Edward. **Freedom of the Press.** Minneapolis, MN: Lerner Publications Company, 1990.

A book for young readers, this work introduces the history of the freedom of expression and how the U.S. press has been conducted and treated since the colonial days. Libel, censorship, and pornography are key issues presented.

Francois, William E. **Mass Media Law and Regulation,** 3d ed. Columbus, OH: Grid, 1982.

Compiles a thorough coverage of news and broadcast court decisions and federal regulations. Analysis of the decisions and rules is provided with quotes from the cases.

Friendly, Alfred, and Ronald L. Goldfarb. **Crime and Publicity: The Impact of News on the Administration of Justice.** New York: Twentieth Century Fund, 1967.

One of the better texts on the conflict inherent between the rights of a free press and the duty of the government to ensure a fair trial for all, this was written by a trial lawyer and a newspaper executive. Particular attention is paid to the process of influencing juries with pretrial publicity.

Friendly, Fred W. **The Good Guys, the Bad Guys and the First Amendment: Free Speech vs. Fairness in Broadcasting.** New York: Random House, 1975; New York: Vintage, 1978.

This is must reading for anyone interested in the broadcast industry's rights and responsibilities under the First Amendment. Friendly is the foremost scholar on broadcasting and the former head of CBS News. His considerable insight and expertise make this a powerful book that is also very readable.

————. **Minnesota Rag: The Dramatic Story of the Landmark Supreme Court Case That Gave New Meaning to Freedom of the Press.** New York: Random House, 1981.

The noted journalist Fred Friendly deftly describes the monumental *Near v. Minnesota* case that established the doctrine of prior restraint. Written in a very lively style, this is a fascinating account of the anti-Semitic publication that rankled local authorities. This is must reading for anyone studying freedom of the press.

Gora, Joel M. **The Rights of Reporters: The Basic ACLU Guide to a Reporter's Rights.** New York: E. P. Dutton & Company, 1974.

One of the ACLU handbooks on individual rights, this provides reporters answers to common questions about their rights regarding news gathering, libel, and censorship. One chapter discusses the special problems of underground presses.

Hohenberg, John. **Free Press/Free People: The Best Cause.** New York: Columbia University Press, 1971.

One of the better historical texts, this book discusses the history and development of a free press from before the invention of the printing press to the 1970s. Only the lack of current data makes this book somewhat flawed.

Ingelhart, Louis Edward. **Press Freedoms: A Descriptive Calendar of Concepts, Interpretations, Events, and Court Actions from 4000 B.C. to the Present.** New York: Greenwood Press, 1987.

This very ambitious undertaking provides an annotated chronology of events of freedom of the press from 4000 B.C., when the first words were written, to 1985, recording the withdrawal of the United States from UNESCO and South African press controls.

————. **Press Law and Press Freedom for High School Publications.** Westport, CT: Greenwood Press, 1986.

Written before the *Hazelwood* case reached the Supreme Court, this book is nonetheless an excellent coverage of the law governing student publications. The initial federal district court decision on *Hazelwood* is mentioned. Though flawed without a current analysis of this case, the topical approach to this subject is extremely useful.

Kristof, Nicholas D. **Freedom of the High School Press.** Lanham, MD: University Press of America, 1983.

Reports the result of a survey conducted of 500 randomly selected public high school presses. A response rate of 77.7 percent was realized. The author found that most high school papers avoid controversy and that those that do not usually experience censorship.

Kronenwetter, Michael. **Free Press v. Fair Trial: Television and Other Media in the Courtroom.** New York: Franklin Watts, 1986.

Written for students in upper elementary and junior high, this work uses specific cases to demonstrate the conflict between press coverage of a trial and the rights of the defendants. Famous cases such as the Scopes trial, the 1935 Lindbergh kidnapping case, and the Billy Sol Estes trial, a fraud and influence-peddling case linked to President Johnson where cameras were used to record the court's deliberation, are described. This is a useful text for most schools and school libraries.

————. **Politics and the Press.** New York: Franklin Watts, 1987.

In this book designed for upper elementary and junior high readers, Kronenwetter explains the intermingling of the press and politics. Freedom of the press, editorial fairness, and candidate issues are described and discussed. This is an excellent book on this topic for this age group.

Labunski, Richard E. **The First Amendment under Siege: The Politics of Broadcast Regulation.** Westport, CT: Greenwood Press, 1981.

The decisions of the Supreme Court and the influential Court of Appeals for the District of Columbia on FCC regulations are discussed. An argument is made that the courts, especially the D.C. Court of Appeals, have been too active in regulating broadcasting.

Lee, Martin, and Norman Solomon. **Unreliable Sources: A Guide to Detecting Bias in the News Media.** New York: Lyle Stuart, 1990.

The authors contend that the press sides with the conservative establishment far too often. Both authors are affiliated with Fairness and Accuracy in Reporting, a liberal media watchdog. They charge that the press relies too heavily on public relations handouts and official sources.

Levy, Leonard W. **Emergence of a Free Press.** New York: Oxford University Press, 1985.

This is a major revision of Levy's colossal book *Legacy of Suppression* in which he argues that the press was a major force in public affairs, more so than indicated in previous texts, including his own. Levy's substantial scholarship cannot be ignored. This is an important work for all libraries.

————, ed. **Freedom of the Press from Zenger to Jefferson: Early American Libertarian Theories.** Indianapolis, IN: Bobbs-Merrill, 1966.

This historical review of the conduct of the press prior to the Bill of Rights is written by one of the country's foremost media scholars, Leonard Levy. He divides this history into five time periods: the formative period of the *Zenger* case, the revolutionary period, the constitutional period, the New Libertarianism, and a review of Thomas Jefferson's influence.

Manual for Student Expression: The First Amendment Rights of the High School Press. Washington, DC: Student Press Law Center, 1976.

Produced by the premier student press organization, this is the best reference handbook on the rights of student journalists. Editions written since the *Hazelwood* case in 1988 should be consulted.

Montgomery, Kathryn. **Target: Prime Time: Advocacy Groups and Entertainment TV.** New York: Oxford University Press, 1989.

Montgomery provides an in-depth look at the forces within and outside the broadcasting industry that influence its content and responses to society. She makes the case that advocacy groups play a pivotal role in controlling TV content but that deregulation and advocacy group lobbying have caused standards of quality to drop.

Morland, Howard. **The Secret That Exploded.** New York: Random House, 1981.

This is Morland's personal account of government censorship and persecution as the author of the H-bomb article in the celebrated *Progressive* case. It is an unapologetic defense of intellectual freedom and the public's right to government information. This should be required reading for all students of the First Amendment.

Pember, Don R. **Privacy and the Press: The Law, the Mass Media, and the First Amendment.** Seattle: University of Washington Press, 1972.

Pember provides an understanding of the conflict between privacy and reporters' rights in order to create the maximum opportunities for news gathering. Though privacy is a cherished individual right, the intent here is to help increase news-gathering capabilities without treading on individual liberties.

Pool, Ithiel de Sola. **Technologies of Freedom.** Cambridge, MA: Belknap Press of Harvard University Press, 1983.

An engrossing history of the mass media and their regulation, this volume goes beyond print and broadcasting issues to describe and analyze cable TV and electronic publishing as well. Easy to read, it is must reading on the impact of the press among all media and especially as a work that covers the new technologies.

Powe, Lucas A., Jr. **American Broadcasting and the First Amendment.** Berkeley: University of California Press, 1987.

A focus on the licensing history and function within the broadcasting industry, particularly by the Federal Radio Commission and then the Federal Communications Commission, is used as a vehicle to demonstrate that broadcasting is treated differently from print media. Powe argues against regulations to create equal treatment of the two media.

The Press and the Courts: Competing Principles. Washington, DC: American Enterprise Institute, 1978.

This is a transcript of a debate between Jack Landam of the Reporters Committee for Freedom of the Press; Edwin Yoder of the Washington *Star;* and two law professors, Ralph Winter of Yale University and Larry Sims of Georgetown University. This lively discussion is a good example of liberal and conservative opinion on freedom of the press.

Rips, Geoffrey, comp. **The Campaign against the Underground Press.** Anne Janowitz and Nancy J. Peters, eds. San Francisco: City Lights Books, 1981.

Although a collection of articles by some noted civil libertarians such as Aryeh Neier, Todd Gitlin, and Angus MacKenzie, this is a somewhat flawed coverage of the repressive climate against alternative and underground presses. The *Lawless State* by Morton Halperin and Gitlin's *The Whole World Is Watching* are better texts.

Rogers, Donald J. **Press versus Government: Constitutional Issues.** New York: Messner, 1986.

Designed primarily for upper elementary and junior high readers, this is an interesting survey of major cases on freedom of the press. Cases such as the Watergate affair, the H-bomb secret, and the *New York Times v. Sullivan* case illustrate how journalistic privilege and press freedoms often conflict with public values and requirements.

Rowan, Carl T. **Broadcast Fairness: Doctrine, Practice, Prospects.** White Plains, NY: Longman Publishing Group, 1984.

Written by a well-known columnist and television commentator, this is one of the best analyses of the fairness doctrine. Rowan favors the doctrine but argues against recent trends in FCC rulings.

Schmidt, Benno, Jr. **Freedom of the Press vs. Public Access.** New York: Praeger, 1976.

A thorough review of broadcast regulations provides an excellent analysis of the relation of the broadcast media to the print media. Schmidt examines the concept that access is more of an obligation of broadcasting than of print media.

Schroeder, Theodore A. **"Obscene" Literature and Constitutional Law: A Forensic Defense of Freedom of the Press.** New York: Da Capo Press, 1972. Reprint of 1911 ed.

In this early treatise against anti-obscenity legislation and repression, the author probes into not just the law of the day, circa 1920, but also the folly of prudery and high-minded keepers of the public morals.

Seldes, George. **Freedom of the Press.** New York: Garden City Publishing Company, 1937. Reprint ed. by Da Capo Press, 1971.

One of the United States's foremost critics of press censorship records a history of repression and self-censorship. Seldes also edited *In Fact,* a journal dedicated to exposing the censored news from whatever source.

Shapiro, Andrew O. **Media Access: Your Right to Express Your Views on Radio and Television.** Boston: Little, Brown, 1976.

A thorough coverage of the law and regulation of citizen use of the broadcast airwaves. Strategies for overcoming major problems in obtaining access are also described.

Smith, Jeffrey A. **Printers and Press Freedom: The Ideology of Early American Journalism.** New York: Oxford University Press, 1988.

A historical account of the conduct of news gathering in colonial and revolutionary times. The author provides insight into the concepts of sedition and libel and their roles in the establishment of the First Amendment.

Sommons, Steven J. **The Fairness Doctrine and the Media.** Berkeley: University of California Press, 1978.

One of the better texts on the fairness doctrine, both the development and the implications of the doctrine are described and discussed.

Zerman, Melvyn Bernard. **Taking on the Press: Constitutional Rights in Conflict.** New York: Harper/Crowell, 1986.

A thorough study of the freedom of the press, from the *Zenger* trial to the press blackout during the invasion of Grenada in 1983. Spiced with photographs and cartoons, this is an excellent source book for most students and scholars alike because of its attention to detail.

Freedom of Association

Abernathy, M. Glenn. **The Right of Assembly and Association,** 2d ed. Columbia: University of South Carolina Press, 1961.

A legal analysis of the right of association defines both the right to assemble and the right of association. Relevant and significant court decisions are described.

Fellman, David. **The Constitutional Right of Association.** Chicago: University of Chicago Press, 1963.

Fellman provides an understanding of the right to association within the context of various organizations, such as the right to belong to a political party and the right to belong to a trade association or union. He also defends the right to associate with a "bad" element.

Hamlin, David. **The Nazi/Skokie Conflict: A Civil Liberties Battle.** Boston: Beacon Press, 1980.

This is the best book on the Nazi march through predominantly Jewish Skokie, Illinois. It is a thorough historical account of the events leading up to the march and the case following, with particular attention paid to a discussion of the First Amendment implications of the case.

Potter, Edward E. **Freedom of Association, the Right To Organize and Collective Bargaining: The Impact on U.S. Law and Practice of Ratification of ILO Conventions No. 87 & No. 98.** Washington, DC: Labor Policy Association, 1984.

The International Labor Organization (ILO) was established as part of the League of Nations to protect unions. This work examines the U.S. concept of freedom of association as it applies to the ILO's conventions on the right to organize (No. 87) and the right to collective bargaining (No. 98). The two conventions are reproduced in their entirety.

Rice, Charles E. **Freedom of Association.** New York: New York University Press, 1962.

Provides a thorough history and analysis of the right to assemble and freedom of association. The origins of the Bill of Rights are discussed with respect to this freedom, as well as Supreme Court decisions. Specific cases and instances, such as the Ku Klux Klan, Communist Party, and criminal syndicalism cases, are also described.

Whitehead, John W. **The Right To Picket and the Freedom of Public Discourse.** Westchester, IL: Crossway Books, 1984.

This thorough treatment of the right to picket includes a historical perspective and an excellent discussion of relevant cases. Whitehead also includes state laws on picketing. He makes a concrete argument linking the right to picket with freedom of expression. The intent is to provide a legal handbook for use by pro-life, anti-abortion activists.

Worton, Stanley N. **Freedom of Assembly and Petition.** Rochelle Park, NJ: Hayden Book Company, 1975.

In this unbridled polemic on one of our basic rights, Worton begins with biblical and historical roots of the freedom of assembly, including an excellent discussion of the Magna Carta. The major issues of petition, assembly, and dissent are described, including the McCarran Act, *Dennis v. United States, DeJonge v. Oregon,* and *Griswold v. Connecticut.*

Periodicals

The following is a selected list of periodicals of relevance to at least one of the four freedoms of the First Amendment. Many are journals of scholarly study or opinion that can be found in many academic or public libraries. Several are the most important publication of an association that has been active in a substantial way with an aspect of intellectual freedom. Not all of these latter journals are accessible through a library service, often being limited to the membership of the association or only available through limited distribution channels. That has been indicated, and such titles can be accessed using a standard library's services.

AFA Journal
American Family Association
P.O. Drawer 2440
Tupelo, MS 38803
Monthly. $15.

The official journal of the American Family Association, it features articles focusing on traditional family values and the portrayal of families on television. It raises concern about television programming and promotes boycotts of products that sponsor programs objectionable to the association.

AIM Report
Accuracy in Media, Inc.
1275 K Street, NW, Suite 1150
Washington, DC 20005
Semimonthly. $35.

The official organ of Accuracy in Media, the *AIM Report* is the vehicle for publishing charges of liberal bias in the other news mediums. It promotes citizen action against news bias, works for public awareness of issues not covered adequately in the major news sources, and publishes what it sees as facts left out of national news stories. The *Report* also features news of the association, symposia, and special projects it conducts and editorial commentary.

Bill of Rights in Action
Constitutional Rights Foundation
601 S. Kingsley Avenue
Los Angeles, CA 90005
Quarterly. Free.

The primary purpose of this journal is to promote the teaching of law-related citizenship skills. It includes articles on civics, history, and government topics and issues and provides activities and questions suitable for classroom use. A recurring feature presents reports of current research in this subject area. This is a very useful periodical for junior and senior high schools and lower division college courses.

Censorship News
National Coalition against Censorship
132 W. 43rd Street
New York, NY 10036
Quarterly. $25.

Censorship News is one of the primary activities of this national coalition of intellectual freedom, civil liberties, and literary groups. It covers the major censorship news stories of the day and reports on a wide variety of challenges to books, films, art, public speakers, broadcasts, and other forms of expression. It is one of a few titles useful for keeping abreast of current censorship complaints.

Center Magazine: A Publication of the Center for the Study of Democratic Institutions
Center for Study of Democratic Institutions
P.O. Box 4068
Santa Barbara, CA 93140
Bimonthly. $30.

Begun as a journal for social change, *Center Magazine* publishes topical articles and a range of political and social issues, including affirmative action, ethics in journalism, the arms race, and constitutional law. It is not primarily concerned with civil liberties but is a strong advocate for intellectual freedom as occasions arise. It is the publication of the Center for the Study of Democratic Institutions, which also publishes *New Perspectives Quarterly*.

Christian Herald
Christian Herald Association
40 Overlook Drive
Chappaqua, NY 10514
Monthly. $15.97.

The *Herald* presents a conservative, family values viewpoint on religious and social issues of the day. Recent topics included marriage, divorce, gay rights, and social activism.

Christianity Today
465 Gunderson Drive
Carol Stream, IL 60188
Biweekly. $24.95.

Christianity Today is one of the better known journals of evangelical and conservative religious thought. Its format emphasizes style and appeals to teenagers. Articles are on social and religious topics with a biblical flavor, and the magazine has touched on censorship issues.

Church and State
Americans United for Separation of Church and State
8120 Fenton Street
Silver Spring, MD 20910
Monthly. $18.

The thrust of this journal's editorial policy is to guard against entanglement by the government in religious affairs. Each article focuses on potential conflicts between religion and the state such as prayer in the schools and government aid to parochial schools.

The Citizen
Citizens Council, Inc.
254 E. Griffith Street
Jackson, MS 39205
Monthly. Ceased Publication.

Advocates the separation of the white and black races and argues against the landmark school desegregation case *Brown v. Board of Education*. The articles are extremely conservative in tone and substance. *The Citizen* was one of the oldest (1956) arch- conservative, anti–racial integration journals in the country. It ceased publication in 1991.

Civil Liberties
American Civil Liberties Union Foundation
132 W. 43rd Street
New York, NY 10036
Quarterly. $20 with membership.

This newsletter publishes the activities of the American Civil Liberties Union (ACLU), the premier civil liberties organization in the United States. News of the legal defenses entered into by the ACLU on a wide variety of freedom of expression, due process of law, equality, and privacy concerns is reported. It also discusses ACLU research and public education projects. This is recommended for those individuals tracking civil liberties cases and news.

Commentary: Journal of Significant Thought and Opinion on Contemporary Issues
American Jewish Committee
165 E. 56th Street
New York, NY 10022
Monthly. $39.

The major publication of the American Jewish Committee, its stated purpose is to combat bigotry, protect human rights, and influence public opinion on problems of concern to the Jewish people. However, most of the articles cover general political and cultural affairs with a moderate to conservative viewpoint. An occasional piece pertaining to the First Amendment is included.

Connexions Digest: A Digest of Resources and Groups for Social Justice
Connexions Information Sharing Service
427 Bloor Street, W.
Toronto, Ont. M551X7 Canada
Quarterly. $25.

This resource guide is designed as a tool for groups working toward social change, human rights, and civil liberties. Each issue is divided into headings such as "Economy/Poverty/Work" and "Human Rights/Civil Liberties," which lists organizations, events, and publications of value to current issues in these topics. Its focus is Canadian sources but it has some U.S. information as well.

Conservative Digest
National Press Building
Suite 800
Washington, DC 20045
Monthly. Ceased Publication.

The *Reader's Digest* of conservative issues, this periodical covers a wide variety of political, social, cultural, and economic topics with a decidedly conservative viewpoint. Some original articles are included, but most are edited versions of stories from other conservative magazines. Recent issues have dealt with pornography crusades, the Concerned Women of America, and abortion issues. It ceased publication in 1991.

Constitutional Commentary
University of Minnesota Law School
229 19th Avenue S.
Minneapolis, MN 55455
Semiannual. $15.

A journal of constitutional law, it is less case oriented than other competing magazines, with articles and commentary on political and historical topics. Each issue includes extensive book reviews. Civil liberties coverage exists when such issues are in the forefront of the news of the courts.

First Principles: National Security and Civil Liberty
Center for National Security Studies
122 Maryland Avenue, NE
Washington, DC 20002
Quarterly. $15.

A newsletter format, *First Principles* produces incisive analysis of covert activities by the CIA and domestic spying by the FBI. Articles also deal with governmental actions restricting the free flow of information and violations of individual rights.

Focus on the Family
Focus on the Family, Inc.
801 Corporate Center Drive
Pomona, CA 91768
Monthly. Free.

Dedicated to presenting facts and opinion on current issues that will strengthen the family and traditional Judeo-Christian values, *Focus on the Family* is the publication of Dr. James Dobson's research organization. Dobson, a member of the Meese Commission, supports traditional family values and combats pornography and obscenity as well as abortion on demand. He also defends other conservative, Christian causes.

Free Inquiry
Council for Democratic and Secular Humanism
P.O. Box 5
Buffalo, NY 14215
Quarterly. $25.

Presenting issues in a popular style, this journal promotes the separation of church and state and the ideals of intellectual freedom. Articles discuss current issues from a philosophical and historical viewpoint on religious beliefs and institutions and humanism.

Freedom To Read Foundation News
Freedom To Read Foundation
50 E. Huron Street
Chicago, IL 60611
Quarterly. Available to Foundation members only.

Affiliated with the American Library Association, this is the foundation's report on its activities in support of libraries and librarians, booksellers, and others involved in censorship cases. It is also one of the better sources for news on censorship incidents. Federal and state legislation of relevance is also described and discussed.

The Guardian: Independent Radical Newsweekly
Institute for Independent Social Journalism
33 W. 17th Street
New York, NY 10011
Weekly. $27.50.

A left-of-center news weekly, *The Guardian* is considered the best of the publications on leftwing or radical organizing. It is primarily news oriented, and features on civil liberties and intellectual freedom appear frequently, but as news permits. *The Guardian* also includes other standard newspaper fare such as an op–ed page and theater and film reviews.

Harvard Civil Rights-Civil Liberties Law Review
Harvard University Law School Publications Center
Cambridge, MA 02138
Semiannual. $24.

Considered the most outstanding journal on civil rights and civil liberties, its regular articles are more general interest than case law oriented. The analysis of current civil liberties issues provides the best arguments for examining governmental policy and the impact of Court decisions.

Heritage Today
Heritage Foundation
214 Massachusetts Avenue, NE
Washington, DC 20002
Bimonthly. Price included in $25 membership fee.

The primary publication of the conservative, public interest group the Heritage Foundation, *Heritage Today* reviews the activities of the foundation and features articles on topics of concern. The foundation promotes a conservative view on free enterprise, limited government, individual liberty, the national defense, and traditional family values. Though the emphasis is on limiting government and maintaining national defense, this is a significant voice in the conservative movement and its reports on individual liberty have a strong impact on a significant number of individuals.

Human Rights: Official Publication of the ABA Section on Individual Rights and Responsibilities
American Bar Association Press
750 N. Lake Shore Drive
Chicago, IL 60611
Three times per year. $18 to nonmembers.

This journal is the official organ of the American Bar Association's Section on Individual Rights and Responsibilities. Each issue presents articles of current issues on a variety of topics affecting civil liberties including the First Amendment and the rights of the accused. Some issues focus on one subject.

Index on Censorship
Fund for Free Expression
485 Fifth Avenue
New York, NY 10017
Ten times per year. $24.

In this leading chronicle of current issues on censorship, all forms of expression including books, art, films, and cases of dissident writers are covered. It has an intellectual focus with occasional articles on difficulties in the United States.

Interracial Books for Children Bulletin
Council on Interracial Books for Children, Inc.
1841 Broadway
New York, NY 10003
Eight times per year. $16.

A major book selection tool, this journal provides judgments on racial and sexual themes in children's literature. The primary focus is concerned with the portrayal of stereotypes, societal biases, and areas of concern to minorities. Two regular features, "Bookshelf" for books and "Media Monitor" for Hollywood and classroom films, contain short reviews concerning racial and sexual images and the depiction of minorities. There are usually six to ten articles in each issue, often with a poem or excerpt from a banned author's work. A short country-by-country record of current events is included in an index format. Excellent for journalism majors and appropriate for public and college libraries.

Journal of Church and State
Baylor University
J. M. Dawson Studies in Church and State
P.O. Box 380
Waco, TX 76798
Three times per year. $20 to individuals; $25 to institutions.

Presents a more scholarly approach to the issues of the separation of church and state. Recommended for academic libraries.

Journal of Criminal Law and Criminology
Northwestern University Law School
357 E. Chicago Avenue
Chicago, IL 60611
Quarterly. $30.

This is primarily a journal for criminologists. The winter issue of each year includes a lengthy "Supreme Court Review" of commentary on cases before the Court. These analyses are grouped by each of the amendments of the Bill of Rights. An occasional article of direct significance to the First Amendment will also appear.

Journal of Law and Religion
Hamline University School of Law
Council on Religion and Law
1536 Hewitt Avenue
St. Paul, MN 55104
Semiannual. $12.

A more specialized journal than similar titles, this scholarly publication provides excellent research articles on legal issues and religious institutions. It also publishes an annual survey of trends and developments on religious liberty.

Klansman
Empire Publishing Company
P. O. Box 700
Gulf, NC 27256
Bimonthly. Write to request price.

The oldest and most well-known publication of the Ku Klux Klan, it features articles and editorials on Klan activities and current social and political concerns from a Klan perspective.

Mel Gabler's Newsletter
Educational Research Analysts (E.R.A.)
P.O. Box 7518
Longview, TX 75607-7518
Semiannual. Donation requested.

A substantial voice on the selection of school textbooks, *Mel Gabler's Newsletter* is the primary vehicle for groups and individuals concerned about the lack of traditional values in modern school textbooks. Begun as an attempt to influence the selection of textbooks for the public schools of Texas, the newsletter has been so successful it has sparked nationwide textbook reviews for liberal bias and secular humanism. The newsletter reports reviews of textbooks with commentary on the level of objectionable content, as well as important omissions of facts as noted by E.R.A.

The Nation
Nation Associates, Inc.
P.O. Box 1953
Marion, OH 43305
Weekly. $36,

A consistently liberal editorial policy has been enhanced by the leadership of Victor Navasky, one of the most prolific writers on liberal issues, especially intellectual freedom. *The Nation* is an excellent news and opinion journal, with investigative reports from a liberal perspective and political commentary. It is one of the few national journals of general interest that frequently includes articles on intellectual freedom.

National Review: A Journal of Fact and Opinion
National Review, Inc.
150 E. 35th Street
New York, NY 10016
Fortnightly. $57.

The National Review has been the best conservative opinion journal since its founding in 1955. It is the conservative counterpart of *The New*

Republic and *The Nation.* Feature articles cover a wide range of social, political, and economic topics, often on the Supreme Court and the First Amendment. The writing style is witty, iconoclastic, and well done. It also includes some of the best political cartoons with a conservative focus.

New American
Review of the News, Inc.
395 Concord Avenue
Belmont, MA 02178
Weekly. $39.

This publication is affiliated with the John Birch Society and provides political commentary on social, political, cultural, and religious events. Its format is similar to *Time* and *Newsweek,* but its content is very conservative and anticommunist. Recent issues covered the "science of creationism." It is dedicated to promoting Christianity and combatting communism.

New Perspectives
U.S. Commission on Civil Rights
U.S. GPO
Washington, DC 29492
Irregular. Free.

This is the official publication of the U.S. Commission on Civil Rights, formerly known as the *Civil Rights Digest.* It is currently in suspension but plans have been announced for new issues. It publishes articles about discrimination, but occasionally items on individual rights are included.

New Perspectives Quarterly
Center for the Study of Democratic Institutions
P.O. Box 4068
Santa Barbara, CA 93140
Quarterly. $35.

This is an excellent publication on issues facing democracy and freedom of expression throughout the world but especially in the United States. The graphics, typography, and writing style are superior. There are regular columns commenting on major events throughout the world. This is highly recommended for all libraries and the general reader.

The New Republic
New Republic, Inc.
1220 19th Street, NW
Washington, DC 20036
Weekly. $69.97

One of the best liberal journals, it began as a supporter of President Woodrow Wilson's reform administration. It has remained an iconoclastic journal of opinion, savaging both Left and Right as it sees fit. Many articles deal directly with current events relevant to the First Amendment, though a wide variety of topics are included. It now includes more of a balance of opinion, with moderate conservatives as well as liberals as regular authors.

New York Law School Journal of Human Rights

New York Law School
57 Worth Street
New York, NY 10013
Semiannual. $18.

This law journal focuses on cases before the Supreme Court of relevance to civil rights and civil liberties. First Amendment law is covered as such cases come before the Court, and the articles are in-depth legal analyses.

News Media and the Law

Reporters Committee for Freedom of the Press
800 18th Street, NW, Suite 300
Washington, DC 20006
Quarterly. $20.

This is the principal journal of one of the leading intellectual freedom organizations in the United States. Each issue contains approximately 25 short articles on legal issues of freedom of the press. Relevant case citations are included in each article. A subject classification groups the articles under such headings as "Libel and Privacy," "Prior Restraints and Secret Courts," and "Confidentiality of Sources." It is useful for both legal research and readers interested in First Amendment rights.

Newsletter on Intellectual Freedom

American Library Association
50 E. Huron Street
Chicago, IL 60611
Bimonthly. $30.

A publication primarily aimed at library professionals and individuals concerned about libraries, this is still one of the best sources of censorship news. Each article features at least one topical article, plus news and analysis of recent Supreme Court decisions. More important, there is a concise report on recorded censorship incidents of the most recent past, grouped by type of media. A "success stories" section describes situations where principles of intellectual freedom were upheld after a challenge.

Obscenity Law Bulletin
National Obscenity Law Center—Morality in Media, Inc.
475 Riverside Drive, Suite 239
New York, NY 10115
Bimonthly. $10.

This publication is designed to assist law enforcement officials and district attorneys, primarily, in the prosecution of obscenity cases. A publication of Morality in Media, an anti-pornography organization, it covers major legislative efforts and Supreme Court decisions and activities. It is also useful for local grassroots groups interested in combatting pornography.

Our Right To Know
Fund for Open Information and Accountability
145 W. 4th Street
New York, NY 10012
Quarterly. $12 to individuals; $25 to institutions.

This journal promotes the right to freedom of information and government publications. Its articles are concise reports on government accountability, secrecy issues, and the Freedom of Information Act. It is recommended for all public and college libraries.

Phyllis Schlafly Report
Eagle Trust Fund
P.O. Box 618
Alton, IL 62002
Monthly. $20.

The voice of Phyllis Schlafly and her Eagle Forum, the report discusses news items on a wide variety of social, political, and economic topics. It promotes traditional family values, especially in the schools, through actions for and against textbooks, teaching methods, and library books. It takes a strong stand against feminism and the Equal Rights Amendment. This is one of the most important conservative newsletters because of the visibility and impact of Phyllis Schlafly's activities.

The Progressive
The Progressive, Inc.
409 E. Main Street
Madison, WI 53703
Monthly. $30 to individuals; $50 to institutions.

One of the oldest liberal political magazines, *The Progressive* is a prime force within the left wing. Its articles focus on civil rights, foreign policy, and environmental issues, and it regularly features well-known names, particularly Nat Hentoff on intellectual freedom.

Propaganda Review
Media Alliance
Ft. Maston Building D
San Francisco, CA 94123
Quarterly. $20.

This unique title chronicles the use of propaganda throughout the world. The purpose is to show, through current events and philosophical commentary, how the news is manipulated and controlled.

Public Eye: A Journal of Social and Political Issues Concerning Repression in America
National Lawyers Guild Civil Liberties Committee
14 Beacon Street, Suite 407
Boston, MA 02108
Irregular. $8 to individuals; $15 to institutions.

As its subtitle suggests, *Public Eye* is a liberal watchdog publication. Its features track governmental abuse of individual rights. It is very useful for its coverage of conservative and rightwing attacks on groups and individuals such as censorship incidents.

Religious Freedom Reporter
Center for Law and Religious Freedom
Christian Legal Society
P.O. Box 1492
Merrifield, VA 22116
Monthly. $95.

The primary focus of this journal is on church-state law. It organizes state and federal cases and decisions under more than 100 subjects, including the Constitution, education, family law, religion in public institutions, media and broadcasting, and social/ethical issues. This is one of the best sources for objective information on the relationship of church and state and current issues in this topic. References to law-review articles are included with a description of each case.

Social Philosophy and Policy
Basil Blackwell Ltd.
108 Cowley Rd.
Oxford OX41JF England
Semiannual. $27 to individuals; $70 to institutions.

An excellent publication for examining a more theoretical approach to current social topics, including civil rights and civil liberties. Its focus is not on intellectual freedom, but when included, the writings provide a strong, research-based discussion on philosophical arguments for and against current trends.

The Spotlight
Cordite Fidelity, Inc.
300 Independence Avenue, SE
Washington, DC 20003
Weekly. $32.

The primary publication of the Liberty Lobby, it serves up ultra-conservative editorials and articles on national defense and U.S. politics. It often features opinions on the influence of Israel in U.S. foreign and domestic policy. It supports a variety of conservative causes in its editorial policy and contents.

Student Press Law Center Report
Student Press Law Center, Inc.
1735 I Street, NW
Washington, DC 20006
Three times per year. $15.

The official organ of the Student Press Law Center, this is the best source for news on the censorship of student journalism. Each article is relatively brief and written in a newsworthy style. The journal also includes resources available to student journalists and news of the center's activities.

Utne Reader: The Best of the Alternative Press
Lens Publishing Company, Inc.
1624 Harmon Place, Suite 330
Minneapolis, MN 55403
Bimonthly. $24.

Digests and compiles articles and issues from over 1,000 primarily alternative presses, magazines, and newsletters. With a liberal editorial policy, *Utne Reader* is one of the better sources for news on censorship incidents.

7

Selected Nonprint Resources

Films, Videocassettes, and Filmstrips

THERE ARE NUMEROUS FILMS, VIDEOS, and filmstrips with an intellectual freedom theme that provide a unique format for conveying information on and the concepts of this topic. Such media often give a more experiential view and can portray these issues in a more graphic manner. The following films and videos are the more important and relevant works on intellectual freedom and free expression. This chapter also includes databases that are the most relevant, CD-ROM products, and appropriate television programs.

Alexander William Doniphan
Type: $3/4''$ and $1/2''$ black & white videocassette
Length: 51 min.
Cost: Purchase $49.95
Source: Social Studies Schools Service
10000 Culver Boulevard
P.O. Box 802
Culver City, CA 90232-2436
(800) 421-4246

This film depicts the life of Alexander Doniphan, a frontier lawyer who defended the religious and political rights of Mormon settlers. Peter

Lawford plays Doniphan who also must struggle with his conscience over his orders, as a military commander, to execute Mormon founder Joseph Smith.

Archbishop O'Connor Scores Pornography as Major Threat to Family Life/Father Ritter Fights "Teen Sex Industry" in New York City

Type: 1/2" color videocassette
Length: 47 min.
Cost: Purchase $20
Date: 1989
Source: Keep the Faith Inc.
             P.O. Box 8261
             North Haledon, NJ 07508
             (800) 221-1564

Two films in one, this production is designed to present the problems of pornography and the breakdown of moral values. The first half presents Archbishop O'Connor's impassioned argument against pornography. The second half chronicles the courageous work of Father Ritter in New York City.

Bill of Rights in Action: Freedom of Religion

Type: 3/4" or 1/2" color videocassette
Length: 21 min.
Cost: Purchase $250
Date: 1969
Source: Barr Films
             12801 Scharbarum Avenue
             P.O. Box 7878
             Irwindale, CA 91107
             (800) 262-2557

The freedom of religion as guaranteed by the First Amendment is explained from a constitutional and social perspective. The film uses a blood transfusion case involving Christian Scientists to show the dilemmas the free exercise of religion can cause.

Bill of Rights in Action: Freedom of Speech

Type: 1/2" color videocassette
Length: 21 min.
Cost: Purchase $240
Date: 1982

Source: Barr Films
12801 Scharbarum Avenue
P.O. Box 91107
Irwindale, CA 91107
(800) 262-2557

The demonstration of freedom of speech is shown through a dramatized event. An unpopular speaker is convicted of disturbing the peace. The film focuses on the complex problems of free speech.

Bill of Rights in Action: Freedom of the Press
Type: 3/4″ or 1/2″ color videocassette
Length: 18 min.
Cost: Purchase $285
Date: 1973
Source: Phoenix/BFA Films and Video, Inc.
468 Park Avenue South
New York, NY 10016
(212) 684-5910

This film depicts the issues of the freedom of the press with a fictionalized incident. The facets of this freedom are shown through a story of a reporter's attempt to keep his source confidential.

Books Our Children Read
Type: 3/4″ or 1/2″ color videocassette
Length: 28 min.
Cost: Purchase $79
Date: 1984
Source: Films Incorporated Educational
5547 North Ravenswood Avenue
Chicago, IL 60640-1199
(800) 323-4222

Discusses book censorship through the portrayal of an actual censorship attempt. Documents the challenge to Robert Peck's *A Day No Pigs Will Die* in a southern Ohio community, including interviews with parents, students, and teachers.

Case History of a Rumor
Type: 3/4″ or 1/2″ black & white videocassette
Length: 52 min.
Cost: Purchase $250
Date: 1963

Source: Carousel Film and Video
260 Fifth Avenue
New York, NY 10016
(212) 683-1660

Follows the events of a rumor that an anticommunist military maneuver was a plot to overthrow the government. The film shows how hate and prejudice can threaten freedom.

Censorship in a Free Society
Type: 3/4" or 1/2" color videocassette
Length: 30 min.
Cost: Purchase $49.95
Date: 1976
Source: American Humanist Association
7 Harwood Drive
P.O. Box 146
Amherst, NY 14226-0146
(800) 743-6646

Features a debate between Emmett Lyrrell, editor of *The Alternative* magazine, and the attorney for Larry Flynt, publisher of the men's magazine *Hustler,* on the limits of obscenity and the threat of censorship. Both men offer similar views against censorship, though differences on limitations are evident.

Censorship or Selection—Choosing Books for Public Schools
Type: 3/4" or 1/2" color videocassette
Length: 60 min.
Cost: Purchase $153.50
Date: 1982
Source: Medical and Society Seminars
Graduate School of Journalism, Columbia University
New York, NY 10027
(212) 854-4150

This film reproduces in condensed form a seminar of school book selection topics for school administrators that was presented at the 1982 National School Boards Association conference. The discussion covers required classroom readings, school library acquisitions and withdrawals, and the legality of teaching scientific creationism. Recommended for teachers and school authorities.

The Challenge of Ideas
Type: 16mm black & white film
Length: 30 min.
Cost: Purchase $190

Date: 1961
Source: U.S. National Audiovisual Center
8700 Edgeworth Drive
Capital Heights, MD 20743-3701
(301) 763-1896

Produced by the U.S. Defense Department, this highly patriotic film highlights the differences between the U.S. form of government and that of the Soviet Union of the early 1960s. The lack of individual rights in the Soviet Union is an integral part of the film.

Charge and Countercharge—A Film on the Era of Senator Joseph R. McCarthy

Type: 16mm black & white film, 1/2″ black & white videocassette
Length: 43 min.
Cost: Rental $60; purchase $595 (film), $395 (video)
Source: Cinema Guild
Division of Documents Associates
1697 Broadway
New York, NY 10019
(212) 246-5522

Using historical news and film footage, this production recalls the life of Wisconsin Senator Joseph McCarthy, architect of the political repression of the 1950s. The hearings on Communist influence in the army and the Hollywood blacklisting issues are primary facets of the film.

Church, State and the First Amendment

Type: 3/4″ or 1/2″ color videocassette
Length: 30 min.
Cost: Purchase $49.95
Date: 1972
Source: American Humanist Association
7 Harwood Drive
P.O. Box 146
Amherst, NY 14226-0146
(800) 743-6646

The separation of church and state is debated in this production between Edd Doer, editor of *Church and State* magazine, and Glenn Archer, from Americans United Foundation. The basic freedom of religion tenets of the First Amendment are discussed in philosophical and moral terms.

Clown of Freedom

Type: 1/2″ color videocassette
Length: 27 min.
Cost: Rental $19; purchase $29.95

Date: 1974
Source: Paulist Productions
           P.O. Box 1057
           Pacific Palisades, CA 90272
           (310) 454-0688

This drama portrays the political repression in Third World countries through a story about a street theater troupe leader in a fictitious Latin American country. The theme is intended to show the inner strength of prisoners of conscience.

Combating Pornography
Type: 3/4″ color videocassette
Length: 30 min.
Cost: Purchase $24.95
Date: 1987
Source: Broadman
           127 Ninth Avenue N.
           Nashville, TN 37234
           (800) 458-2772

Uses religious and moral teachings to condemn pornography. Demonstrates the ill effects of pornography on society and argues for its abolishment.

The Constitution: For Adults Only?
Type: 1/2″ color videocassette
Length: 30 min.
Cost: Purchase $189
Date: 1989
Source: Zenger Video
           10200 Jefferson Boulevard
           P.O. Box 802
           Culver City, CA 90232
           (800) 421-4246

The rights of youth are compared with adult rights in this well-prepared documentary. A wide range of viewpoints are presented, including interviews with former Chief Justice Warren Burger, several youths who have been incarcerated, and a 20-year-old lawyer. One focus of the film is on school issues such as school newspaper censorship, dress codes, and distribution of contraceptives. An interview is also conducted with students at a high school that bans dancing, interspersing clips from the hit movie *Footloose.*

A Crime against Women
Type: 3/4″ black & white videocassette
Length: 55 min.

Cost: Purchase $40
Date: 1979
Source: Women in Focus
           849 Beatty Street
           Vancouver, BC V6B2M6 Canada
           (604) 682-5848

Describes and illustrates the methods used by feminist groups to combat pornography. Argues that a stand against pornography must be taken because pornography is degrading to women.

Dangerous Songs: Censors, Rock and the First Amendment
Type: 1/2" color videocassette from filmstrip
Length: 18 min.
Cost: Purchase $63
Date: 1991
Source: Zenger Video
           10200 Jefferson Boulevard
           P.O. Box 802
           Culver City, CA 90232
           (800) 421-4246

Describes the controversy over explicit language in rock music lyrics and sexually explicit rock music videos and album covers. The film introduces both sides of the arguments and presents members of the Parent's Music Resource Center arguing for record labeling. The ethical and constitutional issues of such labeling schemes are described.

The Day They Came To Arrest the Book
Type: 1/2" color videocassette
Length: 47 min.
Cost: Rental $50; purchase $495
Date: 1989
Source: Film Fair Communications
           175 Lexington Avenue
           New York, NY 10016
           (212) 889-3820

In story form, the issues of freedom of speech and censorship are poignantly presented. *The Adventures of Huckleberry Finn* is introduced to Gordon's history class. He becomes angered by the use of the word "nigger" in Twain's tale and refuses to read the remainder of the book or remain in class. The dilemma for Gordon is eventually solved with a thorough examination of the historical era in which the story takes place.

Death of a Porn Queen
Type: 1/2" and 3/4" color videocassette
Length: 58 min.

Date: 1988
Cost: Purchase $59.95 (½″), $79.95 (¾″)
Source: PBS Video
            1320 Braddock Place
            Alexandria, VA 22314
            (800) 424-7963

Chronicles the life and death of the pornographic film star Shauna Grant (formerly Colleen Applegate of Farmingdale, MN). Describes her ambitions to become a movie star and her trials in Hollywood attempting to start a legitimate career. Details the events leading up to her suicide at age 20 after her involvement in the pornographic film industry.

Ethics in Advertising

Type: ¾″ or ½″ color videocassette
Length: 30 min.
Cost: Purchase $100
Date: 1970
Source: Nebraska Educational TV/Council for Higher Education
            P.O. Box 831
            Lincoln, NE 68501
            (402) 472-3611

This excellent educational presentation provides a very useful coverage of the limits of commercial speech. Federal and industry-imposed regulations are covered. The film also discusses truth in advertising and standards of taste.

Ever Changing, Ever Free

Type: 16mm color film
Length: 11 min.
Cost: $190
Date: 1974
Source: U.S. National Audiovisual Center
            8700 Edgewood Drive
            Capital Heights, MD 20743
            (301) 763-1896

The U.S. Bill of Rights is heralded as the guarantee for individual rights, but the film also stresses that these rights operate within a framework of order and restrictions. This production emphasizes the glory of the Bill of Rights and our form of government.

The Facts of Love in the Library: Making Sexuality Information Relevant and Accessible to Young People

Type: ½″ color videocassette
Length: 20 min.

Cost: Purchase $75
Date: 1987
Source: A.L.A. Video
           320 York Road
           Towson, MD 21204-5179
           (800) 441-TAPE

Featuring young-adult librarian Patty Campbell, this dynamic production discusses the inclusion of materials on sexuality in library collections. Topics included are methods of evaluating these materials,
successful programs for promoting them and tips on planning to gain
community support. An introduction by Dr. Ruth Westheimer is also
included.

Fahrenheit 451
Type: $3/4''$ or $1/2''$ color videocassette
Length: 111 min.
Cost: Purchase $29.95
Date: 1966
Source: Zenger Video
           10200 Jefferson Boulevard
           PO Box 802
           Culver City, CA 90232
           (800) 421-4246

Directed by Francois Truffaut, this is the film version of Ray Bradbury's
classic science fiction novel on censorship. Starring Oscar Werner and
Julie Christie, it depicts a futuristic society that burns books to control
people's minds. The hero is a government book burner who defects to a
small minority who memorize classic literature to preserve it.

The First Amendment and the Ku Klux Klan
Type: $1/2''$ color videocassette
Length: 12 min.
Cost: Purchase $60
Date: 1989
Source: Zenger Video
           10200 Jefferson Boulevard
           P.O. Box 802
           Culver City, CA 90232
           (800) 421-4246

As technology has grown, so have the controversies over its use. This
film describes the furor over the use by the Ku Klux Klan of a public-
access TV channel. The issues of censorship, morality, and the rights of
the cable company and the Ku Klux Klan are presented and discussed.

The First Freedom

Type: 1/2" color videocassette
Length: 58 min.
Cost: Purchase $49
Date: 1989
Source: Films Incorporated Educational
            5547 North Ravenswood Avenue
            Chicago, IL 60640-1199
            (800) 323-4222

Based on the book *The Struggle for Democracy* by Benjamin Barber and Patrick Watson, this is an excellent film on the freedom of expression. Comparisons are made about the level of expressive rights in the United States, Canada, Great Britain, and Mexico.

Footloose

Type: 3/4" or 1/2" color videocassette
Length: 106 min.
Cost: Purchase $14.95
Date: 1984
Source: Movies Unlimited
            6736 Castor Avenue
            Philadelphia, PA 19149
            (800) 523-0823

This teen dance picture was a box office hit about a rural community that banned dancing and rock music. The protagonist, played by Kevin Bacon, moves into town with his mother from Chicago and pressures the town fathers to allow a prom. The most influential minister, portrayed by John Lithgow, makes an impassioned plea to several townspeople to stop burning library books in one scene. The film holds a PG rating.

Fred Friendly—Journalist

Type: 3/4" or 1/2" color videocassette
Length: 30 min.
Cost: Purchase $100
Date: 1977
Source: Nebraska Educational TV/Council for Higher Education
            P.O. Box 8311
            Lincoln, NE 68501
            (402) 472-3611

An interview with Columbia University journalism professor and former CBS News president Fred Friendly, this film is an excellent introduction into the climate of news reporting of the 1950s, the abilities of Edward R. Murrow, and the political repression of the McCarthy era. Friendly also describes the emergence and value of public broadcasting.

Free Press, Free Trial

Type: 16mm color film
Length: 30 min.
Cost: Rental $12.15; purchase $250
Date: 1975
Source: Indiana University
Audio-Visual Center
Bloomington, IN 47405
(812) 855-8087

The conflict between a fair trial and press coverage is examined in this film. Vice-president Spiro Agnew's claim that unfair press coverage biased the jury in his trial is discussed, as well as coverage of a Houston mass murder case.

Free Thought and the Mass Media

Type: 3/4" or 1/2" color videocassette
Length: 30 min.
Cost: $49.95
Date: 1973
Source: American Humanist Association
7 Harwood Drive
P.O. Box 146
Amherst, NY 14226-0146

An interview with former FCC commissioner Nicholas Johnson highlights concerns about television programming. Johnson argues for more diversity and creativity.

Free To Believe

Type: 1/2" color videocassette
Length: 56 min.
Cost: Purchase $159
Date: 1987
Source: Films for the Humanities and Sciences
P.O. Box 2053
Princeton, NJ 08540
(800) 257-5126

One of the *We the People* series, this film is narrated by ABC News anchor Peter Jennings. It describes the Alabama textbook controversy and the constitutional issues raised. Judge Brevard Hand, who ruled that the *Impressions* textbook series introduced the religion of secular humanism into the schools, is interviewed. Parents, teachers, and students also present their viewpoints.

Freedom of Expression

Type: 16mm color film, color videocassette
Length: 29 min.
Cost: Purchase $400 (film), $180 (video)
Date: 1987
Source: Agency for Instructional Technology
            Box A
            Bloomington, IN 47402
            (800) 457-4509

Using dramatic episodes to illustrate free expression, this film explores the constitutional guarantee of free speech. Each scene gives the viewer a dilemma caused by the exercise of speech and suggests what the law will allow.

Freedom of Speech and Press

Type: 3/4" or 1/2" color videocassette
Length: 30 min.
Cost: Purchase $375
Date: 1979
Source: Dallas County Community College District
            4343 North Highway 67
            Mesquite, TX 75150
            (214) 324-7784

This is a good example of comparisons of court decisions on the First Amendment. It shows how the Court has produced different standards over time, with a changing court makeup and under varying circumstances.

Freedom To Speak: People of New York vs. Irving Feiner

Type: 3/4" or 1/2" color videocassette
Length: 23 min.
Cost: Purchase $149
Date: 1969
Source: Britannica Films
            310 South Michigan Avenue
            Chicago, IL 60604
            (800) 554-9862

Depicts the events leading to the major Supreme Court case on "provocative" words, *Feiner v. New York.* Shows how the expression of dissent can cause public disorder and reviews the Court's decision to ban such speech if the speaker incites a riot.

Freedoms

Type: 16mm color film, 3/4" or 1/2" color videocassette

Length: 23 min.
Cost: Purchase $520 (film), $365 (1/2″ video), $395 (3/4″ video)
Date: 1984
Source: Barr Films
            12801 Scharbarum Avenue
            P.O. Box 7878
            Irwindale, CA 91107
            (800) 234-7878

A patriotic story of a boy who learns to appreciate the U.S. form of government. The focus is on the individual rights guaranteed by the Bill of Rights.

George Mason
Type: 3/4″ or 1/2″ color videocassette
Length: 51 min.
Cost: Purchase $49.95
Date: 1965
Source: Social Studies Schools Service
            10000 Culver Boulevard
            P.O. Box 802
            Culver City, CA 90232-2436
            (800) 421-4246

Portrays the life of George Mason, a little-known but driving force for the Bill of Rights during the 1787 Constitutional Convention. Based on John F. Kennedy's *Profiles in Courage,* the film discusses constitutional guarantees of individual rights.

God and the Constitution
Type: 1/2″ color videocassette
Length: 60 min.
Cost: Purchase $59.95 (1/2″); $79.95 (3/4″)
Date: 1987
Source: PBS Video
            1320 Braddock Place
            Alexandria, VA 22314
            (800) 424-7963

Noted journalist Bill Moyers interviews two constitutional scholars on freedom of religion. Martin Marty, Professor of History of Modern Christianity at the University of Chicago, presents the more conservative viewpoint and Leonard Levy, editor of the *Encyclopedia of the American Constitution,* offers up the more liberal position. Topics include prayer in the schools, religious symbols on municipal property, and the tax-exempt status for religious institutions.

The History of Pornography

Type: 1/2" Videocassette, color
Length: 45 min.
Cost: Purchase $180
Date: 1987
Source: Focus International
           14 Oregon Drive
           Huntington Station, NY 11746
           (516) 549-5320

This pictorial review of the production of pornography highlights ancient historical beginnings as well as current materials and themes. The difficulties pornography has experienced over the years is also discussed.

The History of Religious Freedom

Type: 1/2" color videocassette
Length: 30 min.
Cost: Purchase $24.95
Date: 1989
Source: Broadman Productions
           127 Ninth Avenue
           Nashville, TN 37234
           (800) 251-3225

Though limited to a discussion on Protestant faiths, this production eloquently traces the history of religious persecution in Europe of the most well-known Protestant faiths. It describes the flight of prominent religious leaders to America throughout the 18th and 19th centuries and the establishment of these faiths in America. There is also a discussion of the Constitution's guarantee of religious freedom.

Individual Rights

Type: 3/4" or 1/2" color videocassette
Length: 30 min.
Cost: Purchase $375
Date: 1981
Source: Dallas County Community College District
           4343 North Highway 67
           Mesquite, TX 75150
           (214) 324-7784

This instructional program on the First Amendment shows the role the Supreme Court plays in interpreting the four freedoms. Recommended for classroom use in civics and government courses.

Inherit the Wind

Type: 3/4" or 1/2" black & white videocassette
Length: 127 min.

Cost: $20
Date: 1960
Source: Zenger Video
            10200 Jefferson Boulevard
            P.O. Box 802
            Culver City, CA 90232
            (800) 421-4246

Directed by Stanley Kramer and starring Spencer Tracy as Clarence Darrow and Frederic March as William Jennings Bryan, this blockbuster movie recreates the famous Scopes trial. Useful for a discussion on the teaching of evolution in the public schools.

It's Only Rock and Roll
Type: 1/2" color videocassette
Length: 45 min.
Cost: Purchase $395
Date: 1991
Source: The Media Guild
            11722 Sorrento Valley Road
            Suite E
            San Diego, CA 92121
            (619) 755-9191

Originally, an "ABC After School Special," this video presents the story of a teen rock band under pressure to write and perform sexually explicit music. After the group, Hallie's Comet, loses a Battle of the Bands to another group with raunchy lyrics, they modify their act with more vulgar language and a more revealing outfit for the female lead singer. After some success, they realize they have been used by a sleazy rock music promoter and break away to reform a new career with a hit song about freedom and rock music.

Journalistic Freedom
Type: 3/4" or 1/2" color videocassette
Length: 30 min.
Cost: Purchase $100
Date: 1973
Source: Nebraska Educational Television/Council
            on Higher Education
            P.O. Box 8311
            Lincoln, NE 68501
            (402) 472-3611

Re-creates the events leading to the incarceration of journalist Peter Bridges in 1972. Bridges refused to reveal the source for a story, and the film explores the dilemma among freedom of the press, shield laws, and judicial procedures.

Justice Black and the Bill of Rights

Type: 16mm color film, ³/₄″ or ¹/₂″ color videocassette
Length: 32 min.
Date: 1969
Cost: Rental $73 (film); purchase $550 (film), $330 (video)
Source: Phoenix/BFA Films
            468 Park Avenue South
            New York, NY 10016
            (212) 684-5910

A thought-provoking interview with Supreme Court Justice Hugo Black, this production provides a forum for discussion on the absolutist theory of individual rights. CBS news correspondents Eric Severeid and Martin Agronsky are the interviewers. An excellent slice of constitutional and Supreme Court history.

Justice Is a Constant Struggle

Type: ¹/₂″ color videocassette
Length: 28 min.
Cost: Rental $40; purchase $295
Date: 1988
Source: University of California at Berkeley, Extension Media Center
            2176 Shattuck Avenue
            Berkeley, CA 94704
            (510) 642-5578

Narrated by the oral history author Studs Terkel, this video chronicles the accomplishments of the National Lawyers Guild and the role it has played in support of civil liberties. It describes the work the Guild did in opposing the Army–McCarthy hearings and the investigations of the U.S. House Un-American Activities Committee (HUAC) during the 1950s and 1960s. Recent issues the Guild has been involved with include the labor movement and sanctuary for Latin American political refugees.

Mr. Justice Douglas

Type: 16mm color film, ³/₄″ or ¹/₂″ color videocassette
Length: 52 min.
Cost: Rental $45; purchase $330
Date: 1974
Source: Carousel Film and Video
            260 Fifth Avenue
            New York, NY 10016
            (212) 683-1660

An interview with Supreme Court Justice William O. Douglas provides an insight into one of the great liberal justices and the decisions of the Court since 1940. Eric Severeid of CBS News is the interviewer.

News—A Free Press

Type: 16mm color film, ³/₄″ or ¹/₂″ color videocassette
Length: 15 min.
Cost: Rental $20; not available for purchase
Date: 1977
Source: Indiana University
            Audio-Visual Center
            Bloomington, IN 47405
            (812) 855-8087

This educational film is suitable for showing how a free press operates under the constraints of fairness. Discusses the need for a free flow of information and objectivity in the press.

A Night in the Art Gallery

Type: 16mm color film, ³/₄″ or ¹/₂″ color videocassette
Length: 18 min.
Cost: Rental $40; purchase $375 (film), $195 (video)
Date: 1984
Source: Filmakers Library, Inc.
            133 East 58th Street, Suite 703A
            New York, NY 10022
            (212) 805-4980

This short, animated film presents a different view of censorship and political repression. It satirizes China's Cultural Revolution and the political repression it produced.

Noam Chomsky, Parts I & II

Type: ¹/₂″ and ³/₄″ color videocassette
Length: 60 min.
Cost: Purchase $59.95 (¹/₂″), $79.95 (³/₄″)
Date: 1990
Source: PBS Video
            1320 Braddock Place
            Alexandria, VA 22314
            (800) 424-7963

Bill Moyers interviews "America's Leading Dissenter," Noam Chomsky. Chomsky discusses his life and political philosophies as well as the events of the Vietnam War protests in which he was intimately involved. Chomsky believes that there is a decline in political democracy in America and provides his arguments in this regard.

Of Monkeys and Men

Type: 16mm color film
Length: 30 min.

Cost: Rental $12.15; purchase $250
Date: 1968
Source: Indiana University
           Audio-Visual Center
           Bloomington, IN 47405
           (812) 855-8087

Records the events of the 1925 Scopes trial and provides background for a discussion on the controversy of teaching evolution in the public schools. John Scopes and others are interviewed, as well as a presentation of several speeches of leading Tennessee politicians of the time.

The Pentagon Papers
Type: 3/4" or 1/2" color videocassette
Length: 14 min.
Cost: $99
Date: 1973
Source: Videocassette-Journal Films, Inc.
           930 Pitner Avenue
           Evanston, IL 60202
           (800) 323-5448

The nature of government information and the demand for a free flow of information are demonstrated in this film on the Pentagon Papers case. The free speech implications of the government's decision to withhold information on a public policy matter are discussed.

Point of Order
Type: 1/2" black & white videocassette
Length: 107 min.
Cost: Purchase $79.95
Date: 1961
Source: Zenger Video
           10200 Jefferson Boulevard
           P.O. Box 802
           Culver City, CA 90232
           (800) 421-4246

This is a documentary of the Army–McCarthy hearings into the allegation of Communist influence in the U.S. Army made by Wisconsin Senator Joseph McCarthy in the 1950s. An introduction by the actor Paul Newman provides the stepping-off point to this collection of newsreel footage.

Porky's II: The Next Day
Type: 3/4" or 1/2" color videocassette
Length: 100 min.

Cost: Purchase $29.98
Date: 1983
Source: Movies Unlimited
           6736 Castor Avenue
           Philadelphia, PA 19149
           (800) 523-0823

This is the sequel to the first of a three-part teen sex farce popular in the early 1980s. Though there is little educational value in the film, it is one of the few popular movies appealing to teenagers with a censorship theme. The main plot centers around a reactionary physical education teacher who demands the school's production of a Shakespearean play be banned or expurgated. The film is rated R.

Pornography: The Double Message

Type: 3/4″ color videocassette
Length: 28 min.
Cost: Rental $55; purchase $300
Date: 1985
Source: Filmakers Library, Inc.
           133 East 58th Street
           New York, NY 10022
           (212) 808-4980

This highly acclaimed production examines the correlation between pornography and criminal behavior. It reports on several studies that show that images of rape, domination, and violent pornography create an insensitivity toward rape victims. The program includes some sexually explicit material.

Rate It X

Type: 16mm film, 1/2″ color videocassette
Length: 93 min.
Cost: Rental $225 (film) and $150 (video); purchase $350 (film and
           video)
Date: 1986
Source: Women Make Movies
           225 Lafayette Street, Suite 206-7
           New York, NY 10012
           (212) 925-0606

This documentary on sexism examines the treatment of women in a wide range of activities. A narrator/interviewer visits a bank, toy stores, a fundamentalist church, and a suburban baker who makes a torso-shaped cake. One major facet of the film is an examination of the treatment of women as projected in the images at the country's largest sex emporium.

Red Squad

Type: 3/4″ black & white videocassette
Length: 45 min.
Cost: Rental $70; purchase $375
Date: 1972
Source: Cinema Guild
         Division of Document Associates
         1697 Broadway
         New York, NY 10019
         (212) 246-5522

A humorous look at police surveillance and the illegal spying on ordinary citizens. The film chronicles the New York City Red Squad, a police unit founded in 1912 to combat subversives. It depicts the filmmakers becoming a target of the squad as well.

Release of Information—Or Knowing When To Open Your Mouth and Close the File

Type: 3/4″ color videocassette
Length: 39 min.
Cost: Purchase $95
Date: 1978
Source: U.S. National Audiovisual Center
         8700 Edgeworth Drive
         Capital Heights, MD 20743-3701
         (301) 763-1896

Designed as an instructional film to aid citizens in the procurement of government files through the Privacy Act of 1974 and the Freedom of Information Act. Other provisions for obtaining information on drugs, alcohol, sickle cell anemia, and the Veterans Administration are also addressed.

Religious Deception in the Schools

Type: 3/4″ color videocassette
Length: 60 min.
Cost: Purchase $19.95
Date: 1983
Source: Video Bible Library, Inc.
         Box 17515
         Portland, OR 97213
         (206) 892-7707

Argues that secular humanism as a religious precept is being indoctrinated into the minds of schoolchildren. Interviews with teachers, students, and religious leaders are included in the program.

Religious Liberty
Type: 3/4″ or 1/2″ color videocassette
Length: 30 min.
Cost: Purchase $49.95
Date: 1972
Source: American Humanist Association
            7 Harwood Drive
            P.O. Box 146
            Amherst, NY 14226-0146
            (800) 743-6646

Features a debate between Glenn Archer, director of Americans United for Separation of Church and State, and Stanley Lowell, editor of *Church and State* magazine. Both speakers make strong cases for maintaining the integrity of the traditional constitutional relationship of church and state.

A Respectable Lie
Type: 3/4″ color videocassette
Length: 30 min.
Cost: Purchase $40
Date: 1980
Source: Women in Focus
            849 Beatty Street
            Vancouver, BC U6B2M6 Canada
            (604) 682-5848

A feminist film about the exploitation of women in the pornography industry. The methods for hiring women to perform in sex films are described.

School Prayer, Gun Control and the Right To Assemble
Type: 3/4″ or 1/2″ color videocassette
Length: 60 min.
Cost: Purchase $29.95
Date: 1984
Source: Films Incorporated Educational
            5547 North Ravenswood Avenue
            Chicago, IL 60640-1199
            (800) 323-4222

Using a hypothetical community, the problems of the First and Second Amendments are brought to light. The role of the Supreme Court in determining public policy is interwoven into the story line.

Seasonal Differences: Constitutional Rights
Type: 1/2″ and 3/4″ color videocassettes
Length: 45 min.

Cost: Purchase $395 (1/2″), $425 (3/4″)
Date: 1988
Source: Barr Films
12801 Schabarum Avenue
P.O. Box 7878
Irwindale, CA 91706-7878
(800) 234-7878

This film dramatizes the difficulties some students experience in standing up for their religious freedom and First Amendment rights. Mark, a Jewish student, files a complaint with his high school principal over the display of a Nativity scene on school grounds. His friend Dana, a Christian, at first clashes with him over the complaint and organizes a counter-protest. As the situation gets out of hand, Mark experiences anti-Semitic threats and discrimination. Dana sees the trouble this has brought to his friend and offers to help make peace with the student body.

The Secret File
Type: 1/2″ color videocassette
Length: 58 min.
Cost: Purchase $79
Date: 1987
Source: Films Incorporated Educational
5547 North Ravenswood Avenue
Chicago, IL 60640-1199
(800) 323-4222

This is a chronicle of the true story of Penn Kimball, a university professor who discovered that a secret file had been kept on him by the U.S. government. Using the provisions of the Freedom of Information Act, Kimball learned that the file had been started because he was considered a subversive. The events surrounding his attempt to clear his name are presented, and a discussion on government spying is provided.

Sex for Sale—The Urban Battleground
Type: 3/4″ or 1/2″ color videocassette
Length: 45 min.
Cost: Purchase $29.95
Date: 1977
Source: CRM/McGraw-Hill Films
2215 Faraday Avenue
Carlsbad, CA 92008
(619) 237-1010

Addresses the problems of sex-oriented businesses and prostitution in most major cities. Discusses the problems of pornography and urban decay and the myth of victimless crimes such as prostitution. Documentary footage from major urban centers is shown.

The Speaker—A Film about Freedom

Type: 16mm color film, $3/4''$ color videocassette
Length: 42 min.
Cost: Purchase $545 (film), $475 (video)
Date: 1977
Source: American Library Association
        50 East Huron Street
        Chicago, IL 60611
        (800) 545-2433

Loosely based on the work of Dr. William Shockley, a scientist who believes in the genetic inferiority of nonwhite races, *The Speaker* demonstrates the need for and difficulties in defending intellectual freedom. A hypothetical high school speakers committee invites such a scientist to make a presentation. The film demonstrates various stereotypical arguments against controversial speakers.

The Supreme Court's Holy Battles

Type: $1/2''$ and $3/4''$ color videocassette
Length: 60 min.
Cost: Purchase $59.95 ($1/2''$), $79.95 ($3/4''$)
Date: 1989
Source: PBS Video
        1320 Braddock Place
        Alexandria, VA 22314
        (800) 424-7963

A series of interviews examines and discusses a variety of religious freedom topics. Noted politicians, scholars, and historians present various political and constitutional viewpoints, as well as students' and citizens' opinions. Public funding of church-supported educational institutions, tax exemptions for religious institutions, school prayer, and the U.S. motto "In God We Trust" are covered in these discussions.

Sympathy for the Devil

Type: $3/4''$ or $1/2''$ color videocassette
Length: 110 min.
Cost: Purchase $29.95
Date: 1970
Source: Movies Unlimited
        6736 Castor Avenue
        Philadelphia, PA 19149
        (800) 523-0823

An early rock-and-roll musical, this film provides a vehicle for director Jean-Luc Goddard's views on contemporary problems such as crime, pornography, black power, and fascism. The film stars Mick Jagger and the Rolling Stones, who also provide much of the soundtrack.

To Speak or Not To Speak
Type: 16mm color film
Length: 11 min.
Cost: Purchase $195
Date: 1972
Source: International Film Bureau
332 South Michigan Avenue
Chicago, IL 60604-4382
(800) 432-2241

Uses animation to show that people who do not inform themselves about politics are in danger of allowing a dictatorial government. Instead of narration, the characters' words and symbols are animated.

United States Supreme Court—Guardian of the Constitution
Type: 16mm color film, 3/4″ or 1/2″ color videocassette
Length: 24 min.
Cost: Purchase ($575 (film), $300 (video)
Date: 1973
Source: Encyclopaedia Britannica Educational Corp.
425 North Michigan Avenue
Chicago, IL 60611
(800) 554-9862

An excellent history of the Supreme Court, this film depicts significant cases from the Court's beginning in 1789 to the early 1970s. Former Vice-president Hubert Humphrey describes the role of the Court in protecting individual rights in the latter part of the production.

U.S. v. Nixon
Type: 1/2″ color videocassette
Length: 15 min.
Cost: Purchase $69
Date: 1986
Source: Zenger Video
10200 Jefferson Boulevard
P.O. Box 802
Culver City, CA 90232
(800) 421-4246

News footage and interviews present the celebrated executive-privilege case *U.S. v. Nixon*. As the Watergate scandal unfolded, special prosecutors Archibald Cox and Leon Jaworski attempted to obtain documents from President Nixon. Claiming the documents were confidential communications vital to the leadership of the nation, Nixon denied access on the grounds of executive privilege. The Court's reversal of Nixon's refusal and the outcome of the case are detailed.

What Johnny Can't Read
Type: ³/₄" or ¹/₂" color videocassette
Length: 13 min.
Cost: Rental $175; purchase $175
Date: 1980
Source: Carousel Films, Inc.
241 East 34th Street, Room 304
New York, NY 10016
(212) 683-1660

Mike Wallace interviews a Texas housewife who has monitored school textbooks for objectionable material for over 18 years. In this film that was originally broadcast as a *60 Minutes* report, Ms. Gabler answers critics who say she is practicing censorship.

Words To Live By
Type: ¹/₂" color videocassette
Length: 45 min.
Cost: Purchase $395
Date: 1990
Source: Pyramid Films
Box 1048
Santa Monica, CA 90406
(800) 421-2304

Originally a CBS "School Special," this video dramatizes the problems students have in exercising their freedom of the press. Two high school students are suspended for publishing and distributing an underground newspaper. They learn of the price they must pay for freedom of the press, but the school authorities discover they must follow the laws of their state and the Constitution.

Databases

The following databases provide useful resources and services for research on the topic of intellectual freedom. This is not an exhaustive list, but major databases from law, news, and social science research are included. These three subject areas provide a basis for research in this topic.

BNA ONLINE
Bureau of National Affairs, Inc.
1231 25th Street, NW
Washington, DC 20037
(202) 452-4132

Open to anyone, this database makes several Bureau of National Affairs publications available in electronic format. It can be accessed through numerous vendors, and its scope includes federal legislation, information on intellectual property, current issues, and many business services. Of the 80 databases, the most useful for this area of study are BNA California Case Law Daily, which covers significant court cases from the state and federal courts; BNA New York Case Law Daily, which is similar to the above; and the BNA Washington Insider, which includes the opinions of the Supreme Court, the table of contents of the *Federal Register,* and brief synopses of congressional hearings and floor action. Also useful are Individual Employment Rights, covering privacy issues and other employee rights, and U.S. Law Week, a comprehensive report on all Supreme Court activities.

BNA PLUS
Bureau of National Affairs, Inc.
1231 25th Street, NW
Washington, DC 20037
(202) 452-4323

Open to all BNA subscribers on a fee or no-charge basis and open to all nonsubscribers on a fee-only basis. BNA PLUS is a customized research and document delivery service. Services include annotated bibliographies, information packets, current topics, analytic reports, and commercial database searches. Also, government information is available on a rush delivery service and there is a "Congress on Diskette" database containing facts on all members of Congress.

Congressional Information Service, CIS/Index
Congressional Information Service, Inc.
4520 East-West Highway, Suite 800
Bethesda, MD 20814-3389
(301) 654-1550

CIS/Index as well as ASI (American Statistics Index) are accessible online through DIALOG Information Services. This is an index service to all U.S. congressional publications and legislation. It also accesses demographic statistics, international statistics, state constitutional revision documents, and Supreme Court records and briefs. CIS offers custom searches from these databases. It is also affiliated with Greenwood Press, a major publisher of texts in this subject area.

DIALOG Information Services
3460 Hillview Avenue
Palo Alto, CA 94304
(415) 858-3785

All services are available to any person or agency through a purchase order or on a subscription basis. Many libraries offer DIALOG services to qualified patrons. The KNOWLEDGE INDEX version is available for home or business use via personal computing. DIALOG is one of the largest online information retrieval systems in the world. It contains holdings of over 370 databases. Some of the more useful ones for research in this topic are America: History and Life, CIS/Index, Legal Resource Index, SOCIALSCI SEARCH, and U.S. Political Science Documents.

HUMAN RIGHTS INTERNET (HRI)
Harvard Law School
Pound Hall, Room 401
Cambridge, MA 02138
(617) 495-9924

Services on a fee-only basis. Though this database service is international in scope and covers all issues of human rights, intellectual freedom concerns form a significant portion of the data available. HRI is an international communications network gathering information on the condition of human rights in over 90 countries. It publishes the *North American Human Rights Directory* in addition to many international directories. The online service maintains and provides searches from the HRI Bibliography and HRI Organizations databases. The HRI Bibliography is a citation service to all articles and work in the Human Rights Internet Reporter.

LEGAL FORUM
CompuServe Information Service
5000 Arlington Centre Boulevard
P.O. Box 20212
Columbus, OH 43220
(614) 457-8600

All services are available without restrictions, commercially online via CompuServe, Inc. Also known as LAWSIG, LEGAL FORUM is an interactive forum for the legal profession and interested individuals. It serves as an active message base and holds data libraries on topics such as current legal issues, law school information, and public domain software.

LEGI-SLATE
111 Massachusetts Avenue
Washington, DC 20001
(202) 898-2300

This service is available by subscription only. LEGI-SLATE is designed to track federal legislative and regulatory information. There are six services: (1) Congressional Service, for congressional bills data, (2) Bill Text

Service, for full-text, online, of all bills and resolutions since the 99th Congress, (3) Federal Register Service, (4) Member Profile and Rating Service, for data on representatives and senators, (5) News Journal, which includes reports from the *Washington Post*, the *National Journal*, and the *Congressional Quarterly Weekly Report*, and (6) Press Briefing Service, for full-text of transcripts of White House press conferences and briefings.

PAIS INTERNATIONAL
Public Affairs Information Service
521 West 43rd Street
New York, NY 10036-4396

This database can be accessed through BRS Information Technologies, BRS/AfterDark, Data-Star, DIALOG, and DIALOG's KNOWLEDGE INDEX. PAIS INTERNATIONAL is an online compilation of the print publications *PAIS Bulletin* and *PAIS Foreign Language Index*. The INTERNATIONAL also provides additional descriptions and abstract-like notes. This is one of the better bibliographic resources for government information and social science research.

WESTLAW
West Publishing Company
50 West Kellogg Boulevard
P.O. Box 64526
St. Paul, MN 55164-0526
(612) 228-2500

WESTLAW is available by contract with the West Publishing Co. This is the computer-assisted legal research service of the largest legal publisher in the United States. It is the best legal information service, though the LEXIS service of the Lawyers Cooperative is a very competitive product. It contains access to all federal and state case law and has topical materials, including a major source of First Amendment law. The Index to Legal Periodicals is also included online.

WILSONLINE
H. W. Wilson Co.
950 University Avenue
Bronx, NY 10452
(800) 367-6770

Wilson products are available without restrictions. Two of the many databases on WILSONLINE that are useful for research are the *Index to Legal Periodicals* and the *Social Sciences Index*. These are online versions of the printed indexes of the same name. The *Index to Legal Periodicals* is also available on WESTLAW and LEXIS.

CD-ROMs

CD-ROM products offer another useful source of bibliographic information for research. CD-ROMs provide relative ease of acquisition, similar to printed reference sources, and the power of computerized searching. The following are a select number of available CD-ROM products of some relevance to study and research on intellectual freedom.

Congressional Masterfile 2

Publisher:	Congressional Information Service
Distributor:	Congressional Information Service
	4520 East-West Highway, Suite 100
	Bethesda, MD 20814
	(800) 638-8380
Equipment:	IBM PC-AT or compatible
Drive:	Any reader meeting High Sierra standard
Software:	Quantum Access
Price:	Current subscription $1760; retrospective subscription $8800
Updates:	Quarterly

This product is a complete index and abstract service of all congressional publications since 1970. Congressional Masterfile 1 is the same product for publications from 1789 to 1969. Congressional hearings, reports, documents, and committee prints are among the many items covered.

The Constitution Papers

Publisher:	Electronic Text Corp.
Distributor:	Software Resources; CALI, Inc.
	CALI Inc.
	526 East Quail Road
	Orem, UT 84057
	(801) 226-6886
Equipment:	IBM PC-XT/AT or compatible
Drive:	Hitachi, NEC, Sony, Toshiba
Software:	Word Cruncher
Price:	$495 Software Resources; $99, CALI
Updates:	None

This unique product holds the full text of all the constitutions of the 13 original states, the U.S. Constitution, the Magna Carta, the Federalist Papers, *Common Sense* by Thomas Paine, the Codfishery Debates, and a number of documents on colonial and Revolutionary War history and the Constitutional Convention.

National Newspaper Index

Publisher: Information Access Co.
Distributor: Information Access Co.
326 Lakeside Drive
Foster City, CA 94404
(800) 227-8431
Equipment: IBM or compatible
Drive: Hitachi or Sony
Software: Proprietary
Price: $3200
Updates: Monthly

This is the CD-ROM index to five major newspapers: the *New York Times, Wall Street Journal, Christian Science Monitor, Washington Post,* and *Los Angeles Times.* This is a very useful source for searching censorship incidents on a national scale as well as for identifying legal and social trends in intellectual freedom.

PAIS on CD-ROM

Publisher: Public Affairs Information Service
Distributor: Public Affairs Information Service
512 West 43rd Street
New York, NY 10036
(212) 736-6629
Equipment: IBM PC-XT/AT, PS/2, or compatible with 640K RAM
Drive: Sony, Hitachi, Phillips, or Microsoft Extensions
Software: Online Computer Systems
Price: $1795
Updates: Quarterly

This is the CD-ROM version of PAIS INTERNATIONAL, the online database containing *PAIS Bulletin* and *PAIS Foreign Language Index.* It is a bibliographic index to social and public policy literature published throughout the world in English, French, German, Italian, Portuguese, and Spanish.

Social Science Index

Publisher: H. W. Wilson Co.
Distributor: H. W. Wilson Co.
950 University Avenue
Bronx, NY 10452
(800) 367-6770
Equipment: IBM PC with hard disk and 640K RAM
Drive: Hitachi, Sony, or Phillips
Software: H. W. Wilson
Price: $1295
Updates: Quarterly

The CD-ROM version of the major index of social science publications, this covers over 300 English-language titles. Subjects include economics, geography, health, planning, and sociology.

U.S. Civics/Citizenship

Publisher:	IBM version, Quanta Press
Distributor:	Jason Enterprises
	218 Pine Street
	Buffalo, NY 14024
	(716) 852-6711
Equipment:	IBM PC-XT/AT, PS 2, or compatible
Drive:	Hitachi, NEC, Phillips, Sony, Toshiba, AMDEK, Denon, Chinon, Panasonic, Dagger, and various Juke Boxes
Software:	TestWare (Unibase)
Price:	$99
Updates:	Unscheduled
Publisher:	Macintosh version,Wayzata Technology
Distributor:	Wayzata Technology
	P.O. Box 225
	Farmington, MN 55024
	(612) 460-8438
Equipment:	Apple Macintosh
Drive:	Sony
Software:	Proprietary
Price:	$99
Updates:	Annual

Designed to assist persons seeking U.S. citizenship, this CD-ROM has a reference manual for citizenship instructors that is useful for all civics classes. The information included covers U.S. history and government structure and details the Constitution and Bill of Rights. It was compiled by the U.S. Immigration and Naturalization Service.

Television Programs

Several television shows are designed to present conservative and liberal opinion on a wide variety of topics. Most often in a talk show or debate-like format, these programs are not only an exercise in free speech but also often feature issues directly related to the four freedoms of the First Amendment. Some of these programs, especially the investigative "magazines," are designed to be more informational than debate oriented. The following are by no means all of the most relevant shows but represent some of the best and more well-known ones.

Crossfire
Michael Kinsley and John Sununu, hosts
CNN, 7:30 p.m. EST (check local listings for exact time) Formerly a debate between liberal Michael Kinsley, editor of *The New Republic*, and conservative Patrick Buchanan, John Sununu replaced Buchanan as the conservative voice while Buchanan ran for the Republican presidential nomination against President George Bush in 1992. With Sununu in the right-hand seat, the program features sharp, rapid-fire, and often angry debates on current political and social issues. Occasionally Robert Evans or Bob Novak fills in as the conservative commentator.

Firing Line
William F. Buckley, Jr., host
PBS, Sundays, 6:00 p.m. EST (check local listings for exact time)

One of the oldest informational news and viewpoint talk shows, *Firing Line* has been hosted by conservative writer and editor of the *National Review* William F. Buckley, Jr., since it began in 1971. Though not all programs are on political issues or content directly relevant to the First Amendment, this is one of the best programs for viewpoints, especially by conservatives, on a wide variety of topics.

McLaughlin Group
John McLaughlin, host
PBS, Sunday afternoons or Friday evenings (check local listings for exact times)

In this conservative-liberal debate on current political issues, including congressional and Supreme Court events, conservative commentator John McLaughlin hosts several commentators, with liberals such as Morton Kondracke and Fred Barnes of the *New Republic* and conservatives such as Patrick Buchanan before his run for the Republican presidential nomination in 1992. The debates are often strong, opinionated, and occasionally a free-for-all. Other commentators include Eleanor Clift and Jack Germond.

Nightline
Ted Koppel, host
ABC, weeknights, midnight EST

Considered to be one of the best news-interview shows, *Nightline* features a wide variety of social, political, and economic topics. *Nightline* has gained a reputation for extremely timely coverage and analysis of current, "hot" topics. For example, one program interviewed the current president of L. Ron Hubbard's Church of Scientology with an analysis and criticism of the church's fundraising methods and theology.

A Question of Balance
Fred Friendly, host
PBS, weeknights, various times (check local listings for exact times)

This "town meeting" format is hosted by the eminent broadcast journalist Fred Friendly and features prominent individuals, conservative to liberal, on major, current constitutional issues. Friendly uses a Socratic method to draw opinions out of the panelists. For example, one show featured Nat Hentoff, Dinesh D'Souza, several students and professors from Stanford University, the presidents of Yale University and Bard College, and several others on the multicultural–hate speech regulations such as university rules prohibiting racial epithets or university policies that include a list of words not permitted to be spoken on college campuses.

60 Minutes
Mike Wallace, Morley Safer, Ed Bradley, and Leslie Stahl, hosts
CBS, Sundays, 7:00 p.m. EST

The oldest and one of the best investigative news-gathering shows, *60 Minutes* has set the industry standards for this type of programming. The show is divided into four segments, three on a topic of political or social concern and the fourth, generally, humorous commentary by Andy Rooney. This and other investigative shows are known to challenge local, state, and federal governmental authorities to address individual grievances.

Tony Brown's Journal
Tony Brown, host
PBS, Sundays, 11:00 a.m. (check local listings for exact time)

This interview-news program is designed to discuss current political and social issues of interest, primarily, to Black Americans. It features journalist Tony Brown interviewing prominent individuals before a live audience. This is one of the best programs on issues relevant to Black Americans.

20/20
Hugh Downs and Barbara Walters, hosts
ABC, Fridays, 10:00 p.m. EST

This investigative news show features two of the most widely known and highly respected news reporters, Hugh Downs and Barbara Walters. Though not as well known for tough investigative journalism as *60 Minutes,* *20/20*'s format is similar and also features segments that address grievances against local, state, and federal governmental authorities.

Educational Software and Simulation Games

The following educational software can be used in a classroom setting to teach at least one aspect of intellectual freedom.

The Amendments to the Constitution

Software:	5 1/4″ or 3 1/2″ floppy disk
Hardware Requirements:	IBM PC, PC XT, PCjr., PC AT and compatibles; color graphics adapter
Memory Requirements:	16K
Operating System:	PC-DOS 2.0 or greater, MS-DOS
Date:	1984
Cost:	Disk, $69.95
Source:	Classroom Consortia Media Inc.
	57 Bay Street
	Staten Island, NY 10301
	(718) 447-6777
Grade level recommendation:	6–12

This program is designed to introduce the contents of the amendments of the Constitution and to the procedures for the amendment process. The Bill of Rights receives extensive coverage. Students interact with situations that apply to each amendment. A demo disk is available.

The Bill of Rights

Software:	5 1/4″ or 3 1/2″ disk
Hardware Requirements:	Apple II+, IIe; IBM PC
Memory Requirements:	64K
Operating Language:	BASIC
Date:	1987
Cost:	Disk, $45
Source:	Oronoque Computer Concepts Inc.
	RFD #1
	Williamstown, VT 05679
	(802) 433-6022
Grade level recommendation:	7–12

Students access the Bill of Rights through a computer database that includes twenty actual case studies from American history. The user is asked to find explanations for each case with information located on these individual rights. A printout of results is produced at the end of the exercise.

Case Study: Tinker vs. Des Moines

Software:	5 1/4″ or 3 1/2″ disk
Hardware Requirements:	Apple II+, IIe; IBM PC

Memory Requirements:	64K
Operating Language:	BASIC
Date:	1984
Cost:	Disk, $45
Source:	Oronoque Computer Concepts Inc.
	RFD #1
	Williamstown, VT 05679
	(802) 433-6022
Grade level recommendation:	7–12

Introduces the student to the landmark student rights case *Tinker v. Des Moines Independent School District.* Using the classic case-study method, the student identifies the legal issues of importance. The program asks the student to render an opinion after examining the Constitution and legal precedents provided. A database of useful Constitutional phrases is also included. A printout is produced at the end of the exercise.

The Constitution and the Government of the United States

Software:	3 program disks and 3 backup disks
Hardware Requirements:	Apple II, II+, IIe, IIc
Memory Requirements:	None
Operating System:	Apple
Date:	1987
Cost:	All disks and six booklets, $179
Source:	Educational Activities, Inc.
	1937 Grand Avenue
	Baldwin, NY 11510
	(516) 223-4666
Grade level recommendation:	7–12

This program provides excellent coverage of the U.S. Constitution with emphasis on government powers and individual rights. Each disk contains four lessons, a court case option, a glossary of terms used in the lesson, and instructions. Scores and progress are shown in a report card at the end. The program keeps a record of the results and can store up to fifty student records.

Constitutional Trivia

Software:	5 1/4" or 3 1/2" disk
Hardware Requirements:	Commodore 64
Operating System:	Commodore
Memory Requirements:	64K
Date:	1986
Cost:	Disk, $25

Source: Micro Learningware
P.O. Box 9762
Ambay, MN 56010-9762
(800) 222-5113
Grade level recommendation: 5–12

This challenging program has two versions that ask the student to answer a series of multiple choice questions on every major aspect of the U.S. Constitution, including the Bill of Rights. The teacher has the option of setting the program for content accuracy over speed. A complete summary of the student's performance is provided at the end.

Decisions, Decisions: Television: A Study of Media Ethics

Software:	5 1/4″ or 3 1/2″ disk
Hardware Requirements:	Apple II, II+, IIe, IIc; IBM PC, PC jr.
Operating System:	Apple or MS-DOS
Memory Requirements:	64K
Cost:	Disk, $89.95
Source:	Tom Snyder Productions Inc.
	90 Sherman Street
	Cambridge, MA 02138
	(800) 342-0236
Grade level recommendation:	5–12

Designed for use by teachers, this program is very useful as a history tool and as a tool for journalism classes. The content emphasis is on the dilemma between citizen privacy and news gathering. The instructional value extends to critical thinking and problem-solving skills. The program requires extensive teacher-student interaction.

Intolerable Acts

Software:	5 1/4″ or 3 1/2″ disk
Hardware Requirements:	Apple II+, IIe; IBM PC; Printer
Operating Language:	BASIC
Memory Requirements:	64K
Cost:	Disk, $45
Source:	Oronoque Computer Concepts Inc.
	RFD #1
	Williamstown, VT 05679
	(802) 433-6022
Grade level recommendation:	7–12

An excellent history tool on the American Revolution and the Intolerable Acts, including the quartering of troops and the closing of Boston Harbor in reprisal for the Boston Tea Party, this program also provides students with an understanding of the importance of individual rights. The student is asked to apply one of the acts to an actual situation. The explanation of the event they describe is then printed out as a record for the teacher.

U.S. Constitution

Software:	5 1/4″ or 3 1/2″ disk
Hardware Requirements:	IBM PC and compatibles, PCjr., PC XT, PC AT; CGA card
Operating System:	PC-DOS 2.0 or greater; MS-DOS
Operating Language:	C
Memory Requirement:	128K
Cost:	Disk, $69.95
Source:	Classroom Consortia Media
	57 Bay Street
	Staten Island, NY 10301
	(718) 447-6777
Grade level recommendation:	6–12

This courseware package has a strong emphasis on the amendments to the U.S Constitution. Each amendment is keyed to descriptive graphics. The student is faced with two crossword puzzles and a set of multiple-choice questions. The program includes case studies designed to simulate trials based on the Amendments. After examining the positive and negative options, the user is required to make a decision.

Glossary

absolute privilege   A defense against libel. Three types of communication are absolutely immune from charges of libel: (1) privileged communications, such as those between husband and wife, doctor and patient, lawyer and client, and minister and parishioner; (2) communications involving prior consent, where a person agrees to an act that subsequently libels him or her; and (3) political broadcasts.

absolutism test   A constitutional test for free speech whose proponents, most notably justices Hugo Black and William O. Douglas, argue that the government has absolutely no power to restrict or abridge expression. The absolutist test has never been validated in any court case.

actual malice   A test for libel. A defamatory statement must be made with knowledge that it is false or with reckless disregard for the truth to be libelous in those situations where such actual malice must be shown, most notably when statements are made about public officials or public figures.

advocacy of action   To promote or call for conduct or action to be taken. The Supreme Court has made a distinction, for free expression purposes, of the advocacy of illegal acts between mere advocacy of ideas, which is protected, and advocacy of action. To hold ideas or to express ideas that, if carried out, would be illegal but without promoting such action is a protected form of dissent. For example, to express the belief that the government should be overthrown is constitutionally protected speech, but to advocate an actual act that would overthrow the government is unprotected speech.

amicus curiae brief   A "friend of the court" legal argument, an amicus curiae brief is a legal document filed before a court that is hearing a case.

The brief is written by a person or group who wishes to support one side in the case. The amicus curiae brief is not filed by the principal participants in the case but by a person or group who hopes to influence the outcome. Many federal and state cases, especially the appeals courts and Supreme Court cases, have amicus curiae briefs filed in important constitutional cases such as First Amendment issues.

art porn   Pornographic films of the 1970s that were considered to be more acceptable than the usual pornographic film. Art porn never realized the acceptability that was expected after the initial success of the first major art porn film *Deep Throat*. Though *Deep Throat* was seen by millions of men and women, the phenomenon died after *Behind the Green Door* and *The Devil in Miss Jones* failed to capitalize on similar audience popularity within the next two years.

Article 19   The section of the United Nations Universal Declaration of Human Rights that embodies the concept of intellectual freedom into international law. Adopted in 1948, it is not guaranteed by legal treaty but is considered de facto international law. Article 19 is also the name of an international human rights organization.

average person   A legal concept required as part of the *Roth, Miller,* and *Memoirs* standards to prove obscenity. In each of these tests, an "average person" is an adult member of society, not part of an identifiable group normally understood to be susceptible to the influence of obscenity, such as minors or sex offenders, who applies contemporary community standards to judge whether or not something is obscene.

aversion   A defense against obscenity charges, "aversion" is the argument that the average person would be so disgusted by the alleged obscene item that the item would not excite or titillate him or her. The argument is used to attempt to show that only those groups with a proclivity toward that type of book or film would be interested in it and that such works would not corrupt or ensnare the average person.

bad tendency test   A constitutional test of free expression that states that any form of speech that has a tendency to lead to substantial evil can be prohibited. This test was established in *Gitlow v. New York* (1925) but has been rejected as a valid test in subsequent court cases.

balancing test   A constitutional test of free expression. When the right to free speech runs into conflict with other rights, such as the right to privacy or a fair trial, then the competing rights must be balanced or weighed to determine which has priority. This has the effect of prohibiting certain acts of free expression that would be protected under normal circumstances but are not protected when in conflict with these certain other rights.

Bill of Rights Generally, the first ten amendments to the United States Constitution listing individual rights. However, many states have a bill of rights with similar individual freedoms in their respective state constitutions.

blacklisting Generally, the act of excluding qualified persons from their work or social engagements because their views or beliefs are considered unacceptable. The most well known case of blacklisting occurred during the early 1950s against writers and actors in Hollywood. The U.S. House Un-American Activities Committee and Senator Joseph McCarthy conducted hearings into Communist influence in Hollywood. Those writers and actors who were hostile to the committee during testimony found limited opportunities for work afterward. Movie producers and studios were influenced by Congress, informants, and noted lobbying groups to make such blacklists.

book burning A severe act of censorship. The decision to burn books is an attempt to eradicate entirely any of the ideas contained within. There have been many acts of book burning throughout history, particularly against religious and scientific works considered heretical by the Christian church. The most famous incidents of book burning in modern times were those mounted by the German Nazi party in the 1930s to eliminate political viewpoints opposed to Nazi policies and theory. As a result, recent decisions by school and government authorities to remove objectionable books by burning them have been met by accusations of Nazism by foes of censorship.

bowdlerize Derived from the English family of Bowdler, it is the act of expurgating or removing words or parts of a work because of objectionable language or ideas. Several Bowdler family members were active in the eighteenth and nineteenth centuries arguing for the censorship of many works. Thomas Bowdler wrote *The Family Shakespeare* and *The Family Gibbon,* editions of the works of William Shakespeare and Edward Gibbon with offensive language removed and with sections rewritten to be more suitable to an assumed audience.

certiorari A legal order from a higher court to a lower court to, literally, deliver the documents in a case. A ruling by the higher court granting certiorari is needed before a case on any matter can be decided by the higher court. If the higher court denies certiorari, the decision of the lower court is final.

chilling effect A legal argument against an act of censorship or an alleged act of censorship. The argument is made that such censorship would cause other creators of similar works, including books, art, or films, to limit what they create in the future for fear it might be censored.

Such a "chilling effect" would eliminate creative works not yet made that otherwise might not be ruled obscene or unacceptable.

chopping The military slang for censorship. Chopping is the process used by military authorities to screen information, even unclassified information, that is being produced by and for journalists. Requests for information are put under an elaborate assessment, with each assessment called a "chop," before being processed and disseminated.

classification at birth The concept within the classification of secret documents that certain works within classified areas, such as nuclear weapons and espionage, are automatically protected and classified before they are actually examined and given a formal classification level. This is the means of protecting sensitive documents prior to any actual official examination of the nature of their secrecy.

classification of documents The method for restricting the dissemination of secret or sensitive government documents and information only to people legally permitted to see those documents. There are four levels of document classification: confidential, secret, top secret, and special intelligence. A "confidential" classification allows the broadest range of individuals able to view the document, ascending up to the strictest category, "special intelligence," which limits severely the number of individuals able to read that document. The nuclear order of battle, or the SIOP (Single Integrated Operational Plan), is an example of a "special intelligence" document. A fifth category, "for official use only," does not classify secret documents but eliminates public dissemination through the Freedom of Information Act.

clear and present danger A criterion in the constitutional test of the exercise of free expression that states that acts or words cannot create a dangerous situation that will bring about "substantive evils" that the government has the right to prevent. Prior to 1969, the "clear and present danger" needed only to be probable to deny the right to express that form of expression. Beginning with the case *Brandenburg v. Ohio* (1969), the danger needs to be imminent.

commercial speech Advertisements and other forms of speech designed to promote a product or service for profit. The Supreme Court has ruled that commercial speech does not enjoy the same protection as speech directed at public issues. Reasonable regulations of commercial speech can be made to control it for the public good.

comstockery Named for Anthony Comstock, the United States' preeminent nineteenth-century anti-pornography crusader, it is an excessive concern with morality and its decline to the point of attacking legitimate books, art, and other activities with false obscenity charges.

George Bernard Shaw coined the phrase, saying to the *New York Times*, "Comstockery is the world's standing joke, at the expense of the United States."

contemporary community standards A central part of the test for obscenity under the *Roth, Miller,* and *Memoirs* rulings, it requires a work to be judged by current, modern-day understandings of what is acceptable to the average person within a community. Under the *Roth* test, the "community" was considered by the Court to be a national standard. With the advent of the current *Miller* test, the "community" is much more local in nature and is defined to be the state or a region within a state.

contempt A restriction on free speech, a person is cited with contempt as a result of words or actions that would unreasonably interfere, in an immediate way, with the administration of justice. Inside a courtroom, a criticism of the judge or other courtroom officer could be considered grounds for contempt and punishable. Outside the courtroom, similar criticism would have to pass other constitutional tests to be declared unprotected.

criminal syndicalism Criminal or illegal anarchy or the act of advocating rebellion, incitement to revolution, or the violent overthrow of the government. Many of the state criminal syndicalism acts made it illegal to exercise free speech in these areas of political discourse.

defamation A form of unprotected speech, defamation is the printed or written or spoken word that tends to injure a person's reputation, causing him or her to be subjected to public hatred or ridicule or financial loss. It can also call into question a person's character, integrity, or morality. In the United States, a remedy for being defamed can be brought into court through a suit for financial reward; however, the Supreme Court has restricted such charges to private citizens. Public officials and public figures must first prove actual malice before an award for defamation can be given.

derivative classification The process within the government of conferring a classified status onto a document or project that would normally not have a classification level by adding data or documents that are classified. When a project that is nonclassified uses classified materials, the entire project then becomes as protected as the classified documents. A prime example was the Pentagon Papers, which originally were not classified until secret documents and information were incorporated into them.

equal-time rule A regulation of broadcasting under the Federal Communications Act of 1934 by which all radio and television stations that offer broadcast time to any candidate for political office must offer equal time to all bonified candidates for that office. Broadcasters do not have to seek out all qualified candidates but must give time if requested. Stations may also choose to offer no time to all candidates instead.

erotica   Literary or artistic works with sexual themes or images that would tend to arouse sexual desire or love. Erotica is not necessarily pornographic or obscene. To be obscene, the work would have to be judged so using a constitutional test.

evolution   The theory that all things in the animal and plant kingdoms have their origins in preexisting types and that the differences between the original types and current species are due to adaptations and modifications that have changed over time through successive generations. The validity of the theory of evolution has been questioned and has been the source of many censorship attempts. Several states had, until recently, laws forbidding the teaching of evolution in public schools.

executive privilege   The principle that the president of the United States does not have to reveal discussions or information communicated in confidence. The principle of executive privilege was first established in the landmark case *Marbury v. Madison* in 1803.

fairness doctrine   A regulation of broadcasting under the rules of the Federal Communications Commission by which radio and television stations must provide "balanced" programming on controversial public issues. This rule is different from the equal-time rule, which deals with access to broadcasting by political candidates, by prohibiting the broadcast of only one point of view or slanted reports of one belief. The fairness doctrine is only used in the evaluation for the re-authorization of a station's license.

fighting words   A form of unprotected speech, fighting words are words that are "personally abusive epithets" that, when said to the ordinary citizen, will most likely tend to inflict injury or cause an immediate breach of the peace. The concept of "fighting words" was established in the case *Chaplinsky v. New Hampshire* in 1942. Fighting words are not necessarily vulgar or obscene, but the emphasis is on whether they are deemed to be able to cause an immediate breach of the peace.

First Amendment   The first of 26 changes or additions to the U.S. Constitution. Added in 1791 as part of the Bill of Rights, it guarantees all citizens four basic intellectual freedoms: freedom of religion, freedom of speech, freedom of the press, and freedom of assembly and association.

forecast rule   A criterion needed to prohibit certain exercises of free expression in public schools. School officials must show that a substantial disruption of or material interference with school activities could be predicted or forecast before they can legally prohibit exercises of free expression. The most important case using the forecast rule is *Tinker v. Des Moines Independent Community School District* (1969).

Helsinki Accords   The human rights agreement of the 1975 Conference on Security and Cooperation in Europe (CSCE). The Helsinki Accords were of prime importance because of the Soviet bloc nations' initial willingness to participate in the improvement of East-West relations and in their tacit support for the documents. The accords include, in Point VII, a commitment to "respect for human rights and fundamental freedoms, including the freedom of thoughts, conscience, religion and belief."

Hicklin **rule**   The first constitutional test for obscenity, the *Hicklin* rule was created in the British case *Regina v. Hicklin*. Under this test, an entire publication could be deemed obscene even if only a single passage in an otherwise unobjectionable work was ruled obscene. Furthermore, it need only be shown that the material be a corrupting influence on impressionable groups, such as youth, to be considered a problem for general reading audiences. Though this was a British case, the argument was used as the test for U.S. publications until it was overturned in *Roth v. United States* in 1957.

hot news   A defense against libel charges. "Hot news" is news that needs to be disseminated to the public without delay. A newspaper can use this defense to show that there was not enough time to investigate the truth or falsehood of a report. If the concept of "hot news" is not proven, then the newspaper would be guilty of reckless disregard for the truth and subject to libel punishment.

incitement   To induce another person to commit a criminal act. In First Amendment cases, this can extend to inflammatory speeches. There is a difference between "incitement" and "advocacy" in such cases. Advocacy of a criminal act does not mean that the act will occur. In incitement, to be illegal, it must be shown that such acts were encouraged to occur immediately and that a clear and present inducement to commit the illegal act existed. The case of *Yates v. United States* (1957) best demonstrates the Court's thinking on incitement.

labeling   The assignment of a code, name, or symbol to categorize or otherwise indicate the level and type of objections to a work. The movie rating code is a form of labeling that indicates the relative level of violence and/or sexual themes that might be included in the film. Books are sometimes labeled to indicate content, and some book labels are designed to show which ones may contain something controversial and the nature of that controversy.

libel   A form of unprotected speech, libel is a defamatory word or words that are either written or broadcast. A defamatory word or statement does not have to be false to injure someone but instead needs to be shown to have a harmful effect, more a "breach of the peace," causing pain and suffering to at least one person. The falsity may, however, make it a more serious case. There is a difference between criticism and defamation. Criticism is an expression of opinion based on facts that provide grounds for a difference of opinion and that do not attack a person's private or personal affairs. Defamation attacks the personal qualities of the character of an individual.

libel per quod   One of two types of libel, libel per quod is a defamatory statement that is not immediately understood to be libelous but becomes so when the facts associated with the statement become known. In this type, defamation is dependent on the context in which the statement was made.

libel per se   One of two types of libel, libel per se is a defamatory statement that is obvious or is immediately understood to be libelous.

loyalty oath   A signed statement, carrying the force of law for false swearing, that is designed to establish loyalty to the nation and its democratic principles and to exclude anyone from employment who may hold ideas advocating the overthrow of the established form of government by violence or force, which generally means anyone who holds communist beliefs. Loyalty oaths as a condition of employment existed in various forms, usually for teachers and other public employees, but have been struck down by the Supreme court as unconstitutional.

McCarthyism   Named for Joseph McCarthy, U.S. senator from Wisconsin from 1947–1957, it is a term still used to indicate an anticommunist or antiliberal campaign that is marked with inaccurate or unjust allegations or actions. Also, it has been invoked to label or denounce any repressive attack on ideas or beliefs.

malice   As part of a libel charge, malice involves an evil intent or a motive caused by spite, personal hatred, ill will, recklessness, or a willful and wanton disregard for the rights of a person being defamed. It needs to be shown that the libelous statement is false. Malice in a libel suit constitutes the most serious type of libel.

marketplace of ideas   The theory of free expression espoused by John Milton, which emphasizes that ideas must be allowed to enter the marketplace untouched so people can pick and choose from the contrasting beliefs on their own. This theory assumes that truth will win over falsehoods in the end due to the competition inherent in the marketplace.

Memoirs **standard** A revision of the *Roth* test for obscenity, the *Memoirs* standard has three elements to prove that a work is obscene: (1) the dominant theme of the work, taken as a whole, appeals to prurient interest in sex, (2) the work is patently offensive because it violates contemporary community standards on the depiction of sexual matters, and (3) the work is utterly without redeeming social value. This test was set down by the Supreme Court in the case *A Book Named "John Cleland's Memoirs of a Woman of Pleasure" v. Attorney General of Massachusetts* (1966). Each of the three elements has to be judged separately and one cannot outweigh the others.

Miller **standard** A constitutional test, the *Miller* test is the current judicial standard for judging obscenity. It has three components: (1) the average person would view the work, using contemporary community standards, as appealing to prurient interest, (2) the work describes or shows sexual conduct in a patently offensive way as defined by an applicable state law, and (3) the work, taken as a whole, lacks serious literary, artistic, political, or scientific value. The *Miller* test changes the national consensus of the *Roth* and *Memoirs* tests to a state consensus and provides for a more strict evaluation of the value of the work than the concept of "utterly without redeeming social value."

nodis A term used in the classification of government documents, nodis prohibits distribution of sensitive documents to anyone except to the individual or individuals for which it was originally intended.

noforn A term used in the classification of government documents, noforn restricts distribution of such documents to U.S. citizens only.

obscenity Generally, any written or visual work that offends moral standards or incites to lust or depravity. A legal definition has been considered difficult to formulate and apply fairly to all possible works. The three main standards, or tests, in the history of obscenity cases are the *Hicklin* standard, the *Roth* standard and its revision under the *Memoirs* standard, and the *Miller* standard. The current definition is covered in the *Miller* test delineated in *Miller v. California* (1973).

offensive words Words that offend certain listeners but are not obscene under any legal test for obscenity or unprotected speech as defined by constitutional tests, such as "fighting words," are considered "offensive words" and are protected by the Constitution. The case of *Cohen v. California* (1971) is a primary example of an offensive words case.

overbreadth A law or statute making illegal certain actions or words that are actually protected by the Constitution. When a law is "overbroad" it generally includes words or actions that can be made illegal along with those that cannot, making the whole law unconstitutional. This is an argument made in cases involving the Bill of Rights. Lawmakers must be careful in writing such laws to include only what can legally be prohibited.

pandering   The act of advertising or attempting to capitalize on a work by appealing to potential buyers using the work's erotic or sexual content. Pandering is not used as a test for obscenity, but if it is shown, it can be sufficient to convict on obscenity charges in cases with works not easily determined to be obscene based on their content. The case of *Ginzburg v. United States* (1966) is the most important one defining pandering in obscenity cases.

patent offensiveness   A term used in the *Memoirs* and *Miller* standards for proving obscenity. The concept under *Miller* usually applies to hard-core pornography. The Supreme Court used the *Miller* case to provide some examples of what was to be considered "patently offensive" but left any actual definition up to the individual states.

personal-attack rule   A regulation of broadcasting under the Federal Communications Commission's rules, the personal-attack rule requires radio and television stations to notify any person or group of the existence of a broadcast with a personal attack against them and offer them an opportunity to respond. The most important case upholding this rule is *Red Lion Broadcasting Company v. Federal Communications Commission* (1969).

podsnappery   Meaning excessive concern for supposedly impressionable children and youth, the term is derived from the Charles Dickens character Mr. Podsnap, in his *Our Mutual Friends*. Dickens wrote the character as a satire on the prevailing prudery of contemporary Victorian literary criticism.

political hyperbole   Political statements that if taken literally would be illegal but that stated in the heat of political debate without any intent to commit an illegal act are hyperbole and therefore are not illegal in this context.

preferred position   The concept that the rights and freedoms guaranteed by the First Amendment are of primary importance and that any restriction of these rights due to legislative preferences does not take precedent over the "preferred position" these rights hold in our legal system. To restrict a right or freedom under this concept, there has to be a clear and substantial reason to do so.

prior restraint   The removal or attempt to remove an exercise of free speech or press before it is made or before it is distributed, without a proper judicial determination using due process to establish that exercise as unprotected or not. This concept was first developed in the case *Near v. Minnesota* (1931), and it prohibits authorities from stopping speeches, published works, or other types of expression from being made or delivered until the courts can decide whether the expression is illegal. Once a type of speech or material has been judged as unprotected, prior restraint can occur.

provocative words Words that, when stated, create a dangerous situation or a clear and present danger. Provocative words need not be obscene or offensive. For such words to be illegal, the speaker must contribute substantially to the creation of the disorder provoked. If the crowd or public substantially creates the disorder after hearing words that may be provocative, those words are protected. The case *Terminiello v. Chicago* (1949) defined the concept of provocative words.

prurient interest Defined by U.S. law as "having a tendency to excite lustful thoughts." This concept is an integral component of the *Roth, Memoirs,* and *Miller* tests for obscenity.

public figure A person who has achieved prominence in society either by fame or notoriety acquired or by becoming very involved in a public controversy. I˞ tʰˑ latter, a person is considered a public figure only for that controversy. The pˑʳrpose of defining a "public figure" is to establish the limits of libel. Tʰe courts have ruled that public figures and public officials have less causˑˑ to claim defamation, at least regarding acts committed as a public figure or official, than an individual citizen because the public has a right to know as much information as possible on topics of public interest.

public official A person who holds a position, or appears to hold a position, within the hierarchy of government with substantial responsibilities. Not all government employees can be considered public officials. The case *New York Times Company v. Sullivan* (1964) is the most important case defining a public figure and a public official.

public place Any place open to the public. For the purpose of exercising one's First Amendment rights, the courts have placed some restrictions on what can constitute a public place or public forum to conduct such an exercise. Courthouses, jails, public transport vehicles, and military bases are open to the public, but due to the nature of their purposes, free speech and press issues can be regulated or restricted on their premises. Doorbells at private residences are also public places if the purpose for ringing them is to engage in political, charitable, or religious solicitation but not if it is for purely commercial solicitation.

qualified privilege A limited right of a news medium to publish or broadcast an impartial report of judicial, legislative, executive, or other public proceeding. In a libel case against a news organization, the doctrine of "qualified privilege" can be used as a defense if the libel charges come from a published news story that is from an impartial report of public proceedings.

reasonable belief   An argument for proof of libel. A false statement concerning public officials can be punished if "an ordinary, prudent man" might be able to ascertain the statement as true. The Supreme Court has rejected this argument and has established the doctrine that public officials must show "actual malice" by the person or group making the statement.

reckless disregard   In a libel case, if a person or group fails to attempt to ascertain the truth of a statement before publishing or repeating it, when there is sufficient time to take the precaution of checking the statement's accuracy, then a "reckless disregard" for the truth was committed. Only if the information concerned "hot news," leaving little time to check for accuracy, could a charge of reckless disregard be dismissed.

retroactive classification   A concept of classification of government documents that considers previously unclassified materials, including those published and circulated to the public, as secret and due restrictions because of their content or topic. Such material is considered to be eligible for withdrawal from all files and collections.

right to reply   The right to respond to charges in a newspaper that have assailed one's personal character or that have charged malfeasance in office. The Supreme Court rejected this concept to protect a free press, because such a right may limit what is published in order to avoid controversy.

robust debate   The ability of individuals in society to thoroughly discuss topics of substantial interest and concern. The doctrine of robust debate prohibits a charge of libel where the concerns of society outweigh a person's interest in maintaining his or her good name.

***Roth* standard**   A constitutional test for obscenity, the *Roth* standard requires that it be demonstrated that a work have as a dominant theme, when taken as a whole, that appeals to prurient interests as perceived by the average person applying contemporary community standards. The effect of *Roth* was to reject the *Hicklin* standard that a work could be declared wholly obscene for containing only one obscene passage. *Roth* itself was rejected in the 1973 *Miller* test.

scienter   The amount of knowledge that an individual must have to be held responsible under the law for the consequences of an action or statement made. A person has to have a reasonable amount of knowledge that such an action or statement is illegal. In the case of obscenity, as an example, a bookseller must be aware that the contents of the book are obscene before he or she can be convicted of selling obscenity.

secular humanism   A term applied by some groups to mean any educational philosophy that rejects the primacy of absolute values and does not base its principles in a literal reading of the Bible. The charge of secular humanism is often used by such groups as justification for removal of books, textbooks, and courses on a wide variety of subjects, including evolution, sex education, and critical appraisals of government scandals and the arms race.

sedition   To advocate the overthrow of any government in the United States by violence or force, to write or publish any work advocating the overthrow of any government in the United States by violence or force, or to organize any group for this purpose. Sedition is defined and made illegal by the Smith Act of 1940 and its amendment in 1948.

shield laws   Laws designed to protect journalists from being forced to reveal the identity of confidential sources used to obtain information for news stories.

single instance rule   This states that the publication of just one defamatory statement, a "single instance," calling into question the competency of a professional person is not sufficient to prove libel. The single instance rule is a defense when professionals such as doctors or lawyers are involved; however, it is not a defense for questioning unethical business practices.

social exchange   The theory of free expression developed by John Stuart Mill that emphasizes that citizens can only trade false ideas for true ones if, and only if, they can hear all ideas. This theory recognizes the importance of providing all people with a wide variety of political, moral, and aesthetic ideas.

social utility   The theory of free expression developed by Zechariah Chafee, Jr., which recognizes two types of expression: expression that serves individual interest and expression that serves the interest of society. Chafee considered the latter type to be far more important and believed it should be restrained only when the public safety is endangered.

symbolic speech   Conduct performed to communicate an idea. Symbolic speech usually does not involve the spoken word, but it is a representation of an idea. The conduct and the communication of an idea must be directly linked or else the conduct is not legally considered protected symbolic speech.

threatening words   Words not otherwise prohibited as "fighting words" but that pose a danger, when taken literally, to the life or safety of an individual. Threatening words can be unprotected by the First Amendment if an actual intent to injure can be shown.

time-place-manner   The legally permissible restrictions that can be placed on what is considered the exercise of otherwise absolute freedoms. Under the concept of time-place-manner, an authority can regulate when, where, and the format for allowing free speech activities but not the content of such activities.

Ulysses **standard**   A constitutional test for obscenity in which a work must be determined to have a "libidinous" effect on a person with average sex instincts. The *Ulysses* standard was established in the case of *United States v. One Book Entitled Ulysses* (1934), and it was the first break with the *Hicklin* rule. The *Ulysses* standard rejected the test permitting isolated passages to determine the obscene nature of a whole work. This concept has never been overturned but instead has been incorporated in all subsequent standards.

unofficial classification   A method used for withholding government information from journalistic inquiries by claiming the requested document has been classified as secret when it has not been.

unprotected speech   Any form of speech, spoken or symbolic, that is not considered constitutionally acceptable or protected by the First Amendment to the U.S. Constitution. Unprotected forms of speech include obscenity, libel, slander, defamation, fighting words, situations where a clear and present danger can be shown, child pornography, and commercial speech that is proven to be false.

vagueness   Use of terms in a statute that are not defined enough or do not provide enough guidance as to what is permitted and what is illegal. A charge of "vagueness" is usually coupled with the concept of overbreadth and often is used as a defense against laws regulating or restricting speech.

widest latitude   The concept that legislators must be given the greatest opportunity to discuss matters of national and state policy in order to preserve a representative government. Even though a state may require an oath of allegiance not required of private citizens, legislators cannot be subjected to a higher standard of speech, so that legislators can take positions that will fully inform their constituents.

Index

Abernathy, M. Glenn, 226
Abington School District v. Schempp, 11, 56, 71
Abortion, 51
Abrams v. United States, 77, 78
Absolute privilege, 279
Absolutism test, 279
Academe, 168
Academic freedom, 18–19, 45, 50
Academic Freedom, 188
Accuracy in Academia, 59
Accuracy in Media (AIM), 59 , 135
ACLU. *See* American Civil Liberties Union
Action for Children's Television (ACT), 135–136
Actual malice, 279
Adams, John, 75
Adderley v. Florida, 127
Adler v. Board of Education, 125
The Adventures of Huckleberry Finn, 27
Advertising, 248
Advocacy of action, 279
AFA Journal, 227
African-Americans, 176. *See also* National Association for the Advancement of Colored People (NAACP)
The AIM Report, 59, 228
Alderman, Ellen, 170
Alexander William Doniphan, 241–242
Alien and Sedition Acts, 38, 41, 75–76. *See also* Sedition Act
Alien Registration Act, 81–82
Aliens and Dissenters, 211
All in the Family, 61
Alternative Press Index, 163
The Amendments to the Constitution, 274

American Bar Association. Section on Individual Rights and Responsibilities, 136
American Booksellers Association, 63
American Booksellers Foundation for Free Expression, 63
American Broadcasting and the First Amendment, 211, 224
American Civil Liberties Union, 39–40, 53, 55, 57, 61, 136–137, 186
American Family Association, 64
American Heroes, 201
American Legion, 30
American Library Association, 41, 55, 62, 137–138
American Library Association. Office for Intellectual Freedom, 60, 187
American Newspaper Publisher's Association Foundation, 138
American Revolution, 7, 276–277
An American Tragedy, 28, 76
American Union Against Militarism, 53
Americans for Constitutional Freedom, 138–139
Americans for Decency, 139
Americans for Religious Liberty, 139
Americans United for Separation of Church and State (AUSCS), 140
Amicus curiae brief, 279–280
The Anatomy of AIM, 220
The Anatomy of Censorship, 193
Anderson, Arthur J., 187
Anthony Comstock: Roundsman of the Lord, 189
Anti-Defamation League of B'Nai B'Rith, 140

Antisemitism, 140
Apostles of Culture, 198
Archbishop O'Connor Scores Pornography as Major Threat to Family Life/Father Ritter Fights "Teen Sex Industry" in New York City, 242
Archer, Jules, 170
Areopagitica, 4
Arnold, O. Carroll, 181–182
Art and Pornography, 210
Art Censorship, 191
Art porn, 280. *See also* Pornography
Article 19: International Centre on Censorship, 140–141, 170, 280
Articles of Faith, Articles of Peace, 183
Associated Press v. Walker, 90, 91
Association of American Publishers (AAP), 141
Association of American Publishers. Freedom to Read Committee, 60, 62
Attacks on the Freedom To Learn, 1985–1986, 210
Attacks on the Freedom To Learn, 1990–1991 Report, 187
Attorney General's Commission on Pornography, 48–49, 56
Authors League of America, 141–142
Average person, 280
Aversion, 280
Awards. *See* Carl Sandburg Freedom To Read Award; Playboy Foundation's First Amendment Award; Robert B. Downs Intellectual Freedom Award

Bad tendency test, 280
Bagdikian, Ben H., 218
Baker, C. Edwin, 187
Baker v. F&F Investment, 115
Balancing test, 280
Baldwin, Roger Nash, 39, 53–54, 57
The Banned Books of England and Other Countries, 192
Banned Books, 387 B.C. to 1978 A.D., 200
Banned Films, 194
Banned Posters, 212

Bannerman, Hazel, 43
Barnes v. Glen Theatre, 51, 107
Barron, Jerome A., 171, 218
Bartlett, Jonathan E., 171
The Battle for Religious Liberty, 182
The Battle for the Mind, 184
The Battle of the Books, 190
Beauharnais v. Illinois, 84–85
Behind the Green Door, 29, 46
The Believer and the Powers That Are, 185
Belknap, Michael R., 187
Beman, Lamar T., 171
Bender, Paul, 173
Bennett, James R., 161
Berger, Melvin, 187
Bergna v. Stanford Daily, 120
Berkowitz, David, 51
Berninghausen, David K., 54, 171
Berns, Walter, 171–172
The Best Defense, 56
The Best Lawyers in America, 166
Bibliographies, 161–162
Bicknell v. Vergennes Union High School Board, 103–104
The Big Chill, 210
Bill of Rights (England), 6
Bill of Rights (states), 67
Bill of Rights (U.S.), 6, 7, 37, 38, 170, 172, 175, 175–176, 177, 178, 179, 180, 228, 234, 248, 252–253, 274–275, 281
  adoption of, 8
  organizations, 144–145
The Bill of Rights (software), 274
The Bill of Rights: Its Origin and Meaning, 172
The Bill of Rights: Original Meaning and Current Understanding, 175
Bill of Rights in Action, 228
Bill of Rights in Action: Freedom of Religion, 242
Bill of Rights in Action: Freedom of Speech, 242–243
Bill of Rights in Action: Freedom of the Press, 243
Bill of Rights Reader, 177
Birth of a Nation, 29 , 30, 39
The Birth of the Bill of Rights, 179
Black, Henry Campbell, 166

Black, Hugo Lafayette, 10–11, 15,
    54, 57, 71, 85, 124, 172, 173,
    181, 256, 279
Blacklisting, 281
Blacks. *See* African-Americans
Black's Law Dictionary, 166
Blanding, Richard, 38
Blanshard, Paul, 188
Bloom Clive, 193
BNA ONLINE, 265
BNA PLUS, 266
*Board of Education, Island Trees Union
    Free School District No. 25 v. Pico*,
    18, 47, 104–105
Board of Regents v. Roth, 97
Bollinger, Lee C., 188
Bond v. Floyd, 89–90
Book burning, 40, 281
Book Burning, 216
*A Book Named "John Cleland's Memoirs
    of a Woman of Pleasure" v. Attorney
    General of Massachusetts*, 44,
    90–91
Book Selection and Censorship, 196
*Book Selection and Censorship in the
    Sixties*, 207
Book Selection and Intellectual Freedom,
    62, 207
Bookbanning in America, 208
Books Our Children Read, 243
Borden, Morton, 182
Born Secret, 219
Bosmajian, Haig, 188–189, 218
Bowdlerize (term definition), 281
The Bowker Annual, 166–167
Boyz N the Hood, 51
Bradley, Gerald V., 182
Brandeis, Louis, 2, 56
Brandenburg v. Ohio, 45, 75, 93
*Brandywine-Main Line Radio v. Federal
    Communications Commission*, 24,
    115–116
Brant, Irving, 172
Branzburg v. Hayes, 22, 116
Bridges v. California, 15, 82
Broadcast Fairness, 224
Broadcasting rules, 23–24
Broderick, Dorothy M., 55, 189
Broun, Heywood, 189
Brown, Claude, 30
Brown v. Board of Education, 56

Bryan, William Jennings, 40, 79
Bryson, Joseph E., 189
Buckley, William F., Jr., 189–190
Burger, Warren, 56, 58, 103
Burress, Lee, 190, 203–204
Burstyn, Varda, 190
Burstyn v. Wilson, 85
Busha, Charles, 172, 190
Buzzard, Lynn R., 182
Byerly, Greg, 161

Cable TV, 113
Caesar's Coin, 184
Cahn, Edmond, 172
*The Campaign against the Underground
    Press*, 224
Campbell, Douglas S., 218–219
Canavan, Francis, 172
Candidate-access rule, 23
Candy, 28
Cantwell v. Connecticut, 11, 42, 69, 123
Capaldi, Nicholas, 190
Carl Sandburg Freedom to Read
    Award, 61
Carlin, George, 47
Carlisle, Belinda, 58
Carmilly-Weinberger, Moshe,
    190–191
Carnal Knowledge, 29, 46
Carter, Jimmy, 23
Casanova's Homecoming, 76
The Case against Pornography, 202
Case History of a Rumor, 243–244
Case law citations, 67–68
Case Study: Tinker vs. Des Moines,
    274
Catch-22, 30
Catcher in the Rye, 30, 42–43
Catholic League for Religious
    Freedom and Civil Rights, 142
The Catholic Viewpoint on Censorship,
    197–198
Catton, Bruce, 1
CD-ROMs, 268–271
Celebrating Censored Books, 203–204
The Censor Marches On, 196
Censors in the Classroom, 203
Censorship, 162, 167, 167–168, 168,
    169, 171, 178, 186–218, 228,
    233, 240, 244, 249, 257,
    258–259

Censorship (*continued*)
  defined, 26
  literature, 27–29, 42–43
  motion pictures, 29–30, 39, 85,
    194, 211. *See also* Motion Picture
    Code
  organizations, 140–141, 153–154,
    157
  periodicals, 29, 32
  sex education pamphlet, 27
  sources of, 26
Censorship (Berger), 187
Censorship (Ernst), 195
Censorship (Taylor), 215
*Censorship: Evidence of Bias in Our
  Children's Textbooks*, 216–217
Censorship: For and Against, 200–201
*Censorship: Research and Public Policy
  Implications*, 210
*Censorship: The Knot That Binds Power
  and Knowledge*, 203
Censorship and Freedom of Expression,
  191–192
Censorship and Selection, 212
The Censorship Debate, 186
Censorship in a Free Society, 244
Censorship in America, 202
Censorship in Public Libraries, 215–216
Censorship Landmarks, 193–194
Censorship, Libraries and the Law,
  188–189
Censorship Litigation and the Schools,
  191
Censorship News, 228
The Censorship of Books, 193
Censorship of the Movies, 211
Censorship or Selection, 244
The Censorship Papers, 198
Center for Constitutional Rights, 142
Center Magazine, 228–229
Central Intelligence Agency, 22
Certiorari, 281
Chafee, Zechariah, Jr., 4, 173
The Challenge of Ideas, 244–245
Chandler, Ralph C., 167
Chandos, John, 191
Changing Channels, 219
Chaplinsky v. New Hampshire, 16, 42,
  82
Charge and Countercharge, 245
Charles II, King of England, 6

Charren, Peggy, 219
Chicago Seven, 46, 55
Chicago Tribune, 63
Child pornography, 20, 32, 49. *See
  also* Pornography
Child Protection Acts, 49, 106
Children's Legal Foundation,
  142–143
Children's literature, 145
Children's rights, 142–143, 170, 246
Chilling effect, 281–282
A Chilling Effect, 197
Chomsky, Noam, 257
Chopping, 282
Christian Broadcasting Network, 62
Christian Crusade, 143
Christian Herald, 229
Christianity Today, 229
Christiano, David, 165
Church and State, 229
Church, State and the First Amendment,
  245
Church-State Relationships in America,
  182
Cirino, Robert, 219
Citizen, 56
The Citizen, 229–230
*Citizens Committee to Save WEFM v.
  Federal Communications
  Commission*, 118
Citizens for Decency, 218
Citizens for Decency through Law,
  143
Citizens for Decent Literature, 30,
  143
Citizens for Excellence in Education
  (CEE), 143–144
Civil liberties, 136, 142, 152, 154,
  176, 177, 230, 232, 239, 256
Civil Liberties, 230
Civil Liberties and Industrial Conflict, 54
Civil Liberties and the Constitution,
  176
Civil Liberties in Conflict, 199
Civil Rights Legal Defense Fund, 144
Civil rights, 173, 232, 236
The Civil Rights of Students, 179–180
*Civil Service Commission v. Letter
  Carriers*, 81
Civil Service Reform Act, 47,
  132–133

Clapp, J. 191
Clark, Tom, 71
Classification at birth, 282
Classification of documents, 282
Classified documents, 130–131
Classrooms in the Crossfire, 209
Clear and present danger, 282
Clear and Present Danger, 190
Cleaver, Eldridge, 30
Cleland, John, 27, 38, 44
Cline, Victor B., 191
Clor, Harry M., 191–192
Clown of Freedom, 245–246
Coalition for Better Television, 64, 144
Cogley, John, 182
Cohen, Jeremy, 173
Cohen v. California, 16, 46, 96
Cold War on Campus, 206
Cold War Political Justice, 187
Columbia Broadcasting System v. FCC, 23
Columbia Broadcasting System v. United States, 111
Columbia Journalism Review, 168
Combating Pornography, 246
Commentaries on Obscenity, 213
Commentary, 230
Commentary on the Constitution of the United States, 9
Commercial speech, 20, 282
Commonwealth v. Blanding, 38
Communications Control, 211
Comstock, Anthony, 27, 29, 39, 189, 200
Comstock Act, 38, 39, 76–77
Comstockery, 282–283
Comstockery in America, 200
Concerned Women for America, 144
Confessions (Rousseau), 27
Congress Shall Make No Law, 173
Congressional Information Service, CIS/Index, 266
Congressional Masterfile 2, 269
Connexions Digest, 230
Conscientious objectors, 43, 71–72, 73
Conservatism, 229, 229–230, 231, 233, 235–236, 238, 240
  organizations, 139, 143, 143–144, 144, 145, 146, 148–149, 151, 153

Conservative Digest, 231
Constitution (U.S.), 37, 231, 274, 275–276, 277. *See also* Bill of Rights (U.S.), First Amendment
  and individual rights, 7–8
The Constitution: For Adults Only?, 246
The Constitution and the Government of the United States, 275
The Constitution Papers, 269
Constitutional Commentary, 231
The Constitutional Law Dictionary, 167
The Constitutional Right of Association, 226
Constitutional Rights Foundation, 144–145
Constitutional Trivia, 276
Contemporary community standards, 283
Contemporary Literary Censorship, 199
Contemporary Social Issues, 208–209
Contempt, 283
Control of Information in the United States, 161
Conversions, 195
Cord, Robert L., 182
Cornog, Martha, 192
Cotham, Perry C., 192
Council on Interracial Books for Children, 145
The Courage of Their Convictions, 175–176
Court system, 66–67
  case law citations, 67–68
Cowan, Geoffrey, 192
Cox v. Louisiana, 25
Cox v. New Hampshire, 123
Craig, Alec, 192
Cramp v. Board of Instruction of Orange County, Florida, 126
A Crime against Women, 246–247
Crime and Publicity, 220
Criminal syndicalism, 283
  laws, 75
Criticism and Censorship, 204
Crossfire, 272
Current, 57
Current Law Index, 163
Curry, Richard O., 193
Curry, Thomas J., 183
Curtis Publishing Company v. Butts, 91

D'Souza, Dinesh, 195
Daily, Jay E., 193
Dangerous Dossiers, 207
Dangerous Songs, 247
Daniels, Walter M., 193
Dare to Discipline, 56
Darrow, Clarence, 40, 79
Darwin, Charles, 28, 72
Databases, 265–268
Davis, Derek, 183
Davis, James E., 193
The Day They Came To Arrest the Book, 59, 201, 247
Day, Gary, 193
de Tocqueville, Alexis, 2
Dealing with Censorship, 193
Death of a Porn Queen, 247–248
Debs, Eugene, 77, 78
Debs v. United States, 77, 78
A Decade of Censorship in America, 30, 217
Decent Interval, 55
Decisions, Decisions: Television, 276
Declaration of Independence, 7, 37
Deep Throat, 29, 30, 46, 55
Defamation, 283
Defending Intellectual Freedom, 178–179
Defusing Censorship, 203
DeGrazia, Edward, 193–194
Dejonge v. Oregon, 79, 80
Demac, Donna A., 173, 194
Democratic National Committee v. McCord, 117
Dennett, Mary, 27
Dennis v. United States, 15, 82, 84
Dennis, Everette E., 173
Derivative classification, 283
Dershowitz, Alan, 55–56
Detty, Elizabeth W., 189
The Devil in Miss Jones, 29, 46
Devol, Kenneth S., 219
Devolpi, A., 219
Dial magazine, 63
DIALOG Information Services, 266
Dictionaries, 166–167
Dienes, C. Thomas, 171
Directories, 165–166
A Directory of Religious and Parareligious Bodies and Organizations in the United States, 165

Directory of Religious Organizations in the United States, 165
Dissent, 12–13
  "absolutist" principle, 15
  "advocacy of action," 15, 45, 86
  "advocacy of ideas," 15
  "bad tendency" test, 15, 40, 79, 280
  "balancing" test, 15
  "clear and present danger," 14–15, 16, 39, 78, 282
  fighting words, 16, 42
  offensive words, 16–17
  "preferred position" test, 15
  provocative words, 16
  symbolic speech, 17, 45, 46
  threatening words, 16
Dobson, James C., 56
Don't Blame the People, 219
Doniphan, Alexander, 241–242
Donner, Frank, 194
Donnerstein, Edward, 194
Doran v. Salem Inn, 51
Dornan, Robert, 31
Dorsen, Norman, 173
Douglas, William Orville, 15, 56–57, 85, 112, 174, 256, 279
The Douglas Opinions, 174
Down These Mean Streets, 98
Downs, Donald Alexander, 195
Downs, Robert B., 174
Dreiser, Theodore, 28
Duran Duran, 58
Dworkin, Andrea, 48, 57, 105, 195
Dworkin-McKinnon bills, 57, 105–106

Eagle Forum, 145
Educational Research Analysts, 146
Edwards v. South Carolina, 127
The Effete Conspiracy and Other Crimes of the Press, 218
Elliot, George P., 195
Ellsberg, Daniel, 46
Elmer Gantry, 29
Emergence of a Free Press, 222
Emerson, Thomas I., 174
Emery, Edwin, 219–220
Emord, Jonathan W., 174
The Encyclopedia of Censorship, 167
Encyclopedias, 166–167
The End of Obscenity, 212

Engel v. Vitala, 11, 70 -71
English (language) teachers, 154–155
Enslen, Richard, 167
Epperson v. Arkansas, 45, 72
Epstein, Daniel, 220
Equal-time rule, 23, 283–284
Ericsson, Samuel, 182
Ernst, Morris L., 195–196
Erotica, 284
Espionage Act, 29, 77, 78
Essay Concerning Human Understanding, 6
The Establishment Clause, 184
Estrin, Herman A., 220
Ethics in Advertising, 248
European Convention on Human Rights, 43
Evans, J. Edward, 183, 196, 220
Ever Changing, Ever Free, 248
Evergreen Review, 30
Everson v. Board of Education, 10
Evolution, 284. *See also* Scopes v. State
Executive Orders concerning classified documents, 130–131
Executive privilege, 284
Expanding Liberties, 177

The Face on the Cutting Room Floor, 213
The Facts of Love in the Library, 248–249
Fahrenheit 451, 249
Fairness doctrine, 23–24, 284
The Fairness Doctrine and the Media, 225
Family, 137, 227, 231
Fanny Hill. See *Memoirs of a Woman of Pleasure; A Book Named "John Cleland's Memoirs of a Woman of Pleasure" v. Attorney General of Massachusetts*
Farmers Educational and Cooperative Union of America v. WDAY, 87, 112
FCC v. Pacifica Foundation, 24, 47
Fear of Art, 190
The Fear of the Word, 209
Federal Advisory Committee Act, 131–132
Federal Anti-Obscenity Act. *See* Comstock Act

Federal Censorship, 210
Federal Communications Act, 23, 40–41, 110
Federal Communications Commission, 23, 40–41
Federal Communications Commission v. Pacifica Foundation, 119
Feiner v. New York, 16, 84
Fellman, David, 226
Feminists, Pornography and the Law, 162
Ferlinghetti, Lawrence, 196
Fielding, Henry, 27
Fighting Faiths, 211
Fighting for the Minds of Our Children, 56
Fighting words, 284
Films. *See* Censorship—motion pictures; Films, videocassettes, and filmstrips; Motion Picture Code
Films, videocassettes, and filmstrips, 241–265
Filmstrips. *See* Films, videocassettes, and filmstrips
Final Report, July 1986, 216
Firing Line, 272
First Amendment, 1, 38, 65–66, 67, 169, 171–172, 173, 174, 175, 177, 178, 179, 180, 181, 254, 261–262, 284
   freedoms covered, 8–9
   historical background, 5–8
   organizations, 138–139, 146–147, 156
The First Amendment: The Legacy of George Mason, 180
The First Amendment and the Future of American Democracy, 171
The First Amendment and the Ku Klux Klan, 249
The First Amendment Book, 181
First Amendment Congress, 146–147
The First Amendment, Democracy and Romance, 180
First Amendment Freedoms, 177
The First Amendment in a Free Society, 171
The First Amendment under Siege, 222
The First Freedom (book), 59 , 201–202

The First Freedom (film), 250
The First Freedom Today, 174
The First Freedoms, 183
The First Liberty, 184–185
First Principles, 231
Fischer, Louis, 179–180
Fiske, Marjorie, 196
500 Years of Conflict, 208
The Flight from Reason, 54, 171
Focus on the Family, 56, 231
Foerstel, Herbert C., 196–197
Foolish Figleaves? Pornography Figleaves? Pornography In and Out of Court, 205
Footloose, 250
For Adult Users Only, 200
Forbidden Books in American Public Libraries, 1876–1939, 198
Forecast rule, 284–285
Foreign Agents Registration Act, 81
Forer, Lois G., 197
Fowler, Dorothy G., 197
Francois, William E., 220
Frank, John P., 197
Franklin, Bruce, 55
Fred Friendly—Journalist, 250
Free Inquiry, 232
Free Press Association, 147
Free Press, Free Trial, 251
Free Press/Free People, 221
Free Press v. Fair Trial, 222
Free Speech: A Philosophical Enquiry, 212–213
Free Speech and Its Relation to Self–Government, 178
Free Speech in the United States, 173
Free Speech Yearbook, 167
Free Thought and the Mass Media, 251
Free To Believe, 251
Freedman, Warren, 197
Freedman v. Maryland, 89
Freedom
    definitions, 1–2
    as provided for in U.S. Constitution, 1
Freedom and Censorship of the College Press, 220
Freedom and Culture, 217
Freedom and Taboo, 211–212
Freedom at Risk, 193
Freedom Council, 62

Freedom of Access to Library Materials, 179
Freedom of Assembly and Petition, 227
Freedom of assembly. *See* Right to assembly
Freedom of association. *See* Right to assembly
Freedom of Association, 226
Freedom of Association, the Right To Organize and Collective Bargaining, 226
Freedom of expression. *See* Academic freedom, Freedom of speech
Freedom of Expression (book), 188
Freedom of Expression (film), 252
Freedom of Expression: Purpose as Limit, 172
Freedom of Information Act, 44, 131, 260, 262
Freedom of Information Center, 147
Freedom of religion, 1, 8–11, 42, 68, 179, 181–186, 229, 232, 234, 239, 242, 245, 253, 254, 261, 263
    case citations, 68–74
    organizations, 139, 140, 142
Freedom of Religion, 183
Freedom of speech, 1, 8–9, 12–13, 74, 167, 170, 171, 173, 174, 174–175, 175, 177, 178, 179, 186–218, 236, 242–243, 250, 252, 258
    academic freedom, 18–19, 45, 50
    case citations, 74–108
    commercial speech, 20, 82–83
    dissent, 12–13, 14–17
    libel, 12, 13–14
    obscenity, 13, 19–20
    protected speech, 12
    slander, 12
    symbolic speech, 17, 45, 46
    unprotected speech, 12
Freedom of Speech, 196
Freedom of Speech and Press, 252
Freedom of Speech and Press in America, 175
Freedom of Speech in the United States, 215
Freedom of Speech on Private Property, 197
Freedom of the High School Press, 222

Freedom of the press, 1, 8–9, 108, 168, 170, 171, 175, 178, 218–226, 240, 243, 251, 255, 257
  broadcasting, 23–24
  case citations, 108–122
  and freedom of speech, 20–21
  and libel, 21
  news, 21, 22–23
  organizations, 146, 147, 148, 156, 157, 157–158, 158–159
  politics, 22
Freedom of the Press (Evans), 220
Freedom of the Press (Seldes), 63, 225
Freedom of the Press: A Bibliocyclopedia, 162
Freedom of the Press: An Annotated Bibliography, 162
Freedom of the Press for Whom?, 218
Freedom of the Press from Zenger to Jefferson, 223
Freedom of the Press vs. Public Access, 225
Freedom, Technology and the First Amendment, 174
The Freedom To Lie, 214–215
The Freedom To Publish, 218
The Freedom To Read, 188
Freedom to Read Foundation, 60, 148
Freedom to Read Foundation News, 232
Freedom To Speak, 252
Freedom under Fire, 178
Freedom Versus Suppression and Censorship, 190
Freedom, Virtue and the First Amendment, 171–172
Freedoms, 252–253
Fried, Richard M., 197
Friendly, Alfred, 220
Friendly, Fred W., 220–221, 250
Frohnmayer, John, 31
Frohwerk v. United States, 77, 78
Fund for Free Expression, 148

Gardiner, Harold C., 197–198
Gardner, Gerald C., 198
Garrison, Dee, 198
Garrison v. Louisiana, 13–14, 88
Geisendorfer, James V., 165
Gellathy, Peter, 198

Geller, Evelyn, 198
The Genius, 28
George Mason, 253
Gertz v. Robert Welch, Inc., 99–100
Gilbert v. Minnesota, 2
Gillette v. United States, 73
Gillmor, Donald M., 173
Gilmore, Donald H., 198–199
Ginsberg v. New York, 20, 91
Ginzburg, Ralph, 44
Ginzburg v. United States, 90
Girodias, Maurice, 28
Gitlow v. New York, 15, 40, 75, 79
Givhan v. Westernline Consolidated School District, 18, 103
Glasser, Ira, 57–58
Glazer, Myron Perez, 199
Glorious Revolution, 6, 37
Go Ask Alice, 30
Go-Go's, 58
God and Man at Yale, 189
God and the Constitution, 253
God, Caesar, and the Constitution, 185
God in the White House, 183
Gold Mountain Records, 58
Goldberg, Arthur, 55
Goldberg, Danny, 58
Goldfarb, Ronald L., 220
Goldwater, Barry, 45
The Good Guys, the Bad Guys and the First Amendment, 220–221
The Good War, 63
Goodman, Michael B., 199
Gora, Joel M., 221
Gordon, Andrew C., 174
Gorman, Carol, 199
Gostlin, Larry, 199
Government Secrecy, 176
Graber, Mark A., 199
The Grapes of Wrath, 29
The Great Rights, 172
The Great Rights of Mankind, 180
Green, Jonathan, 167
Greenawalt, Kent, 200
Greenbelt Publishing Association v. Bresler, 14, 95
Grey, David L., 173
Griffin, Susan, 200
Griffith, D. W., 29, 39
Grosjean v. American Publishing Company, 111

Grove Press, 28, 41
Grove v. Mead School District No. 354, 73–74
The Guardian, 232
Gubar, Susan, 200
The Guide to American Law, 167
Guinness, Os, 183
Guzick v. Drebus, 96

Hague v. Congress of Industrial Organizations, 25, 41, 122–123
Haight, Anne Lyon, 200
Haiman, Franklyn S., 174–175
Hamlin, David, 226
Hamling v. United States, 99
Hand, Brevard, 62–63
Hand, Learned, 77
Handbook of Free Speech and Free Press, 171
Haney, Robert W., 200
Hannegan v. Esquire, 111–112
Hard Times, 63
Harding, Warren G., 78
Hargis, Billy James, 45
Hart, Harold H., 200–201
Harvard Civil Rights-Civil Liberties Law Review, 232
Harvey, James A., 162
Hatch Act, 81
Hawkins, Gordon, 201
Hayden, Trudy, 201
Hays Office, 40. See also Censorship—motion pictures
Hazelwood School District v. Kuhlmeier, 18, 32, 49, 121–122
Healy v. James, 19, 128
Hefner, Hugh, 29, 43
Heinz, John P., 174
Heller, Joseph, 30
Helm, Lewis M., 175
Helms, Jesse A., 31, 50, 58
Helsinki Accords, 285
Hemingway, Ernest, 29, 63
Hemmer, Joseph J., Jr., 12, 175
Hendrick, Evan, 201
Hentoff, Nat, 58–59, 201–202
The Heritage Foundation, 148–149
Heritage Today, 233
Hicklin rule, 285
Hickock, Eugene W., Jr., 175

The Historic Background of the Bill of Rights, 178
Historical Abstracts, 163
Historical Dictionary of Censorship in the United States, 167–168
The History of Pornography, 254
The History of Religious Freedom, 254
Hoff, Joan, 200
Hoffman, Frank, 162
Hogan, Robert F., 197
Hohenberg, John, 221
Holbrook, David, 202
Holmes, Oliver Wendell, 78, 173
Hot news, 285
House Un-American Activities Committee, 64, 208. See also McCarthy, Joseph
Howl of the Censor, 196
Hoyt, Edwin P., 202
Hoyt, Olga G., 202
Hudnut, William, 48, 57, 105–106
Hudon, Edward G., 175
Hughes, Douglas A., 202
Hughes v. Superior Court of California, 25
Human (and Anti-Human) Values in Children's Books, 202
Human Liberty and Freedom of Speech, 187
Human rights, 43, 44, 163, 165, 166, 233, 237, 266–267
Human Rights, 233
HUMAN RIGHTS INTERNET (HRI), 267
Human Rights Internet Reporter, 163
Human Rights Organization and Periodicals Directory, 165
Humanities Index, 163
Hunter, James Davidson, 183
Hurwitz, Leon, 167–168
Hutcheson, Richard G., 183
Hutchison, E. R., 202

I Am Curious (Yellow), 55
Ice and Fire, 57
Illiberal Education, 195
The Image of the Black in Children's Literature, 55
Impressions series, 49–50, 63
In Fact, 63

In Our Defense, 170
In re Bernstein, 117
In re Bridge, 116
In re Palmetto Broadcasting Company, 112
In re WUHY-FM, Eastern Educational Radio, 114
In the Matter of Pappas, 116
Incitement, 285
Index on Censorship, 233
Index to Legal Periodicals, 164
Indexes and abstracts, 163–165
Individual Rights, 254
Information access, 161, 173, 174, 175, 176, 179, 181, 238, 248–249, 264
  laws, 130–133
  organizations, 147, 153
Information, Freedom and Censorship, 170
Informing the Public, 175
Ingelhart, Louis Edward, 221
Inherit the Wind, 40, 254–255
Inner City Mother Goose, 30
Intellectual freedom, 1–3, 171, 172, 174, 177, 228–229, 235, 237
  and censorship, 26–30
  and communications context, 5
  current issues, 31–33
  defined, 3
  and expression and action, 5
  and federal funding for the Arts, 31
  flag burning, 32
  and marketplace of ideas, 4
  and self-government, 4
  and social exchange, 4
  and social utility, 4
  theories of, 3–5
  under Reagan and Bush administrations, 31
Intellectual Freedom and Censorship, 162
Intellectual Freedom Manual, 187
An Intellectual Freedom Primer, 172
Intellectual Freedom, the Young Adult, and Schools, 217
Intelligence Identities Protection Act, 48
Internal Security Act, 83

International Convention for the Suppression of the Circulation of and Traffic in Obscene Publications, 42
International League for the Rights of Man, 54
International PEN, 59. *See also* PEN American Center
Interpretations of the First Amendment, 180
Interracial Books for Children Bulletin, 233–234
Intolerable Acts, 276–277
Invisible Empire Knights of the Ku Klux Klan, 149
Irons, Peter, 175–176
Irvine, Reed John, 59
Issues of Freedom in American Libraries, 207
It Did Happen Here, 213
It's Only Rock and Roll, 255

Jacobellis v. Ohio, 88–89
Jaifeh, Steven W., 166
James II, King of England, 6
Jansen, Sue Curry, 203
Jefferson, Thomas, 6, 9, 37, 76, 176
Jefferson and Civil Liberties, 177
Jehovah's Witnesses, 11, 41–42, 54, 69–70, 82, 102, 123
Jenkins v. Georgia, 46, 100
Jenkinson, Edward B., 203
Jerry Falwell v. Larry Flynt, 213
Jews, Turks and Infidels, 182
Johann, Sara Lee, 209
John, King of England, 5–6, 37
John Birch Society, 30, 150, 236
Johnson, David L., 215
Johnson, Lyndon, 45
Jones, Frances M., 203
Journal of Church and State, 234
Journal of Commerce and Commercial Bulletin v. Burleson, 108–109
Journal of Criminal Law and Criminology, 234
Journal of Law and Religion, 234
Journalistic Freedom, 255
Joyce, James, 28, 41
Judicial review, 66–67
Justice Black and the Bill of Rights, 256

Justice Hugo Black and the First Amendment, 173
Justice Is a Constant Struggle, 256

Kahane, Jack, 28
Kalish, Abraham, 59
Kalvern, Harry, Jr., 176, 203
Karolides, Nicholas J., 203–204
Katz, Steven L., 176
Kauper, Paul G., 176, 183–184
Keefe v. Geanakos, 93
Keene v. Meese, 48
Keeping America Uninformed, 173
Kelner v. United States, 16, 101
Kendrick, Walter, 204
Kennedy, Caroline, 170
Kennerly, Karen, 59
Kerr, Walter, 204
Keyishian v. Board of Regents, 45, 127–128
Khomeini, Ayatollah, 49
Kilpatrick, James J., 204
Kimball, Roger, 204
Kirk, Jerry, 60, 204–205
Kirkpatrick, R. George, 218
Klansman, 235
Kleeman, Richard, 60
Knights of the Ku Klux Klan, 149–150
Koch, Adrienne, 176
Konigsberg v. State Bar of California, 126–127
Konvitz, Milton, 177
Korematsu v. United States, 54, 124
Kristof, Nicholas D., 222
Kronenwetter, Michael, 222
Kronhausen, Eberhard, 205
Kronhausen, Phyllis, 205
Krug, Judith Fingeret, 60–61
Kruzas, Anthony T., 166
Ku Klux Klan, 149–150, 235, 249
Kuh, Richard H., 205
Kunstler, William, 55
Kunz v. New York, 124

Labeling, 285
Labunski, Richard E., 222
Ladenson, Robert F., 177
Lady Chatterley's Lover, 28, 76
LaHaye, Tim, 184
Lamont v. Postmaster General, 112–113

The Last Temptation of Christ, 30, 64
The Law of Obscenity, 213
Lawhorne, Clifton O., 205
Lawrence, D. H., 28, 205
Lawyers Cooperative Publishing Company, 68
League of Women Voters v. Federal Communications Commission, 121
Lear, Norman Milton, 61
The Learning Tree, 73–74
Leaves of Grass, 28
Lederor, Laura, 205–206
Lee, Francis G., 184
Lee, Martin, 222
Leech, Margaret, 189
Legacy of Suppression, 178
The Legal Aspects of Censorship of Public School Library and Instructional Materials, 189
LEGAL FORUM, 267
Legal Resources Index, 164
LEGI-SLATE, 267
Legman, G., 206
Letelier, Orlando, 59
Letter for Toleration, 6
Letters from a War Zone, 195
Levin, Murray, 177
Levy, Leonard W., 177–178, 184, 222–223
Lewis, Felice Flanery, 206
Lewis, Lionel S., 206
Lewis, Sinclair, 29
Lewis Publishing Company v. Morgan, 108–109
Libel, 13–14, 75, 197, 286
    "actual malice" test, 44
    defined, 12
    organizations, 150
Libel Defense Resource Center, 150
Libel per quod, 286
Libel per se, 286
Liberalism, 235, 236–237, 238, 239
Liberty Denied, 194
The Liberty Federation, 151
The Liberty Lobby, 151
Librarians, Censorship, and Intellectual Freedom, 162
Libraries, Erotica and Pornography, 192
Library Bill of Rights, 41
Library Literature, 164
Library Trends, 169

The Life and Selected Writings of Thomas
   Jefferson, 176
Lightman v. Maryland, 117
Limited-access doctrine, 24
Lindey, Alexander, 196
Linfield, Michael, 178
Linz, Daniel, 194
Literature, Obscenity, & Law, 206
Little Black Sambo, 30, 43
Little Black Sambo: A Closer Look, 218
Lobbying for Freedom, 209
Locke, John, 6, 37
The Lottery, 30
Love and Death: A Study in Censorship,
   206
Loyalty oath, 286
Lynn, Barry, 61–62, 206

MacInnes, Mairi, 206
Madison, James, 6, 8
Madonna, 50–51
Magna Carta, 5–6, 37
Makay, John J., 215
Malice, 286
Manchild in the Promised Land, 30
Manual Enterprises v. Day, 88
Manual for Student Expression, 223
Mapplethorpe, Robert, 31
Marketplace of ideas, 286
Marsh v. Alabama, 54
Marshall, John, 9
Mason, George, 8, 253
Mass Media and the Supreme Court, 219
Mass Media Law and Regulation, 220
The Masses, 29
McBrien, Richard P., 184
McCarran Act, 83
McCarthy, Joseph, 42, 245, 258,
   286. *See also* House
   Un-American Activities
   Committee
McCarthyism, 286
McCollum v. Board of Education, 11
McCormick, John, 206
McCormick, Kenneth Dale, 62
McCoy, Ralph E., 162, 174
McKinley, William, 79
McKinnon, Catherine, 57
McLaughlin Group, 272
McLean, John, 59
The Meaning of Freedom of Speech, 208

Media, 135, 138, 151–152, 218–226,
   228, 237, 251, 276
Media Access, 225
Media Alliance, 151–152
Media Coalition, 152
Meese, Edwin, 29, 48
The Meese Commission Exposed, 61, 207
Meiklejohn, Alexander, 4
Meiklejohn Civil Liberties Institute,
   152
Meinhold v. Taylor, 98
Mel Gabler's Newsletter, 235
Memoirs of a Woman of Pleasure, 27, 38,
   44, 90–91
Meredith, James, 46
The Meritorious Price of Our
   Redemption, 37
Merritt, Leroy C., 62, 207
Meyer v. Nebraska, 78
Miami Herald Publishing Company v.
   Tornillo, 118
Midwestern Television v. Southwestern
   Cable Company, 113
Migdal, Penina, 199
Mighty Mouse, 64
Mill, John Stuart, 4
Miller, Henry, 28, 40, 41
Miller, William L., 184–185
Miller standard, 287
Miller v. California, 19, 29, 47, 98–99
Mills v. Alabama, 22, 113
Milton, John, 4, 286
Milwaukee Social Democrat Publishing
   Company v. Burleson, 109
Minarcini v. Strongsville City School
   District, 101
The Mind Polluters, 60, 204–205
Minersville School District v. Gobitis, 11,
   41–42, 69–70
Minneapolis Tribune, 60
Minnesota Rag, 221
The Miracle, 29, 43
Mitgang, Herbert, 207
Montgomery, Kathryn, 223
Monty Python's Life of Bryan, 30
Moon, Eric, 207
Moore, Everett T., 207
Moral Majority, 106, 152. *See also*
   The Liberty Federation
Morality in Media, 152–153
Moretti, Daniel S., 207–208

Morgan, Richard E., 185
Morland, Howard, 223
Mormon Church, 10, 69, 241–242
Mostel, Zero, 42
Mothers of Invention, 64
Motion Picture Association of
America, 50
Motion Picture Code, 40. *See also*
Censorship—motion pictures
Mr. Justice Black and His Critics, 181
Mr. Justice Douglas, 256
*Mt. Helthy City School District Board of
Education v. Doyle*, 18, 101–102
MTV, 50–51
Murdock v. Pennsylvania, 15, 11, 70
Murphy, Paul L., 178, 208
Musical Majority, 58
*Mutual Film Corporation v. Industrial
Commission of Ohio*, 43

NAACP. *See* National Association for
the Advancement of Colored
People
Nadler, Eric, 208
Naming Names, 208
The Nation, 235
National Association for the
Advancement of Colored People
(NAACP), 25, 30, 40
*National Association for the
Advancement of Colored People
(NAACP) v. Alabama*, 24, 25, 43,
125–126
*National Association for the
Advancement of Colored People v.
Claiborne Hardware Company*, 130
National Association of Pro-America,
153
National Association for the
Advancement of Colored People
(NAACP), 25, 30, 40
*National Broadcasting Company v.
United States*, 111
National Center for Freedom in
Information Studies, 153
National Coalition against
Censorship, 61, 153–154
National Coalition against
Pornography, 60, 154
National Committee against
Repressive Legislation, 154

National Council of Teachers of
English (NCTE), 154–155
National Endowment for the Arts,
31, 50, 58, 168
National Legal Foundation, 62
National Newspaper Index, 269–270
National Review, 235–236
*National Socialist Party of America v.
Village of Skokie*, 129
Navasky, Victor S., 208
The Nazi/Skokie Conflict, 226
Nazis, 40, 129, 155, 226
Near v. Minnesota, 21, 40, 109–110
Negre v. Larsen, 73
The Negro and the First Amendment, 176
Neier, Aryeh, 57
Neiman-Marcus Company v. Lait, 14, 85
Neuborne, Burt, 173
New American, 236
New Order, 155
New Perspectives, 236
New Perspectives Quarterly, 236
The New Politics of Pornography, 195
The New Republic, 236–237
A New Slavery, 54
*New York Law School Journal of Human
Rights*, 237
New York Public Library, 208
*New York State Broadcasters Association
v. United States*, 114
*New York Times Company v. United
States*, 115
New York Times v. Sullivan, 13, 44, 89
New York v. Ferber, 20, 105
Newman, Roger K., 194
News Media and the Law, 237
News—A Free Press, 257
Newsletter on Intellectual Freedom, 60,
62, 237
Newspaper Publicity Law, 109
Newsweek, 30
Nichols, Mike, 29, 46
Niemotko v. Maryland, 124–125
A Night in the Art Gallery, 257
Nightline, 272
Nightmare in Red, 197
Nixon, Richard, 264
No Nukes, 58
Noam Chomsky, 257
Nobile, Philip, 208
Noble, William, 208

Nodis, 287
Noforn, 287
Noonan, James T., Jr., 185
Nordquist, Joang, 208–209
North American Human Rights
   Directory, 166
Norwich, Kenneth P., 209
Norwick, Kenneth P., 209
Noto v. United States, 87
Novik, Jack D., 201

O'Brien, David M., 179
O'Neil, Robert M., 209
Oaks, Dallin H., 185
Obelisk Press, 28, 41
Oboler, Eli M., 2, 178–179, 209
*"Obscene" Literature and Constitutional
   Law,* 225
Obscenity, 13, 19–20, 238, 287. *See
   also* Pornography
   Hicklin rule, 19, 38-39, 41, 43, 76,
      85-86, 285
   Miller, 19, 46
   pandering, 20
   prior restraint, 19-20, 40
   Roth, 19, 38, 43, 44
   youth guidelines, 20
*Obscenity: The Court, the Congress and
   the President's Commission,* 214
Obscenity and Freedom of Expression,
   189
Obscenity and Pornography, 207–208
Obscenity and Public Morality, 191
Obscenity Law Bulletin, 238
Obscenity, Pornography, and Censorship,
   192
*Obscenity, the Law, and the English
   Teacher,* 197
*Oestereich v. Selective Service Board No.
   11,* 91–92
Of Monkeys and Men, 257–258
Offensive words, 287
Ohio v. Osborne, 20, 32, 50
*Oklahoma v. United States Civil Service
   Commission,* 81
Olympia Press, 28, 41
One Man's Stand for Freedom, 172
Origin of the Species, 28
Original Intent, 183
Osanka, Franklin Mark, 209
Osbourne v. Ohio, 107

Ottinger, Richard, 63
Our Children Are Dying, 59
Our Right To Know, 238
Overbreadth, 287–288

PAIS Bulletin, 164
PAIS INTERNATIONAL, 268
PAIS on CD-ROM, 270
Pally, Marcia, 209–210
Palmer, A. Mitchell, 77
Pandering, 288
*Papish v. Board of Curators of the
   University of Missouri,* 117
Parent's Music Resource Center, 48,
   58, 64, 155–156, 247
Parent-Teacher Association (PTA),
   30
Patent offensiveness, 288
Paul, James C. N., 210
Peattie, Noel, 214–215
Peckham, Morris, 210
Peden, William, 176
Pell, Eve, 210
Pember, Don R., 223
PEN American Center, 59, 156. *See
   also* International PEN
Penrod, Steve, 194
The Pentagon Papers, 258
Pentagon Papers case, 46
People for the American Way, 61, 156,
   210
Periodicals, 168–170, 227–240
Perry v. Sindermann, 97–98
Personal-attack rule, 24, 288
Perspective, 179
Perspectives on Freedom of Speech, 215
Perspectives on Pornography, 202
*Perspectives on Pornography: Sexuality
   in Film and Literature,* 193
Peterson, Merrill D., 185
Pfeffer, Leo, 185–186
Phelan, John, 211
*A Philosophy of Free Expression and Its
   Constitutional Applications,* 177
Phyllis Schlafly Report, 238
Pickering v. Board of Education, 92
Pink Flamingo, 30
Pinkus v. United States, 103
Pinochet, Augusto, 59
Playboy Foundation's First
   Amendment Award, 62

Playboy, 29, 30, 43
Pledge of Allegiance, 41–42
Podsnappery, 288
Point of Order, 258
Points of Rebellion, 57
Polenberg, Richard, 211
Police Department of Chicago v. Mosley,
    26, 128–129
Political and Civil Rights in the United
    States, 173
Political Freedom: The Constitutional
    Powers of the People, 178
Political hyperbole, 288
Political Hysteria in America, 177
Politics and the Press, 222
The Politics of Pornography, 212
Pool, Ithiel de Sola, 223–224
Porky's II, 258–259
Pornography, 42, 45, 46, 47, 48–49,
    136, 152–153, 154, 158, 161,
    169–170, 186, 189, 192, 193,
    195, 197–202, 204, 205,
    207–209, 211–214, 216, 242,
    246, 246–247, 247–248, 254,
    259, 261, 262. *See also Art porn,*
    Attorney General's Commission on
    Pornography, Child pornography,
    Erotica, National Coalition Against
    Pornography, Obscenity, President's
    Commission on Obscenity and
    Pornography, Religious Alliance
    Against Pornography
  feminist viewpoint, 48,158,162
Pornography, 199
Pornography: Men Possessing Women,
    57 , 195
Pornography: The Conflict over Sexually
    Explicit Materials in the United
    States, 161
Pornography: The Double Message, 259
Pornography: The Issues and the Law,
    209
Pornography and Silence, 200
Pornography and the Law, 205
Pornography in a Free Society, 201
Pornography, Obscenity, and the Law,
    214
Postal Act, 39, 76, 77
Potter, Edward E., 226
Poulos v. New Hampshire, 125
Powe, Lucas A., Jr., 211, 224

Prayer in schools, 70–71, 261
Preferred position, 288
President's Commission on Obscenity
    and Pornography, 45, 47, 60
President's Council District 25 v.
    Community School Board No. 25, 98
The Press and America, 219–220
The Press and the Courts, 224
Press Freedoms, 221
Press Law and Press Freedom for High
    School Publications, 221
Press versus Government, 224
Presser, Stephen B., 7
Preston, William, 211
The Principles and Practices of Freedom
    of Speech, 189
Printers and Press Freedom, 225
Prior restraint, 288–289
Privacy, 179, 201
Privacy Act, 47, 132, 260
Privacy and the Press, 223
Problems in Intellectual Freedom and
    Censorship, 187
The Progressive, 238
Project Censored, 157
Propaganda Review, 239
Protectors of Privilege, 194
Provocative words, 289
PruneYard Shopping Center v. Robins,
    129
Prurient interest, 289
Public Access to Information, 174
Public Eye, 239
Public figure, 289
Public official, 289
Public place, 289
Public Prayer and the Constitution, 186
The Public Right To Know, 179
Publishers, 141
Publisher's Weekly, 62
Pynchon, William, 37

Qualified privilege, 289–290
A Question of Balance, 273
The Question of Pornography, 194

Racial issues, 145, 233–234, 247,
    263. *See also* Ku Klux Klan;
    National Association for the
    Advancement of Colored People
    (NAACP)

Radicalism, 232
Randall, Richard S., 211–212
Rate It X, 259
Reading, 145, 146, 148, 232, 243
Reage, Pauline, 28
Reasonable belief, 290
Reckless disregard, 290
Red Lion Broadcasting Company v.
    Federal Communications
    Commission, 24, 45, 114
Red Scare, 77
Red Squad, 260
Redrup v. New York, 91
Reems, Harry, 55
Regina v. Hicklin, 19, 38–39, 76
Rehnquist, William, 31, 32, 58,
    100–101
Reichman, Henry, 212
Release of Information, 260
Religion and the Constitution, 183–184
Religion in America, 182
Religious Alliance Against Pornography,
    60, 157
Religious Deception in the Schools, 260
Religious Freedom, 186
Religious Freedom on Trial, 181–182
Religious Freedom Reporter, 239
Religious Liberty, 261
Rembar, Charles, 179, 212
Renstrom, Peter G., 167
The Report of the Commission on
    Obscenity and Pornography, 216
Reporters Committee for Freedom
    of the Press, 157
A Respectable Lie, 261
Retroactive classification, 290
Revenue Act, 7
Reynolds v. United States, 10, 39, 69
Rice, Charles E., 226
Richard I, King of England, 37
Richards, David A. J., 179
Rickards, Maurice, 212
Right to assembly, 1, 8–9, 24–26,
    122, 226–227
case citations, 122–130
The Right of Assembly and Association,
    226
The Right To Picket and the Freedom of
    Public Discourse, 227
The Right To Read, 188
Right to reply, 290

Right-wing Women, 57
The Rights of Reporters, 221
The Rights of Teachers, 212
Rips, Geoffrey, 224
Robert B. Downs Intellectual
    Freedom Award, 61, 64
Robertson, Pat, 62–63
Robotham, John, 179
Robust debate, 290
Rogers, Donald J., 224
Rohrbacher, Dana, 31
Roosevelt, Franklin, 56, 124
Rosenberg, Ethel, 57
Rosenberg, Julius, 57
Roth standard, 290
Roth v. United States, 19, 29, 38, 43,
    44, 56, 85–86
Rousseau, Jean-Jacques, 27
Rowan, Carl T., 224
Rubin, David, 212
Rubin, Rick, 161
Run Home Slow, 64
Rushdie, Salman, 49
Rushdovny, Rousas J., 212
Rushing to Censorship, 206
Rust v. Sullivan, 31, 51, 108
Rutland, Robert Allen, 179

Salinger, J. D., 30, 42–43
Sanderson, Arthur M., 220
Sandler, Martin W., 219
The Satanic Verses, 49
Schauer, Frederick, 212–213
Schenck v. United States, 14–15, 39, 77,
    78
Schimmel, David, 179–180
Schmidt, Benno, Jr., 225
Scholastic Scope, 30
School prayer. See Prayer in schools
School Prayer, Gun Control and the
    Right To Assemble, 261
The Schoolbook Protest Movement, 203
Schroeder, Theodore A., 225
Schultz, Bud, 213
Schultz, Ruth, 213
Schumach, Murray, 213
Schwartz, Bernard, 180
Schwartz, Murray L., 210
Scienter, 290–291
Scopes v. State, 40, 79, 255, 257–258
Seagle, W., 196

Seale, Bobby, 46
Seasonal Differences, 261–262
The Second American Revolution, 186
The Secret File, 262
The Secret Museum, 204
The Secret That Exploded, 223
Secular humanism, 291
Sedition, 291
Sedition Act, 77
See No Evil, 192
Seldes, George, 63, 225
Seldes, Gilbert, 63
Selected Articles on Censorship of Speech and the Press, 171
Selective Service Act, 78. *See also* Conscientious objectors
Sellen, Betty-Carol, 162
Sense and Censorship, 209–210
Separation of Church and State, 182
Seven Dirty Words and Six Other Stories, 214
The 700 Club, 62
Sex for Sale, 262
Sex, Censorship, and Pornography, 198–199
Sex, Literature and Censorship, 205
Sex Magazines in the Library Collection, 198
Shaping the First Amendment, 180
Shapiro, Andrew O., 225
Sharp, Donald B., 213
Shelton v. Tucker, 126
Shepard's United States Citations, 68
Shield laws, 291
Shields, Gerald, 179
Shiffrin, Steven H., 180
Shockley, William, 55
Shumate, T. Daniel, 180
Simon & Schuster v. New York State, 51
Single instance rule, 291
Singleton, John, 51
Sirett, Hazel, 166
Sister Carrie, 28
60 Minutes, 273
Slander, 75
    defined, 12
The Slave Who Bought His Freedom, 59
Slochower v. Board of Higher Education, 18
Smith, Jeffrey A., 225
Smith, Rodney K., 186

Smith Act, 41, 81–82
Smith v. California, 87
Smith v. Goguen, 100
Smith v. United States, 102
Smolla, Rodney A., 213
The Smut Peddlers, 204
Snepp, Frank, 55
Snepp v. United States, 22, 120–121
Sobel, Lester A., 214
Social Education, 169
Social exchange, 291
Social Philosophy and Policy, 239
Social Science Index, 270
Social Sciences Index, 165
Social Sciences Citation Index, 164
Social Service Organizations and Agencies Directory, 166
Social utility, 291
Society, 169–170
Software, 274–277
Solomon, Norman, 222
Sommons, Steven J., 225
Sonderling Broadcasting Corporation, WGLD-FM, 117–118
Soul on Ice, 30
Sourcebook on Pornography, 209
Southern, Terry, 28
The Speaker, 61, 263
Speech and Law in a Free Society, 174–175
Speech, Crime, and the Uses of Language, 200
Spence v. Washington, 100–101
Spitzor, Matthew L., 214
Spock, Benjamin, 55
The Spotlight, 240
Stamp Act, 7
Stand Up to Life, 64
Stanley v. Georgia, 20, 32, 45, 94
Steinbeck, John, 29
Stevens, John D., 180
Stone v. Graham, 73
Story, Joseph, 9
The Story of O, 28
Street v. New York, 17, 46, 94
The Strong Willed Child, 56
Strossen, Nadine, 32
Student Press Law Center, 157–158
Student Press Law Center Report, 240
Students' rights, 179–180, 240
Studs' Place, 64

The Sun Also Rises, 29
Sunderland, Land V., 214
Sunshine Act, 47, 132
Suppressed Books, 192
The Supreme Court and Individual Rights, 181
The Supreme Court and Libel, 205
The Supreme Court and Religion, 185
The Supreme Court and the First Amendment, 175
The Supreme Court and the Mass Media, 218
The Supreme Court Obscenity Decisions, 214
Supreme Court Review, 168
The Supreme Court's Holy Battles, 263
Surveillance in the Stacks, 196–197
Swan, John, 214–215
Sweezy v. New Hampshire, 18, 86
Sylvester and the Magic Pebble, 30
Symbolic speech, 17, 45, 46, 291
Sympathy for the Devil, 263
The System of Freedom of Expression, 174

Take Back the Night, 57 , 205–206
Taking on the Press, 225–226
Target: Prime Time, 223
Target America, 59
Tariff Act, 40, 80
Taylor, Andy, 58
Taylor, C. L., 215
Teachers, 30, 154–155, 197, 212
Technical Report of the Commission on Obscenity and Pornography, 216
Technologies of Freedom, 223–224
Tedford, Thomas L., 215
Teicher, Oren J., 63
Television programs, 271–274
Ten Commandments, 73
Tenured Radicals, 204
Terkel, Studs, 63–64
Terminiello v. Chicago, 16, 83
Texas v. Johnson, 17, 32, 107
Textbooks, 216–217, 235, 251, 265
Theiner, George, 215
They Shoot Writers, Don't They?, 215
Thomas, A. H., 215–216
Thomas, Cal, 216
Thomas v. Collins, 25
Thornhill v. Alabama, 25, 123

Threatening words, 291
Thurmond, Strom, 106
Time, 30
Time-place-manner, 292
Times Film Corporation v. Chicago, 87–88
Tinker v. Des Moines Independent School District, 32, 46, 49, 94–95, 275
Titicut Follies, 30
To Deprave and Corrupt, 191
To Speak or Not To Speak, 264
To the Pure, 196
The Tolerant Society, 188
Toleration Acts, 6
Toleration and the Constitution, 179
Tom Jones, 27
Tony Brown's Journal, 273
Torcaso v. Watkins, 10
Transforming Free Speech, 199
Tropic of Cancer, 28, 40, 41, 76, 202
"Tropic of Cancer" on Trial, 202
Tropic of Capricorn, 28, 41, 76
Truman, Harry, 54, 84
Truth, 2
Twain, Mark, 27
20/20, 273
2 Live Crew, 50
Two Treatises on Civil Government, 6, 37
Tyson, James, Jr., 59

Ulysses, 28, 38, 41
Ulysses standard, 292
Underground Conservative, 59
U.S. Civics/Citizenship, 271
U.S. Commission on Obscenity and Pornography, 216
U.S. Constitution, 277
U.S. Department of Justice. Attorney General's Commission on Pornography, 216
United States of America vs. Sex, 208
U.S. Supreme Court, 67, 168, 175, 181, 218–219, 219, 221, 264. *See also* names of individual justices
United States Supreme Court Guardian of the Constitution, 264
United States v. Caldwell, 116
United States v. Gregg, 110
United States v. Kennerly, 77
U.S. v. Nixon, 264

United States v. O'Brien, 17, 45, 92–93
*United States v. One Book Called
    "Ulysses,"* 41, 80
United States v. Orsini, 119
United States v. Progressive, 120
*United States v. Radio Television News
    Directors Association,* 114
United States v. Seeger, 44, 71–72
*United States v. Southwestern Cable
    Company,* 113
*United States v. Thirty-Seven (37)
    Photographs,* 96–97
Universal Declaration of Human
    Rights, 44
University of Pennsylvania v. EEOC,
    107
Unmailable, 197
Unofficial classification, 292
Unprotected speech, 292
Unreliable Sources, 222
Utne Reader, 240

Vagueness, 292
Valentine v. Chrestensen, 20, 82–83
Van Alstyne, William w., 180
Van Vliet, Don, 64
Vaughan, Robert C., 185
Versions of Censorship, 206
Videos. *See* Films, videocassettes, and
    filmstrips
Village Voice, 58
*The Virginia Statute for Religious
    Freedom,* 185
Vitz, Paul C., 216–217
Voice for Youth Advocates, 55
Voice of Reason, 158
The VOYA Reader, 189

Wagman, Robert J., 181
The Wall between Church and State, 185
Wall of Controversy, 184
Wallace v. Jaffree, 74
*Walz v. Tax Commission of the City of
    New York,* 10
War, 178
Ward v. Illinois, 102
Warren, Earl, 56
Watson v. Jones, 9–10
Watts v. United States, 16, 95
"Wax Museum," 63
Weiss, Ann E., 181

The Well of Loneliness, 76
Welsh v. United States, 72
Wesberry v. Sanders, 54
West Publishing Company, 68
*West Virginia State Board of Education
    v. Barnette,* 11, 42, 70
WESTLAW, 268
What Johnny Can't Read, 265
Where Do You Draw the Line?, 191
The Whistleblowers, 199
Whistleblowers Act. *See* Civil Service
    Reform Act
White Circle League, 84
Whitehead, John W., 186, 227
Whitman, Walt, 28
Whitney v. California, 79–80
Who's Running Your Life?, 170
Who's To Know!, 181
Widest latitude, 292
Widmar v. Vincent, 104
Widmer, Eleanor, 217
Wildmon, Donald E., 64
William of Orange, 6
WILSONLINE, 268
Wiseberg, Laurie S., 166
Wiseman, Frederick, 30
Witness to a Century, 63
Witt, Elder, 168, 181
Woman Hating, 57
Women against Censorship, 190
Women against Pornography (WAP),
    158
Woodhull and Claflin Weekly, 29
Woods, L. B., 30, 217
Woodworth, Mary L., 217
Wooley v. Maynard, 102–103
Words To Live By, 273–274
*Working: People Talk about What They
    Do All Day and How They Feel
    about What They Do,* 63
World Press Freedom Committee,
    158–159
A Worthy Tradition, 203
Worton, Stanley N., 227
*Writer's Guild of America, West v.
    Federal Communications
    Commission,* 119
Writers, 141–142

Yale Law Review, 55
Yarbrough, Tinsley E., 181

Yates v. United States, 82, 86
Yearbooks, 166–168
You Can't Print That, 63
Young, Lisa, 165
Young, Patricia, 162
The Young Adult & Intellectual Freedom, 217
Youngstown Sheet and Tube Co. et al. v. Sawyer, 54
Your Rights to Privacy, 201
Yuill, Phyllis J., 218

Zappa, Frank, 64
Zappa, Moon Unit, 64
Zenger, John Peter, 21
Zerman, Melvyn Bernard, 225–226
Zimring, Franklin G., 201
Zorach v. Clauson, 11
Zurcher, Louis A., Jr., 218
Zurcher v. Stanford Daily, 120
Zykan v. Warsaw Community School Corporation, 104

John B. Harer, a member of the library faculty of Texas A & M University, holds a bachelor's degree in political science and master's degrees in library science and public administration. A brush with book censorship while a junior high school librarian in Williamsport, Pennsylvania, led him to become active in intellectual freedom activities with such organizations as the Pennsylvania School Librarian's Association, the American Civil Liberties Union, and the American Library Association. He is the coauthor of numerous articles on circulation services.